Sounding Imperial

Sounding Imperial

Poetic Voice and the Politics of Empire, 1730–1820

JAMES MULHOLLAND

The Johns Hopkins University Press
Baltimore

Printed in the United States of America on acid-free paper
2 4 6 8 9 7 5 3 1

The Johns Hopkins University Press
2715 North Charles Street
Baltimore, Maryland 21218-4363
www.press.jhu.edu

Library of Congress Cataloging-in-Publication Data

Mulholland, James, 1975–
Sounding imperial : poetic voice and the politics of empire, 1730–1820
/ James Mulholland.
p. cm.
Includes bibliographical references and index.
ISBN-13: 978-1-4214-0854-5 (alk. paper) ISBN-13: 978-1-4214-0855-2
(electronic) ISBN-10: 1-4214-0854-6 (alk. paper)
ISBN-10: 1-4214-0855-4 (electronic)
1. English poetry—18th century—History and criticism 2. Political poetry—History and criticism. 3. English poetry—19th century—History and criticism. 4. Politics and literature—History—18th century. 5. Politics and literature—History—19th century. 6. Politics in literature. 7. Imperialism in literature. I. Title.
PR571.M85 2012
821.709—dc23
2012027075

A catalog record for this book is available from the British Library.

Special discounts are available for bulk purchases of this book. For more information, please contact Special Sales at 410-516-6936 or specialsales@press.jhu.edu.

The Johns Hopkins University Press uses environmentally friendly book materials, including recycled text paper that is composed of at least 30 percent post-consumer waste, whenever possible.

Contents

Illustrations

Acknowledgments

Once, in response to a request for advice about how to revise a dissertation, I replied, almost without thinking, "Don't write lonely." I certainly never have, at any stage in this project. I remember being told as an undergraduate that studying English literature could be a solitary occupation, but luckily for me that has proven untrue. This project began as a course paper for Michael McKeon when I was a graduate student at Rutgers University, and I thank him both for encouraging my initial insights and for generously guiding me since then. Aspiring to the rigor of his thinking and the generosity of his spirit has always improved me as a scholar and a teacher. My committee members at Rutgers University—Michael McKeon, Paula McDowell, Jonathan Kramnick, William Galperin—were a model of how to think about literature. Paula McDowell was a remarkable reader and I greatly appreciate her encouragement since then: it feels as though we have pursued these ideas together. Jonathan Kramnick offered important advice about writing, academe, and publishing that I vividly remember and often share with others. William Galperin added insight to this project from its beginning and helped me to keep its conclusion in view. Brent Edwards indefatigably pushed the concerns of my dissertation in new directions and brought his incisive perspective to every claim I made. The original contours of this project are indebted to his thinking. John Sitter generously provided his expertise about how to expand and improve my dissertation, which I looked back upon until the completion of this book.

My debts to my friends at Rutgers University are too significant to be described adequately. Graduate school never felt like a lonely place, because Hillary Chute, Rick Lee, and Joe Ponce responded with long phone calls, spontaneous reading sessions, afternoon chai, and celebratory dinners, all of which gives some sense of their investment in my intellectual endeavors. This project acquired a lot of its first shape because of their efforts. Kathy Lubey and Kristin Girten were important fellow travelers during this time and afterward; I appreciate their tireless ability to see the promise in my work when I was not always sure of it myself. It was at Rutgers that I came to appreciate the insight and advice of Tanya Agathocleous about publishing, teaching, and being a professor. Asohan Amarasingham, Robert Goldstein, and Andrew Thompson, "ancient friends," have ever been ready to talk about literature even if they did not always understand exactly what I was rambling on about. I met Natalie Phillips at the moment when this dissertation started to become a book, and much of this transition was spurred by her attentive reading.

Not enough can be said about my colleagues at Connecticut College, where I visited for one year, and at Wheaton College in Massachusetts. All of them provided me with a warm environment within which to complete this book. Thanks are owed to David Greven and Alex Beecroft, who have been great friends and interlocutors on everything. At Wheaton, particular thanks go to the members of the Wheaton College Faculty Writing Group, past and present—Francisco Fernandez de Alba, Touba Ghadessi, Alizah Holstein, Yu-Gen Liang, Rolf Nelson, Gail Sahar—who read through this project at many different stages, as well as to Claire Buck, Shawn Christian, Tripp Evans, Paula Krebs, Ellen McBreen, and Josh Stenger. All of them offered friendship, support, and sharp thoughts, and I will remember my years in Providence, Rhode Island, with fondness.

The fellows at the Bill and Carol Fox Center for Humanistic Inquiry at Emory University, where I was in residence during 2009–2010, and the center's staff—Keith Anthony, Colette Barlow, Amy Erbil—and director, Tina Brownley, made Emory a wonderful place in which to overhaul my manuscript. That my time at the Fox Center was one of the most productive of my life is a testament to the place. Special thanks must be reserved for Benjy Kahan, whom I met at the Fox Center and who read the manuscript multiple times, always offering illuminating thoughts. This book is much better because of our collaboration, and it is hard to imagine its existence without his invaluable comments. While in Atlanta I was happy to become friends with Aaron Santesso and Crystal Lake and to renew my friendship with Paul Kelleher; each of them gave me a new perspective on eighteenth-century studies. Crystal read a number of chapters in their final stages and always supplied insights exactly when I needed them.

Several other organizations and fellowships contributed to the completion of this project, including the NYU Long Eighteenth–Century Colloquium (thanks to Paula McDowell and Colin Jennings), Georgia Colloquium in Eighteenth- and Nineteenth-Century Literature (thanks to Chloe Wigston Smith), the Daniel Francis Howard Fellowship at Rutgers University, the David L. Kalstone Memorial Fund, the Marion and Jasper Whiting Foundation Fellowship, and the

Wheaton College Summer Grant. Thanks also to the staffs of the British Library, the National Library of Wales, the National Library of Scotland, the National Gallery of Scotland, and the National Library of Australia for their help in guiding research and finding documents and images. And thanks to Martha Vega-Gonzalez for proofreading, to Chris Hyde for expert help with images, and to Lindsay York for fact-checking.

Portions of Chapter 1 appeared first as "Gray's Ambition: Printed Voices and Performing Bards in the Later Poetry" in *ELH* 75.1 (2008) and pieces of Chapter 3 appeared as "James Macpherson's Ossian Poems, Oral Traditions, and the Invention of Voice" in *Oral Tradition* 24, 2 (October 2009). I thank both of these journals for permission to reprint the material.

Working with the Johns Hopkins University Press has been a wonderful experience; thanks to Matt McAdam, to those in marketing and production, who have been a pleasure to work with, and to the press's anonymous reader, whose extremely detailed report made this into a sharper book. Special thanks must go to Anne Whitmore for her meticulous copy editing, which unfailingly improved my work.

My family—Hugh, Cyndie, Mike, Michelle, Tyler, and Dylan—has always provided me with a place away from this project and some perspective on who I was before it started. They have truly been there the whole way, and "thank you" does not say enough for that. This book is dedicated to Rachel Brewster, for all of those things that mattered beyond this book and thus made it possible.

Sounding Imperial

Introduction: The Global Aesthetics of Poetic Voice

"Poetry," the French philosopher Denis Diderot argues, "must have something in it that is barbaric, vast, and wild."[1] His counterparts in Great Britain found such barbaric wildness in oral traditions near and far. Coming from seemingly primitive speakers whose passionate voices were thought to be natural and authentic, folk traditions felt enlivening and even slightly dangerous. Ancient bards and "noble savages" possessed the "spirit of poetry," exclaimed the eighteenth-century Scottish scholar John Pinkerton, and they expressed it in their "dying sound among the wilds."[2] *Sounding Imperial* analyzes an almost century-long experiment in which British authors revived this unique, endangered spirit and its sound by designing poetic voices that imitated the techniques and attitudes of oral speakers.

This tradition of experimentation with poetic voice occurred in two simultaneous, interconnected literary and cultural transformations. First, an emergent poetics of "printed voice" explored how to present oral voices in literate forms. During the eighteenth century, authors organized new techniques—for example, quotation marks differentiated speakers and certain meters evoked chanting—to suggest that their poems channeled public performances. Second, this new poetics coincided with a reimagining of the author as an intermediary between traditional (often oral) cultures and English literature, seeking out original speakers and appropriating them for readers. As eighteenth-century poets worried that the power of language had declined because of the explosion of print, they sought inspiration in folk culture and foreign speakers to counteract this crisis in vitality. Imitations of Chinese performances, translations of

Persian songs, Indian "tales" in verse, eclogues of Africa or the West Indies, and reworkings of Scandinavian folk songs all are examples of non-European cultures that appeared as topics of eighteenth-century poetry. While the British expanded their dominion in North America, the Caribbean, and Asia, and while they explored the Pacific Islands and Africa, they were also idealizing the oral traditions they found there and impersonating overseas speakers. In this book, I examine the elements that authors developed to convince readers they could hear those distant voices or experience the exoticism of foreign speakers when they read a text. I link these forms of address with literary, social, cultural, and economic changes that motivated an eighteenth-century evolution in the concept of poetic voice and the techniques used to construct it.

Although no text is unmediated, the fantasy of unmediated voices has driven literary experimentation for centuries.[3] As material relations change, so does a culture's imagination of textuality, and it is a central claim of this book that the reexamination of media—oral and written—during the Enlightenment raised anew long-lived questions about the nature of print. Voice is thus a category that needs to be historicized.[4] My study participates in this historicizing of voice. The positive revaluation of oral traditions that occurred in mid-eighteenth-century Britain, the continued culturewide consideration of what mass print and literacy meant to the modern world, and the growing importance of colonialism all contributed to a significant reassessment of poetic voice. Rapid growth in the print industry made texts more readily available. The availability of printed texts created a viable literary marketplace, which in turn supported new notions of professional authorship. At the same time, oral traditions previously thought to be "primitive" were reimagined as heroic and inspiring rather than degraded and uncivilized. Turning uncivilized orality into the type of inspiring barbarism that Diderot championed was one of the most important accomplishments of eighteenth-century poetry.

Oral voices were so appealing because they were seen as wild and passionate, instilling a spirit of communal relationship and promising the intimacy of face-to-face contact. This idealized sense of oral performance as collective belonging offered an antidote to the detachment associated with print circulation. The spread of literacy and the growth of the print marketplace during the eighteenth century only intensified these feelings. "The gradual detachment, through print, of the writer from the present and familiar audience is one of the most far-reaching influences of modern times," Bertrand Bronson comments insightfully. Although an extended reading audience is always in some sense fictional, the conditions of proliferating print meant that the detachment of authors from audiences advanced with "special insistence" during the eighteenth century.[5] Many authors, like Samuel Johnson, embraced the distanced relationship of the professional author, who writes for money and who is beholden to, but also securely removed from, the reading public.[6] However, the smaller group of authors whom I discuss in this book worried that the expressive powers of language had been reduced by the mechanization of print and the progress of civilization. For them, print lacked the affective charge of speech and severed the connection between author and audience. By constructing their poems as wild prophecies, dying speeches, and heroic political addresses, they sought to persuade readers to imagine themselves as auditors and thereby counteract the potential to feel solitary and isolated when reading.

Of course, printed poetry cannot duplicate the auditory dimensions of vocalized sound. It must simulate presence, which requires techniques alert to the representation of different voices. Poetic voice therefore rests at the center—the pivot point—of the relationship between the materiality of print and its metaphorical representation in the cultural imaginary as spoken performance. Most scholars have suggested that these appeals to oral performance were backward-looking attempts to reject modernity or were examples of Britain's "aesthetic imperialism" across the globe.[7] In this model, oral voices and foreign speakers become ways to protest the rationality associated with print by appropriating the authenticity of marginalized cultures. Rather than interpreting eighteenth-century authors as nostalgic for an oral world before print, I understand their poetic experiments to register a new kind of presence in texts and to craft a more intimate relationship with their readers. The dialogue between oral and literate forms was one venue for tinkering with new prototypes of poetic voice and for creating collaborations between what we have until recently considered antagonistic forms of media and modes of cultural belonging. Modern poetic voice, then, must be thought of as textual virtualization, as the disembodiment of a radically singular personal characteristic. Romanticism is often heralded as the era that ushered in the definition of poetic voice as an individualized, interiorized expression of personal identity that is associated with the lyric speaker.[8] But, in the decades before British Romanticism, eighteenth-century authors engaged in similar explorations, which contributed to the arrival of the highly confessional voices of Romanticism's well-known lyrics.

The experimental tradition I discuss was not, however, emblematic of eighteenth-century poetry. It was not understood as an artistic movement at the time, as Margaret Anne Doody claims Augustan poets sensed themselves to be.[9] Moreover, these experiments with poetic voice were unlike many other literary trends contemporary with it, such as the emergence of the novel. Yet it was not subterranean or localized either, in the way of many modern experimental literatures. The authors that I discuss in this project—English poets William Collins and Thomas Gray; Evan Evans, Felicia Hemans, and other Welsh bardic performers; James Macpherson and his Scottish allies; Anglo-Indian poets of colonialism; literary impersonators of Pacific islanders—were eclectic and would be hard-pressed to see themselves as members of the same group or literary collective. Nonetheless, they shared cultural representations and literary devices, and often revised and alluded to the same texts, revealing a common interest in resolving difficult questions about how to animate and reenergize printed poetry. The period's intense awareness of the importance of Gray is especially illustrative, elaborating an extensive chain of adaptations and rewritings of his poem "The Bard" and his folkloric imitations (rather than his better-known "Elegy Written in a Country Church-yard").[10] One goal of this book is to join authors and cultures that have as yet been seen as unrelated or even combative, and thus to redraw familiar literary genealogies.

Novelists had their own interest in using the representation of native and foreign voices to address problems of modernity, as the dialect in Tobias Smollet's *Expedition of Humphry Clinker* (1771) and the idiosyncratic form of Laurence Sterne's *The Life and Opinions of Tristram Shandy, Gentleman* (1759–67) amply illustrate. Alexis Tadié argues that the emergence of the novel forced a paradigm shift for orality. He claims that Sterne's work, for instance, exemplifies the novel's use of conversation as a means of "addressing the changing modes of narrative" that amalgamated storytelling conventions with an emphasis on the literacy of the book.[11] The new reading protocols of the novel pushed readers to "apprehend the text with the prerequisites of an oral culture," that is, to "listen in" on characters, "to participate in conversational exchange," which the novel presents as moments of dialogue.[12] The chaotic grammar for reporting speech in prose narrative—the cacophonous italics of Daniel Defoe's texts, the hyphens of Eliza Haywood's novellas, the increasingly standardized use of quotations and speech markers such as "he said"—is mirrored by the poetic experiments I discuss here. But, while the novel promotes this sense of presence primarily in moments of virtualized conversation, poetry offers the immediacy associated with the spatial proximity of oral performance. And, while poetry was not alone in its engagement with orality—one could argue that the dramatic text always theorizes the collision of oral and literate—this type of eighteenth-century poetry was unique in its attempt to prefigure an aesthetic ideology that insisted on the immediacy of its oral voices and exotic speakers.

Srinivas Aravamudan has wondered whether literary study is "overinvested in the book as [a] cultural and aesthetic category."[13] In *Tropicopolitans,* he seeks to undo the idea of literacy and textual voice as equivalent to subjectivity and agency, calling this relation a "factish"—that is, an imperfect concept we employ because it works.[14] Here, I seek to expand the range and register of Aravamudan's question by wondering if we have overemphasized print—in particular, printed prose—in our literary study of colonialism. The result of this overemphasis is evident, I would suggest, in the conclusions we draw about culture and politics from our analysis of the prose techniques that we investigate. By focusing primarily on prose narrative—on characterization in novel discourse or on the first-person reminiscence of travel writing—we have ignored other modes of mediating and encountering foreign voices. Poetic voice channels foreign speakers in ways different from novels; it makes the inhabitation of another's subject position a constitutive part of its form in a manner that eighteenth-century prose does not easily imitate. The alignment of author and speaker permits readers of English poetry to confront foreign perspectives as if they were immediately available, that is, to confront them as if they were actually speaking as their own person, ultimately voicing themselves without the intervention of a narrator, translator, or traveler. This fictive immediacy, when applied to alternate voices, makes them powerfully persuasive and often dangerous acts of appropriation.

Aspects of this experimentation with voice, performance, and subjectivity have been partially addressed over the past two decades by the disparate fields of postcolonial theory, archipelagic British history, book history, and multimedia and sound studies. I strive to synthesize these rarely overlapping fields and to extend their approaches by considering the various places and political climates in which this poetics of voice was forged and the ways in which it was framed. Because these authors were intent on reestablishing intimate connections between themselves and their readers, they searched widely among geographical locations, ethnic groups, and cultural situations to discover new and vigorous types of speakers and perspectives. For them, poetry was always elsewhere; it was in wild northern Scotland, in the hills of Wales, in the sublime vastness of India, in Scandinavia, or in the past, waiting to be salvaged by those with ears attuned to hear it. Likewise, oral traditions were portrayed as part of a past culture or a remote locale, sometimes preserved in documents but just as likely perceived to be in danger of disappearing forever. In seeking these voices from *over there* or *back then,* Britain's authors cast out toward the edges of their empire and into the distant past for alternative models of the poetic speaker.

At its base, the project of this book is to rethink the relationship between the global and the local in eighteenth-century poetry, between Britain's overseas colonies and the formation of the British national voice. Robert Crawford has offered the idea of devolution to consider the interaction among the parts of the British Isles. He writes that by devolving English literature—by looking to its edges, by decentralizing our study of it—we reveal the geographical and cultural margins that organize the emergence of a national British literature.[15] But what if we also devolve English literature beyond the British Isles? What if we travel to Britain's furthest colonies and back again to discover other interacting forces that influenced poetic voice as an evolving eighteenth-century concept? Following the transperipheral travels of poetic voice as it circulated along the edges of Britain and throughout its colonies offers a deeper sense of how oral traditions and foreign voices revived late-eighteenth-century English literature, shaping some of its most crucial literary experiments. Rooted in multiple locations, connecting various cultures, the experiments described in this book show that British poetic voice was always about the political relationship between different cultures flung across the vast expanse of the globe.

LAYERED MEDIATIONS

A poem from 1749 sets out such an experimental agenda in its very title: "An Ode on the Popular Superstitions of the Highlands of Scotland, Considered as the Subject of Poetry."[16] Its author, William Collins, offers the folk traditions and oral tales of the then-remote Scottish Highlands as a new topic for English literature, seeing Scotland as a place of natural wildness. He departs from early-eighteenth-century neoclassicism in favor of different voices, unusual speakers, and alien places. To describe these new subjects, Collins constructs a printed poem that acts as a conduit for the voices of ancient Highland bards. His poem's speaker is presented as a medium for these bards, whose voices the speaker hears, records in his text, and transmits to English readers, who will be "astonished" by the "choral dirge[s]," "strange lays," and "hideous spells."[17] Collins searched for the correct representational form for these wild oral voices, as a means of reinvigorating an English poetry that he feared would never again achieve the greatness of the work of poets from preceding generations, like John Milton and Edmund Waller.[18]

The Highlands Ode exemplifies a tendency found throughout the eighteenth century of locating poetic inspiration elsewhere. The Scotland of Collins's poem is rich with songs, superstitions, and folk traditions that are still "fresh to that soil" (line 13). Unlike England, the Highlands are "Fancy's Land . . . Where still, 'tis said, the Fairy People meet . . . while Airy Minstrels warble jocund notes" (21–22, 25). In Scotland, "Old Runic Bards shall seem to rise around / With uncouth Lyres, in many-colour'd Vest, / Their Matted Hair with boughs fantastic crown'd" (41–43). Minstrels and bards rise from the ground like apparitions to sing old songs on their "uncouth Lyres." The authenticity of these sounds is connected with their geography. Northern Scotland is "hallow'd Ground" littered with the tombs of supernatural "Pigmie-Folk" and the "Rifted Mounds" of ancient monarchs who arise at midnight from the dead to hold an "Aerial council" (151–54). The land offers tangible evidence of its antiquity. These supernatural voices are autochthonous, like the "Old Runic Bards" themselves.

Susan Stewart concludes that Collins's Highlands Ode should be classified as a "distressed genre," a genre intentionally made antique, in which nostalgia is not "for artifacts for their own sake" but is "a nostalgia for context, for the heroic past, for childhood and the collective experiences of preindustrial life."[19] Authors in the eighteenth century, she notes, appealed to those traditions that were not "literature" to mollify a "crisis in authenticity."[20] Such a crisis makes authenticity into a problem that "arises in situations where there is a self-conscious perception of mediation; a sense of distance between one era and another, one world view and another; a sense of historical periodization, transformation, even rupture."[21] The answer to this problem, she suggests, comes in writing "oral genres" that invest literature with a lost presence, a missing context that only orality can repair. British poets felt, she claims, that English poetry was weary or unenergetic, and they were motivated to look elsewhere for access to the "authority of the oral world" in order to "recoup . . . the voice of orality in all its presumed authenticity of its context."[22]

As with other "distressed" genres that Stewart describes (like the forged ballads of Thomas Chatterton and the historical ballads of Walter Scott), I argue that Collins's Highlands Ode is a "machine for recreating context," meaning that it is a highly intricate literary tool for evoking the nostalgia and authenticity associated with the oral past.[23] Collins mixes supernatural figures, ancient voices, and oral storytelling to depict a haunted Scotland that exemplifies this idealization of the preindustrial past. All of the poems I examine in this book are machines for recreating context in much the same way that the Highlands Ode is. In Collins's poem, this machinery consists of multiple layers of mediation between its authors, speakers, and informants. One important layer is the ode's address to John Home, a Scottish playwright who had attempted to stage his plays in London.[24] Unsuccessful, Home returned to Scotland, an occasion that Collins celebrates in the poem as an opportunity to invent a new kind of writing that channels Scottish oral voices.[25] Collins advises Home: "Proceed, in forcefull sounds and Colours bold / The Native Legends of thy Land rehearse / To such adapt thy Lyre, and suit thy pow'rfull Verse" (185–87). He presents Home as an ideal informant on this alien land and portrays him as a more modern version of Scotland's ancient bards, who continued a long chain of transmission that extended back into antiquity. Within the logic of the poem, Home can sing of his native Scotland in ways that Collins cannot. The imaginative renewal that the Highlands Ode hopes to secure originates in the superstitious songs, ancient customs, and oral traditions mediated by Home to Collins's waiting ear—and then by Collins to England's "astonished" readers.

The media transitions implied by this poem are numerous and extremely complex, moving from the orality of folk traditions to the metaphorical "singing" of Home's verse, then to the speaker's "waiting ear" and onward to the eyes of England's readers. Maureen McLane, following Jay Bolter and Richard Grusin, would call this layering "remediation" or "transmediation"—the transformation of oral material into literate features so that the oral is "remediated" into some other form.[26] Readers of Collins's poem do not experience the oral but, rather, a "variety of orality effects" that results from what Friedrich Kittler calls the "transposition of media."[27] Transposing media across genres entails finding some imperfect equivalent for orality in writing. And while a "medium . . . cannot be translated," as Kittler argues, it can be evoked. Thus, in the Highlands Ode it is not the oral that is represented so much as the layers of mediation required to access an idealized oral past.[28] Collins imagines the process of accessing this past—that is, shifting from oral to literate—to be like translating between languages or listening to a beautiful song being sung and making a musical instrument. At the end of the Highlands Ode, the speaker describes his reaction to reading a sixteenth-century translation by Edward Fairfax of the Renaissance Italian poet Tasso:

> How have I sat, where pip'd the pensive Wind
>   To hear his harp, by British Fairfax strung
> Prevailing Poet, whose undoubting Mind
>   Believ'd the Magic Wonders which He sung!
> Hence at Each Sound Imagination glows
> Hence his warm lay with softest Sweetness flows
>   Melting it flows, pure num'rous strong and clear
> And fills th' impassioned heart, and lulls th' Harmonious Ear
>
> (196–203)

Printed poetry morphs into an aural experience. The text supplies a voice that the speaker animates and makes aural, filling his "impassioned heart" and lulling his ear with harmony.

But the relation between the speaker and the text's voice is mediated by Fairfax's translation of Tasso. Collins portrays Fairfax as an instrument maker and his translation as an Aeolian harp by "British Fairfax strung," where the image of weaving and fixing the strings into the frame of a harp depicts the process of translation.[29] Fairfax captured Tasso's voice, which was carried across temporal and spatial boundaries *through* the translated text. Reading Fairfax's translation, the speaker hears Tasso's song and experiences the romance of his "undoubting mind" (199). Similarly, one can hear Home's song, and thus the collective voices of ancient Scottish bards, through Collins's Highlands Ode. The literary revitalization promised by superstitions and "Native Legends" is achieved through the paradoxical presence and mediation of oral traditional voices as printed poetry. This is the experience Collins hopes to give his readers when they encounter his poem.

In the Highlands Ode, therefore, media transmission crosses the boundaries of nation, language, and of oral and literate modes. The relationship between the speaker and Home exemplifies the broader relationship between English authors and the imaginative power of the Highlands that rejuvenated them.[30] Collins's text translates non-English oral traditions (never accessed directly in the poem, except by the inclusion of Scots vocabulary) into a British poetic idiom: folk traditions become English odes; books become harps and lyres; words are like musical strings. Many of these images are quite conventional, but by combining them, Collins created a highly mediated printed poem that claims to originate in the oral performance of a circumscribed community of listeners. His ethnographical interest in northern Scotland and his address to Home fashion the English author as a translator of others' oral voices.[31] Collins rooted his poetic voice in an authentic context and his poem is the conduit through which oral voices can be heard. This was an extremely powerful and complicated position for English authors to occupy, because Britain was at the same time enlarging its overseas empire by quite literally absorbing new speakers into its domains.

Collins's struggle to find forms that could represent oral voices was answered by the machinery of the poem, which seeks to recreate the context of an oral past in a printed text. While these struggles persisted throughout the late eighteenth century, Collins's confident assertion that his poem enabled readers to listen in on ghostly bards and distant singers is characteristic of an enthusiasm for experimenting with presence, as contingent and troublesome as that idea might be for twenty-first-century critics. Like Collins, the other authors analyzed in this book accepted the authenticity and passion of oral voices, while simultaneously understanding the sophisticated means by which that authenticity was constructed. They were self-conscious in their experiments about the technical and cultural effects of mediating oral voices, in ways that we have been prone to associate only with the media savviness of McLuhanite technological modernity. Yet, in the last age before sound recording made possible the mechanical reproduction of speech, eighteenth-century authors tested out print as a way to convey orality's ephemeral voices. Therefore, issues of authenticity, place, literary and cultural translation, speaking and listening, and cross-media intelligibility are all under examination in this book. Collins's poem is akin to a manifesto for this experimental poetics as it would be taken up over the next half-century. These authors searched for their own equivalent to Scotland's "Old Runic Bards" and wondered how best to present those voices in English verse.

NEW VOICE STUDIES

Questions about how to represent voice and how to theorize about it still preoccupy us today in ways that Collins and his contemporaries would have understood. Voice remains a slippery concept, yet it is pervasive in academic study whenever we mention the "speaker" of a poem, ask students to find their voices, describe a political election as citizens making their voices heard, or lament that the disenfranchised are voiceless.[32] In fact, the first decade of the twenty-first century has brought renewed attention to literary voice as a historically contingent concept, inaugurating what could be called the New Voice Studies. Working at the convergence of numerous fields, the New Voice Studies draws liberally from anthropology and folklore; oral, manuscript, and print culture; media theory; and sound studies. It attempts to create culturally and historically informed understandings about the nature of sound, practices of listening, and technologies of vocal reproduction. Among recent examples, Charles Bernstein on "close listening," Gina Bloom on the "motions" of early modern theatrical voice, Steven Connor on ventriloquism as it reflects on the "auditory self," Ivan Kreilkamp on "voice-in-writing" and Victorian literature, Maureen McLane on "balladeering," John Picker on "Victorian soundscapes," Yopie Prins on "voice inverse," Bruce Smith on early modern "acoustic worlds," Garrett Stewart on the "phonotext," and Lesley Wheeler on modern poetry's public performances use voice as an analytic with which to understand the creation of literary texts and the process of reading in a sensate, aural world.[33] These studies mark a radical break from those that came before by taking an abiding interest in the material forms of voice, which collect new metaphors and offer new vantages for these studies.[34]

The New Voice Studies seeks to describe these possibilities by inhabiting overlapping meanings. In this sense, it thinks of voice as a literary form responsive to numerous cultural, social, and political contexts at once. As a field, it approaches these forms as the concretion of those media transpositions that theorists call "remediation," thinking through the ways printed and written texts evoke a human voice. Connor names this process "sound hermeneutics," in which "giving voice . . . is the process which simultaneously produces articulate sound, and produces myself, as a self-producing being." For him, voice is not "something I have" but rather "something I do."[35] The emphasis in his "sound hermeneutics" on the action involved in making voice present is only a slightly different version of what Susan Stewart describes as a new "formalism" that is meant to analyze the aural and oral characteristics embedded within those printed texts that strive to imitate presence and immediacy.[36] Voice is thus a contract between authors and audiences, one negotiated by the text but not generated solely within it. It is also the literary principle that is able to understand and interpret that contract.

By expanding the range of media under critical investigation, while retaining attention to the text as a fabricated object embedded in social and historical contingencies, the New Voice Studies aims to integrate many disciplines and technologies without rejecting the methods of literary criticism from the past half-century. In fact, New Voice Studies responds to many of the upheavals of twentieth-century criticism. There have been three major stages in the modern study of literary voice. The first began in the early twentieth century with scholars like T. S. Eliot and (later) Francis Berry, who asserted that poetic voice was related to the physical attributes of an author. In reproducing an author's voice, the best one can hope, Berry claims, is for a voice that "approaches [the author's] as nearly as possible" when "the poem is said aloud."[37] These scholars associate voice with the physiology of the writer.

The second stage was dominated by the methods of New Criticism, which was a direct response to the physiological notion of voice. New Criticism detaches voice from the author and instead focuses on the rhetoric of speech to describe the action of a poem. William Wimsatt and Monroe Beardsley, for example, insist that when we read "we ought to impute the thoughts and attitudes of the poem immediately to the dramatic *speaker*."[38] Likewise, Ruben Brower argues that every poem is "dramatic" in the sense that "someone is speaking to someone else," and therefore every poem should be understood as a relationship between "the fictional speaker and auditor." "We hear the drama," Brower writes, in the voice of the poem.[39] For New Criticism it is the structure of this drama that is of paramount importance to literary critics; "the character of the speaker, his thoughts and responses, are reflected in style, structure, metaphor."[40] All of these elements are grouped under what Brower calls the "voice" and what Wimsatt calls the "verbal style" of a text. Therefore, New Criticism and the notion of the intentional fallacy are essential to the modern study of poetic voice. In the process of establishing the importance of the text, New Critics separated it from authorial biography and thus solidified the vocabulary of "poetic speaker" and voice, which remains integral to the protocols of close reading.[41] Establishing the self-sufficient text is prerequisite to understanding the speaker as something related to but still exceeding the authorial persona claimed by New Criticism. It turns "speakers" and "voices" into a textual effect.

The third stage of voice studies responded directly to New Criticism's attention to dramatic speaker and poetic voice. Generally, literary theory after New Criticism contextualized speakers and voices within the wider world and its history. Structuralism, like New Criticism, emphasized the importance of form; but rather than focusing on the self-sufficiency of the literary object, it made voice reflective of cultural situations. In structuralism's accounts of orality and oral culture, voice was a sign of presence. For critics like Walter Ong, the spoken word is the primary instrument for sustaining oral cultures. Orality, he argues, is an attempt to establish the presence of the words; "voice is not peopled with presences. It is itself the manifestation of presence."[42] Writing, in contrast, is technical, permanent, an object and a commodity.[43] Poststructuralism's arguments for the constructed nature of the self and subjectivity motivated a reassessment of this transcultural account of voice and of the authenticity of speech. Jacques Derrida and Deconstruction undermined the notion of speech and voice as physical presence.[44] Simultaneously, Mikhail Bakhtin's ideas of dialogism and polyphony sensitized literary criticism to the multifarious voices that make up literature's constitutive intertextuality.[45] The speaker is historically contingent, the product of a variety of forces within an enormous cultural matrix. Feminism, postcolonialism, and ethnopoetics emphasized the politics of voice. Hélène Cixous's notion of *écriture féminine* is predicated on the idea that a woman "must write her self . . . must put herself into the text"—a task accomplished when women seize "the occasion to speak" and make their bodies "heard."[46] This position has been refined by other feminist scholars, like Julia Kristeva, who draws attention to the "signifying practices" in an artistic work that make us believe there is a self that articulates. Ethnopoetics has developed ideas of voice in relation to experiences of colonialism and postcolonialism, such as Kamau Brathwaite's assertion that "nation language" makes suppressed voices heard and Edouard Glissant's insistence upon "creolization" as voices countering established literary norms imposed by outside powers.[47] These attitudes are paralleled in fields like composition studies, writing pedagogy, and narratology, which have focused on the social and grammatical mechanics of voice. Current methods of teaching writing and composition (at least in American higher education), which emphasize authors and the fictional projections they create (still called "speakers" or "narrators"), reaffirm voice as expressions of selfhood structured by discourses and learned techniques.[48] Since the 1960s, narratology has approached voice as a discursive problem and, together with linguistics, has tended to emphasize that voice and the speaking subjects are a product of grammar; cognitive scientists have linked voice to human consciousness and the function of the mind.[49]

By legitimizing their authoritative voice and by exploring the troubles of the authentic self, the burden of representation, and subjectivity, all of these theoretical camps assess the relationship among voice, self, and authority in their own characteristic manner. And all of these recent approaches stress that voice is inherently artificial; print does not speak, ink cannot make noise. Instead, we imagine that they can, in order to describe the emotional experience of reading. The effect of voice, Roland Barthes notes provocatively, is to create an audiotextual "hallucination."[50] One must always be aware of these ideas as metaphors, while remaining sensitive to how poems *formalize* this hallucination. My approach to poetic voice is therefore formal and historical: I unpack the relationship between a text's form and its metaphorics of voicing. In this, I follow the methods of Eric Griffiths, who describes the relationship between author and reader as a "printed voice." The "voice of the poet," Griffiths argues, "is not the voice of the person who is the poet," but rather something decided "in reading a text." "All writing is dramatic" in the limited sense that all "writing is an act of supplication to an imagined voice." Likewise, reading is an act of "imaginative voicing" that turns readers into an audience. In print, the writer and reader do not face each other, causing an ever present loss of community that Griffiths believes manifests itself again in the "further community," the "new life" of a reader who interprets and resuscitates the text.[51] And, like the theory of French scholar Paul Zumthor, which calls for a "poetics of the voice," my approach to the "printed voice" is anchored in the oral and its manifestations as textuality.[52] Zumthor felt that the orality of a text could only be captured as a "*performance*, not an origin," so we must modify our perspective and examine how to "*perform* the text in action."[53] But, rather than emphasize the relationship between the printed text and its more proper oral enunciation, as Zumthor and others have, I examine the performance *on* the printed page as the place to ascertain poetic voice. Metaphor implies and carries with it a formalization and a structure; changing textual strategies are the evidence of voice. Poetic voice *is* how it operates on the page. In this sense, poetic voice becomes a means of thinking *through* the printed text as the linchpin in the relationship between authors and readers, a relationship mediated by cultural genres that themselves must be historicized.

EPHEMERAL AIR, MATERIAL TEXTS

Formal analysis of the type found in the New Voice Studies (and in this book) depends upon a historically informed concept of voice. This history shows that the Enlightenment was a pivotal point in the study of voice, because it was that period which developed scientific explanations of hearing and sound. By 1750, as Jonathan Sterne notes, sound had become firmly established as an "object and a domain of thought and practice."[54] Since the mechanical preservation and reproduction of sound did not exist until the nineteenth century, printed texts are among the few access points we have to oral cultures and to histories of hearing. By attuning ourselves to this sensory history that Sterne describes, we may be able to hear the past of voice in new ways. Exploring the history of voice, including its roots in early modern and Enlightenment scientific, social, political, and literary discourses, can elucidate the peculiarities of these eighteenth-century poetic experiments.

Early modern theories of voice start with breath; Francis Bacon wrote that breath "maketh the *Voice* . . . for all *Speech*, (which is one of the gentlest *Motions* of *Aire*,) is with *Expulsion* of a little *Breath*."[55] "Invisible yet substantial, ephemeral yet transferable," voice was thought to be a "vapor," the effusion of a "leaky body," as Gina Bloom puts it.[56] This attitude made voice seem material yet unstable: it was "alienable from the speaking subject . . . temporarily attached, released, and exchanged *by* bodies," making Renaissance vocality a site of contention over subjectivity and agency.[57] This versatility and exchangeability of voices helped license early modern technological experiments with human speech. The Italian scholar Giambattista della Porta imagined an early version of telephony in 1584 when he suggested that a series of metal pipes could transmit voices over great distances. He also hypothesized an instrument "now upon trial" in which spoken words could be "shut up as in a prison" until the machine was opened again and the words were heard (a premonition of the answering machine).[58] Of course, della Porta was never close to developing the technology needed to realize these objects, but his preoccupation with different means of producing, transmitting, and preserving oral voices is characteristic of this scientific moment.

Nearly one hundred years later in London, the amateur scientist Samuel Morland invented the "tuba stentoro-phonica," a "speaking trumpet" to amplify the voice.[59] Morland's goal was to "magnifie (or rather multiply) the voice," and after testing his trumpet in St. James's Park, he boasted that he could be heard "word for word" from 850 yards away. In his theory of voice, magnification is multiplication, as the voice propagates itself through space by reproducing like an echo. Morland depicts this reproduction as a series of concentric circles that travel like "ripples on a pond," as diagramed in a pamphlet on his experiments (Fig. 1).

French anatomists in the early eighteenth century followed a track similar to that of Morland when they debated whether the voice was a "blown string" extending out into space, a tightening of the air, or perhaps a "lasso or a noose," an idea that anticipated the notion that voice can recall words and make them less ephemeral.[60] The idea that voice can be corralled or hung demonstrates that early experimenters attempted to find metaphorical equivalents for the physical effects of speech. In the late eighteenth century, the German scientist Wolfgang von Kempelen further explored these effects when he produced the first mechanical voice. He fastened a bellows to a box into which he had bored holes to which he attached thin reeds made from ivory. Operating the bellows by hand and covering some of the holes with his fingers, von Kempelen reproduced the sounds of human speech (in German) by forcing air through what he called his "speaking machine."[61]

In the early modern period, hearing was under investigation as well. Theories of sound developed over the period, as anatomists tested the physiology of the ear and philosophers speculated about the nature of waves caused by vibration, similar to the watery ripples represented in Morland's diagram. This ongoing exploration of sound led to attempts at creating hearing aids, such as Robert Hooke's glass ear trumpets, which he crafted in 1668.[62] Hooke imagined the ear as a film that was vibrating like an extremely complex drum skin.[63] His ear trumpets invert Morland's principles, using the speaking tube to capture voice rather than magnify it. Ear trumpets winnowed their way into general life, even

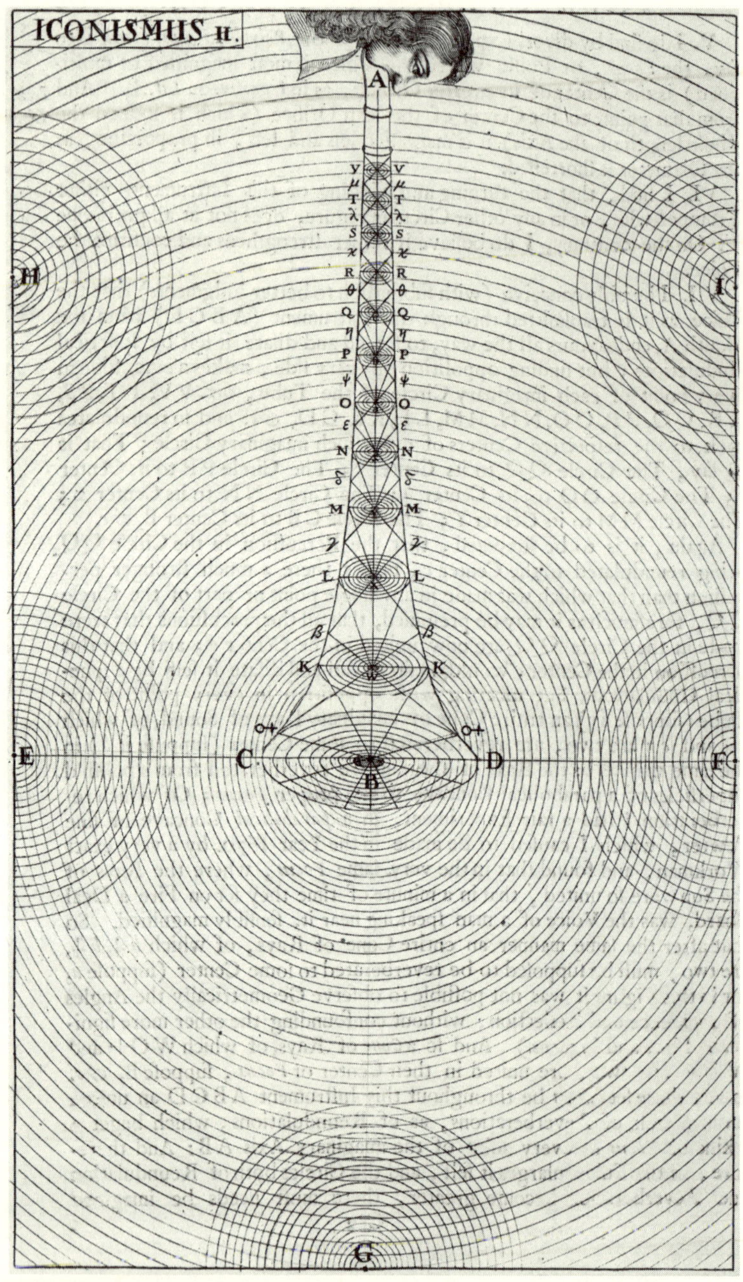

Figure 1. An illustration from Samuel Morland's *Tuba Stentoro-Phonica* (1672) showing something akin to sound waves emanating from his megaphone-like voice. Courtesy of the British Library Board (C.115.t.15).

Figure 2. Engraving of Scottish geologist James Hutton with his ear trumpet, mezzotint by J. R. Smith (1786), after the original by R. Cosway. Courtesy of the Science Museum / Science and Society Picture Library.

appearing as important personal objects, as in the portrait of the Scottish geologist James Hutton. Hutton, a forerunner of Charles Darwin, was hard of hearing for most of his adult life, and his ear trumpet became a constant companion. His deafness was such an identifiable personal characteristic that he had himself painted with his ear trumpet (Fig. 2).[64]

These ideas, gadgets, and experiments show that, long before the phonograph or the telegraph, voice and sound were topics of scientific inquiry and technological innovation.[65] Along with these inventions came new attention to the philosophical relationship between writing and speech. If metal pipes, copper megaphones, and glass trumpets might collect and project the voice, what about the written word? Having inherited ideas that dated back to Plato's *Phaedrus*, Renaissance authors felt that speech was more immediate than writing; Elizabeth I's tutor Roger Ascham taught that "no man can wryte a thing so earnestlye, as whan it is spoken."[66] Erasmus, who had more faith in handwriting than Ascham did, argued in 1528 that handwriting preserves the writer's voice: "when we get letters in their own hand from friends and fellow-scholars, how we welcome them and seem to be listening to their very voices and to be looking at them face to face."[67] For Erasmus, voice conveyed personality, and handwriting converted a person's physical voice into a transportable form, acting upon the reader in the same way as a face-to-face conversation. The early modern connection between letters and voices was so strong that pedagogical techniques arose in which students simultaneously spoke out loud and wrote what they had heard, in an attempt to "imbue [the] hand with the sound of [their] own voice."[68] This inherently metaphysical approach assumes that writing makes human voices present. It was accepted by many that the voice, the handwritten text, and the body were equivalent—even exchangeable—entities.[69]

This strong link between voice and writing differs from the perceived relationship between voice and print.[70] While Renaissance scholars believed that handwriting conveyed someone's personality, making the pen an extension of the human body, print was thought to be the opposite: impersonal and anonymous. The printing press separated the text from the body, creating an alternate persona that, while metaphorically related to the body of its creator, was also understood as being detached from it. This feeling about print had intensified by the eighteenth century, leading many poets to experiment with ways of recreating an intimate connection between author, text, and reader, while still maintaining the benefits of print's alternate personae.

Eighteenth-century poets looked to oral traditions as a way to reestablish this intimate connection. The uninterrupted integration of print into British society brought a "sharper awareness" of oral cultures and orality's special characteristics.[71] During the Enlightenment, the number of media classified as oral was vast and included elements from the many dialect communities throughout the British Isles; songs used during manual labor, recreation, and social rituals; the preservation of regional knowledge through storytelling; and public debates. All of these contributed to what Jay Fliegelman has described as the eighteenth-century's vibrant "culture of performance."[72] This variety was magnified by the fact that in early modern England songs and stories would "migrate promiscuously" between media as they circulated through society, making the "boundaries between speech and text, hearing and reading . . . thoroughly permeable."[73] Early modern reading itself was a "different and much more variegated species" than it is today, because it "centered on hearing the page as much as seeing it."[74] All of this indicates that the relationship between orality and writing in early modern England was "reciprocal," Adam Fox argues, and a hybrid product of "generations of cross-fertilization between oral, scribal, and printed sources."[75] The "cross-fertilization" intensified as print became a more prevalent part of everyday life. Print, rather than undermining or destroying orality, as most scholars claimed until recently, seems in fact to have expanded orality's reach. At the same time, the growth of the literary marketplace led authors to believe that they were in a moment of media shift that concretized orality and literacy as discrete ideas. As Nicholas Hudson contends, "orality is fundamentally a literate concept" that can only originate in the specific conditions that a successful print culture arranged.[76]

A pivotal point in this media shift was the revaluation of oral culture that occurred in the mid-eighteenth century. Paula McDowell reveals that an "increasingly positive idea of oral tradition" emerged from the "originally negative" notions that associated orality with living forms of vulgar speech, often uttered by women like London fishwives or female religious prophets.[77] While gendered notions of orality persisted throughout the period—for example, in the perception that polite women's singing could civilize an otherwise coarse commercial society—differences between "elite" and "non-elite" types of oral tradition continually eroded.[78] As McDowell demonstrates, vulgar orality was "sanitized" in a "close dialectical relationship with ideas about *print*."[79] The sanitized concept of oral tradition combined with a reconsideration of traditional oral performers, like minstrels and bards, to remake orality into something heroic and often masculine, rather than vulgar and feminine. Institutions that supported minstrels and bards, such as aristocratic patronage and national gatherings, dissolved gradually for three centuries. And, while traditional bards remained active during the eighteenth century, especially in more remote parts of Ireland, Wales, and Scotland, the meaning of their bardic performances changed radically. Whereas many observers during the sixteenth and seventeenth centuries saw bards as itinerant vagrants, not unlike the largely female ballad singers who wandered the streets of London singing for pennies, during the mid-eighteenth century bards were reimagined as an element of Britain's noble heroic past, in part because by then they were so rare. The Welsh author Iolo Morganwg seems characteristic of this shift in the perceived value of oral traditions. Morganwg refused to think of oral traditions as "confused" stories or as "*Old wives tales.*" The Welsh bardic traditions that his work invokes (which were almost entirely fabricated) were imagined to be heroic and trustworthy precisely because they were "recited annually" and thus were "guarded" from "deviat[ing] materially from the *Truth.*" The truth is safer, he suggests, in the custody of these oral performances than it is in "letters"—printed type and written script—that "skulk in dens and dark corners; we know not whence they come to light, we often know not how they came into existence."[80] For Morganwg, the public nature of orality, reclaimed from women ("*Old Wives*"), made its traditions more reliable than an unknown manuscript discovered in a dark room. This is a highly ironic position for him to have taken, considering the archival methods he used to create his own performances and his textual representations of ancient Welsh oral traditions (discussed in Chapter 2).

Like the heroic bardic traditions of Britain, other types of oral media (such as ballads, which had been dismissed as low) were, by the end of the eighteenth century, being seen as repositories of national values. While Thomas Percy had relied on manuscripts to compose his *Reliques of Ancient Poetry* (1765), later ballad scholars (for instance, Walter Scott) increasingly turned to oral reciters, whom they believed to be trustworthy sources of knowledge about the past. Oral sources came to be regarded as the most reputable ethnographic authorities.[81] Ballad collectors became ethnographers engaged in fieldwork, collecting evidence and preserving samples of an alien or earlier way of life practiced by what seemed to be a shrinking number of people. This ethnographic approach developed in classical scholarship as well. Thomas Blackwell in 1735 portrayed Homer as a "wandering indigent Bard" whose poems reflected the state of his society, and thirty years later Robert Wood extended Blackwell's conclusion by suggesting that Homer sang rather than wrote his poems.[82] These unorthodox opinions about Homer merged with the fad for medievalism and Celticism to create nostalgia for alternate versions of Britain's past. While the culture of Greece and Rome remained undeniably important to antiquarians throughout the eighteenth century, they also searched for historical British manuscripts, and these revived interest in long-lived British traditions.[83]

The elocution movement also contributed to the positive revaluation of orality. Thomas Sheridan, the most influential eighteenth-century elocutionist, championed the "living tongue," associating speech with passion, with "life, blood, and soul." For Sheridan, even a "man wholly illiterate," with "no other ideas of language, but what he has obtained thro' the ear," can convey his emotions with all the force of "nature."[84] His contemporary Daniel Fenning likewise argued that "each passion" was "expressed by a tone peculiar to itself" and Hugh Blair, a well-known eighteenth-century Scottish academic and writer (discussed in Chapter 3), agreed that "all the great and high efforts of eloquence must be made, by means of spoken, not of written, Language," even as each of them published treatises on oratory.[85] Parliamentary debates were transcribed by hand and circulated throughout England; some political figures, Harold Love notes, would give speeches with this eventual "scribal publication" already in mind.[86] The tenets of the elocution movement "carried over . . . into the realm of silent reading," Jacqueline George claims, creating the expectation that readers might "perform privately, in the theater of their own imaginations."[87] The close relationship between oratory, public performance, and silent reading offered fertile ground for authors seeking to use text as a means of mediating oral voices. In short, oral performance claimed a special prominence in mid- and late-eighteenth-century Britain, and eloquence was associated with the natural power of speech, with the heroic past, and with the changing capacities of readers to imagine reading texts as audible performances.

Not everyone agreed, of course. Samuel Johnson was strong in his denunciation of oral tradition, believing that "speech becomes embodied and permanent" through writing, and without writing, nothing that is not "very short" can be "transmitted from one generation to another."[88] Since, historically, language was spoken before it was written, Johnson intuited that speech was "unfixed by any visible signs, [and] must have been spoken with great diversity" before the invention of writing and print. He believed that this "wild and barbarous jargon" could only be organized and refined by writing; and oral traditions introduced inconsistencies that Johnson, creator of the *Dictionary*, expressly tried to sort out and rationalize using print.[89] Johnson worried, in fact, that the imperial expansion of Britain around the globe further imperiled the purity of the English language by introducing dangerously foreign speech. He remained uncertain whether his incredibly ambitious project to catalog and "fix" the English language could reverse this trend.[90] Such worry demonstrates what many intuited: that the mid-eighteenth century was a transitional moment for those diverse elements that we would now classify as orality—spoken performance, ballad collecting, Homeric scholarship, the elocution movement, medievalism and Celticism, and the heroizing of the bard.

GLOBALIZING POETIC VOICE

The feeling that orality was alien yet original and passionate proved to be a crucial aesthetic for eighteenth-century poetry. From the mid-eighteenth century and into the nineteenth century, authors refined the relationship between orality and ethnographic authority, aligning oral traditions with the exploration of unusual, remote, primitive, often non-European cultures. Whether celebrated as "noble savages" or dismissed simply as uncivilized, the inhabitants of the Americas, the Scottish Highlands, Ireland, central and southern Africa, and various parts of India and the Pacific were described as either preliterate, and thus exclusively oral, or as not yet having progressed beyond a dependence on the oral past. The popularity of stadial theories of history, which perceived societies as moving through ever more sophisticated stages, only confirmed the marginalization and exoticization of the oral, by describing these foreign cultures as mired in earlier periods of civilization.[91] "Orality" thus identified not just a mode or a set of techniques but a precise cultural situation, one which conformed with epistemologies that recognized oral cultures and performance as symbolic of an earlier, more primitive, and at times nobler way of life. By portraying Britain as aware of its heroic oral past, and yet literate, commercial, modern, and imperialistic, unlike many other parts of the world, authors redefined orality as a sign of foreignness and exoticism.

Stadial and climatological theories of human differentiation were attractive to eighteenth-century poets experimenting with voice because they focused on locales and cultures that maintained a more passionate relationship to their surroundings and thus a more natural artistic expression. To adopt these cultures' oral voices and adapt them to printed texts was to access this passion, which had been reduced, they thought, by writing and print. Alterity's alluring suggestion of authenticity is primarily what is under examination in these early versions of what is now termed cross-cultural poetics. These models of ethnic, cultural, and technological difference allowed authors to cast themselves imaginatively out toward other cultures, returning with an understanding of others' legitimacy, which these authors could mediate to their readers, as Collins does in his Highlands Ode. Such authority is predicated entirely on the energy and vibrancy associated with these unusual voices, oral performances, and exotic speakers. The period's obsession with authenticity and voices "going native" was therefore both symptomatic of an eighteenth-century crisis in the legitimacy of print and the system by which to resolve that crisis.

Information about these nonliterate cultures was frequently drawn from travel narratives, from Grub Street's world histories, and from outright literary fantasies. Eighteenth-century authors imagined oral traditions with characteristics, and invested alien cultures with values, that they desired for their poetry. Unsurprisingly, therefore, the sense that primitive societies possessed extraordinarily vigorous languages was widely accepted by English authors. For example, William Warburton argued that the Bible was the "primitive poetry of a primitive people" in his *Divine Legation of Moses* (1741). Continental European philosophers like Giambattista Vico, Étienne Bonnot de Condillac, and Jean-Jacques Rousseau championed living speech over writing, nurturing the idea that primitive languages were part of the "state of nature."[92] The East proved a reservoir of story and fable, as numerous orientalist fictions were translated and then consumed avidly by readers.[93] The Oxford University lecturer Joseph Trapp singled out "Eastern" arts as exemplifying the power of speech, believing that "eastern eloquence abounded . . . with metaphors and bold hyperboles."[94] Thomas Percy called for the reinvigoration of English poetry, arguing in his 1760s translation of the *Song of Solomon* that "cold European imaginations" could benefit from the warmth of Eastern metaphors.[95] Morganwg argued that his native Welsh countrymen were "aborigines" and that their language was the first on earth with a continuous, unbroken tradition. Hugh Blair claimed that the Scots were once "addicted to poetry," which made their compositions "forcible and picturesque."[96] The linguist and legal scholar William Jones (discussed in Chapter 4) suggested repeatedly that a Europe deadened by its obsession with classical Greece and Rome look further east, to Persia and India, for new inspiration.[97] In his 1782 *Essay on Epic Poetry*, William Hayley, a well-published but now overlooked poet, patron (of William Blake, among others), and translator, celebrated the "dark and distant source of modern Verse," which he located in the "Gothic Harp," the "North's wild specters," and the "Runic rhymes of many a *Scald*."[98] These media, he claimed, offered a "vigorous source" from whose "savage strength" English poetry drew "new vigor."[99] While much of the study of exotic cultures was motivated by pseudo-anthropological impulses and by the hunger for more colonial commerce, it was also strengthened by an interest in new aesthetics that might benefit English arts. Authors in this period drew from a variety of cultural idioms, each of which seemed more invigorating, powerful, and natural than polite neoclassicism.

During the mid-eighteenth century, therefore, the idealization of oral culture presented a way to pursue poetic innovation while avoiding the troublesomeness of actually dealing with existing oral practices. This does not mean that eighteenth-century authors were entirely ignorant of oral traditions or of other cultures. Whether oral traditions were brutish and savage or sophisticated and heroic was debated throughout the period. The Enlightenment exploration of the globe and the mechanics of colonialism made oral traditions a useful framework within which to draw cultural comparisons. This book does not seek to exhaust the locations where cultural and literary interactions between the oral and poetic voice were at work. Additional (albeit different) examples might be drawn from the Gaelic songs of Ireland, the syncretic folk practices of West Indian slaves, or the indigenous orators who so fascinated Americans like Benjamin Franklin. Nonetheless, one of the most important claims of this book is that poetry systematically assessed fictional oral speakers as a way to contemplate the affinities and differences among enormously diverse cultures and locations of the modern world.

These fictional speakers, a nascent form of comparative ethnology, served the national and imperial definitions of Britain and Britishness. Fuyuki Kurasawa calls this process the "ethnological imagination," the Western creation of "mythical representations" for non-Western cultures, which he dates to the eighteenth century. This ethnological imagination, Kurasawa argues, "anthropologizes" Western societies "to defamiliarize, to denaturalize, and situate their customs . . . through juxtaposition to a series of non-Western alter egos." At the same time that it created "problematic and flawed," not to mention self-serving, understandings of non-European cultures, it also motivated a "powerful self-critique" of Europe's colonizing nations.[100] Constructing this ethnological imagination was part of a strategy to apprehend European culture by comparing it with those of foreign peoples.[101] As the eighteenth-century author and member of Parliament Edmund Burke wrote with enormous satisfaction: "[W]e possess at this time very great advantages towards the knowledge of human nature. We need no longer go to history to trace in all its stages and periods. . . . now the great map of mankind is unroll'd at once; and there is no state or gradation of barbarism, and no mode of refinement which we have not at the same instant under our view."[102] Burke suggests that there is no longer any need to look into history to find the earliest stages of human life; instead, because of European exploration, historians can just look around the globe at other societies. His comment rightly has been interpreted as reflecting Europe's deeply held sense of superiority over other parts of the world. But it also bears noting that Burke's assertion displays a fundamentally comparative approach to cultural difference. The superiority of English culture is demonstrated not so much by its sophistication or its economic dominance as by the map itself, "unroll'd" so that the "gradation[s] of barbarism, and . . . mode[s] of refinement" are laid out for the English, making them the superlative witnesses to and consumers of the Earth's diverse customs.

Cultural crazes and public mania for the foreign were important influences on the developing ethnological imagination and its unrolled "map." These crazes included the expanding dominion in India and later the celebrity trial of impeached Governor-General Warren Hastings, the controversy over Macpherson's Ossian (poems said to be in the style of an ancient Scottish epic told by the mythological hero Ossian), the Celtic revival from the 1750s onward, and interest in the Pacific between the 1770s and 1790s. Less important to this study, but still significant for the period, are the century-long fascinations with the "oriental" tale, with Native American culture, and with the commercial and scientific exploration of Africa. The simultaneity of these crazes and their geographical diversity show that the British poetic voices of earlier centuries, while no doubt international in orientation, were not as plural, proliferating, and intense as they were in the late-eighteenth-century global world. One small example from Horace Walpole may serve as a larger portrait: after the explorer James Bruce returned in 1774 from Africa, where he had for years been looking for the source of the Nile, Walpole wrote acidly, "Africa is, indeed, coming into fashion. There is just returned a Mr. Bruce, who has lived three years in the court of Abyssinia, and breakfasted every morning with the Maids of Honor on live oxen." He continued, "Otahetie [Tahiti] and Mr. Banks are quite forgotten," referring to Cook's by-then famous expedition to Polynesia and to that voyage's botanist, Joseph Banks, who brought back reports and specimens of its verdancy and descriptions of its inhabitants' rituals.[103] Walpole's letter gives some insight into exactly how the Celtic revival, "Indomania," or the "craze" for the Pacific influenced the global aesthetics of poetic voice.[104] In his reaction, we see how these crazes and manias for the exotic are subject to the vagaries of fashion, coming into and dropping out of the public's attention quickly and capriciously. Yet Walpole also suggests that these locales are ultimately replaceable, even homologous, depending only on the exoticism of their publicity and the timing of the public's attention. Where once Tahiti was fashionable, now Africa is; tomorrow it may be reversed, or interest may move on to India instead.

Furthermore, in reading Walpole's comment we might see that the crazes are also interconnected, informing one another and teaching readers how to have pleasure in each of them. In an expanding literary marketplace, eighteenth-century poets capitalized on these crazes, not so much by offering descriptive scenes of foreign life, as travel narratives often did, but by dramatizing the voices and subjectivity of the speakers found there. The interest in translating cultural differences through literary forms produced what the eighteenth-century antiquarian William Shenstone described as an enormous "appetite" for "foreign poetry," an appetite aided by secondary publications of scholarly tools, such as dictionaries, grammar books, and fantastical world histories that spurred new concern with and comprehension of non-English verse.[105]

A cross-cultural and cross-media poetics based on appealing to oral traditions and foreign voices required the nascent ethnological imagination and the momentum of the cultural craze. Or, to put it differently, the poetics of printed voice adopted Europe's developing ethnological imagination as a way to operationalize its cross-cultural aspects. The experimental tradition uncovered in this book was informed by this ethnological imagination and at the same time rethought its essential components. In particular, I interrogate late Enlightenment ideas of primitivism, the oral-literate binary, the "state of nature," and climatological explanations of cultural difference. The poems in this book respond to broad cultural movements, while helping to represent these outsider cultures collected on the "great map of mankind." In fact, it seems that as the century went on, it became increasingly difficult to tell what it meant to be outside versus inside these cultures; the poems of this study rarely fit easily into imperial models of Britain as possessing a center and a cultural or colonial periphery. There can be no doubt that British authors were keenly aware of the networks and relays of the eighteenth century. London remained the most significant node of them all, as every aspiring English-language author understood, whether they were in Calcutta, Aberystwyth, or Edinburgh. Still, their poetry, engaging with an imagined ethnology, blurs the distinction between cultural categories (oral/printed, primitive/civilized), spatial coordinates (center/edge), and collective identities (colonizer/colonized, British/other) in the effort to create new kinds of voice to circulate across and through the edges of the British empire, often resting in London or other commercial centers before being dispersed again.

Although sincerely interested in translating the differences of alien cultures to English readers, the authors described here were aware of their role in cultural appropriation and the creation of collective identity, acts which were consonant with British nationalism and the colonial project. As Katie Trumpener notes, English literature was a tool by which the aesthetic served imperial ends. While this process is discussed more in Chapter 2, suffice it to say here that Trumpener claims that English literature constituted itself by the "systematic imitation, appropriation, and political neutralization" of cultural movements in the British Isles and the colonies. Bardic nationalism, by contrast, as found in Ireland, Scotland, and Wales, "binds the nation together across time and across social divides; it reanimates a national landscape made desolate first by conquest and then by modernization, infusing it with historical memory."[106] Trumpener's account remains a powerful explanatory system, but her schematization of authentic "bardic nationalists" and appropriative English authors has numbed us to the significance of other exchanges within eighteenth-century British culture. I argue that the local-imperial connections of the cultural nationalist movements that Trumpener brings to our attention demonstrate an evident, if sometimes fraught, collaboration with English literary traditions. These connections between English literature and cultures in Wales, Scotland, and India show that, while literary nationalism occurs under what Trumpener calls the "sign of the bard," the authenticity of bardic voice is consistently made (and remade) in texts: all bardic voices, like all poetic voices, are impersonations. From this vantage, we can work out another set of answers to questions about the role of poetic voice and bardic cultures in the creation of (and resistance to) a British state made up of regional and national cultures. Like Janet Sorensen, I hope to "track the contradictions of the attempts to legitimate the idea of a British national culture" by noting the internal diversity and connections among nationalist and colonial traditions.[107] The international orientation of this experiment with poetic voice provided English literature with new speakers, genres, and models of poetic voice. It also helps to explain why poetry proved to be such fertile ground for the assessment of nationhood.[108] The intra- and international posture of these mediated voices was relational: the link between English literature and marginal cultural nationalism was not a one-way appropriation but the politicized exchange of traditions in uneven hierarchies of power. Understanding the imperial drive of poetic voice refreshes our ideas about eighteenth-century poetry's political purposes and goals.

For the authors involved in this eighteenth-century experiment with poetic voice, the politicized exchange occurred in the printed poem and its renovation of earlier literary techniques and genres. Furthermore, these poems imagine the interactions of these spaces, identities, and cultures through metaphors of speaking and listening, remaking the distant onlookers of Burke's "great map of mankind" into situated listeners and vocalizers. The English poem attuned to these oral voices and foreign speakers promises the impossible—an unmediated experience of other cultures and past voices—while reflecting self-consciously on the tactics and practices by which this supposedly unmediated experience is created in texts and in acts of reading those texts. The English-writing author sits significantly in the middle of this model as a mediating figure required to make these voices intelligible to readers. This is the unspoken obligation of the barbarism and wildness that Diderot championed: there must be an author to tell it to us. The constitutive contradiction of the experimental poetics described in this book is that the authority supplied by ostensibly authentic, immediate oral voices was nonetheless mediated and grounded in the form of the text and in cultural relations and exchanges among the participants of the British state and its growing colonial empire. The poems that I describe in this study aspire to be what they cannot be; they are poems that want to be spoken out loud, like prophecies and pronouncements. They want to channel those exotic speakers—whether ancient Welsh bards or Hindu prophets—that they impersonate. The texts they create, and the readers they attract, are like the Tasso that Collins describes in his Highlands Ode, who "believes the wonders of which he sung." Eighteenth-century poets believed in the wonders of wild, unusual, passionate oral voices, yet they remained keenly aware that these voices were not pure authentic expressions.

This poetics of printed voice exists at the confluence of cultural forces, historical trends, and literary innovations, many of these international and transregional. And, while oral cultures were almost always thematized as historically distant and spatially remote, the texts that I have selected construct a fiction whereby their voices are made immediately available to the speaker via printed literature. The poems rarely engage with dialect or vernacular (though this is an important element of late-eighteenth-century poetry, particularly in Scotland). They also do not display those attitudes and techniques that would become crucial for nineteenth- and early-twentieth-century anthropology, with its emphasis on recording and transcribing of oral performance and folklore in seemingly objective or accurate ways. Eighteenth-century authors and scholars were less concerned with representing the actual practices of oral performance and more interested in creating a satisfying facsimile of what they thought were the stylistic effects of oral performances or the sound of foreign voices rendered in English. These experiments with mediating the voices of oral performance led to consideration of impersonation and ventriloquism as tools with which to revive the past or understand British expansion overseas. Ultimately, then, these appeals to oral voices are insistently about literature: they are a way of maneuvering within the literary by turning to what (and to whom) is perceived as outside of it.

Each chapter of this book emphasizes a different (though related) context in this experiment with printed voice. I begin with Thomas Gray, whose imitations from the late 1750s and 1760s of Welsh bardic voices and Scandinavian folklore serve as an alternate tradition for poetic experimentation with the oral and the alien during the eighteenth century. I show that Gray employed numerous strategies in his poetry to evoke a sense of oral performance. These strategies were not an indication that Gray abandoned the print marketplace, as some scholars have suggested, but rather an attempt to reform it. Gray's "Elegy Written in a Country Church-yard" (1751), "The Bard. A Pindaric Ode" (1757), and his later imitations of folklore, such as "The Fatal Sisters. An Ode" (circa 1761) and "The Triumphs of Owen. A Fragment" (circa 1761–63) reveal, imitate, and evoke bardic voices in innovative ways. In "The Bard," for example, Gray uses quotation marks to differentiate between kinds of voices, and he evokes the prosody of Welsh oral meters. In his imitations from the 1760s, he presents bardic voice without any framing—no quotations marks, no explanation about the speakers—in an effort to supply readers with an unmediated experience of these ostensibly wild, passionate oral voices. I compare Gray's extensive use of quotation marks, point of view, and mode of address with the practices of orators like Thomas Sheridan, Gilbert Austin, and Joshua Steele. Austin and Steele produced fascinating guidelines about how to recite printed poetry like Gray's. I include examples of their curious markings and an assessment of the impulse to "notate" poetry for public performance, and I link these notations with twentieth-century anthropological debates about how best to edit oral texts, for example, of Native American storytellers.

Gray's later poetry, especially "The Bard," was an important origin of the experimental tradition described here, and the voices and scenes of "The Bard" were taken up and adapted by an eclectic group of poets, including Welsh antiquarians who, like Gray, were fascinated by bardic voice. These antiquarians and authors pursued a related set of experimental techniques to imagine Welsh cultural identity as constructed out of the audible voices of the bardic past. Rather than rejecting Gray's representation of Welsh voices, Welsh authors instead borrowed from it. They even cited Gray's poetry as a way to legitimize their own printed voices, and they translated it into Welsh in public performances. These moments of allusion and citation show that collaboration existed between bardic nationalists and those English authors who appropriated from peripheral British cultures. Welsh authors saw the past as oral and audible, making voice, speaking, and hearing significant tropes in the construction of Welsh national identity. Examining the work of Iolo Morganwg shows how oral performance of ostensibly ancient epic poetry was an important part of Welsh cultural nationalism. Likewise, Felicia Hemans sought to create printed versions of fictional public performances to present oral voices. All of these poems addressed in Chapter 2 demonstrate the complex politics involved in fostering Welsh cultural nationalism by collaborating with English literary traditions.

Chapter 3 extends this discussion of the oral past as a means of building national identity by looking at the controversy surrounding James Macpherson's Ossian poems. Examining the Ossian poems as a printed object—as a fabricated thing—reveals that Macpherson's work provided another crucial turning point in the eighteenth-century experiment with reconstructing and mediating oral voices to English readers. I detail how Macpherson's writing creates a sense of oral performance in print by using personification, mode of address, archaic language, obsolete diction, and diacritical indicators like quotations marks. The narrative style of the *Fragments* (1760) and of Macpherson's two-volume expansion of the Ossian myth *Fingal* (1762) and *Temora* (1763) imitates the characteristics of oral discourse. This is particularly apparent in his use of repetition and tense shifts to create what I call "restored voices," those moments when the text approximates the experience of aural reception. Macpherson emulates bardic speech and the intimacy of its implied audiences as a means of creating a participatory mode of reading that aims to turn readers into auditors, a process that I term the "intimate hailing" of his texts. His poems were taken up especially by women writers, who revised and extended the intimate publics that accreted around his collections, demonstrating that women were important contributors to the redefinition of earlier gendered notions of oral performance during the eighteenth century.

The focus of Chapter 4 shifts to experiments with textualized oral performance in one of Britain's colonies. Impersonation and persona take on a greater role as the experiment with voice in print moves overseas to India and as British orientalists adopt foreign voices as a means of comprehending the vast domains that were being organized under the British flag. Chapter 4 takes up Anglo-Indian poems written during the 1770s and 1780s that impersonate Indian speakers. Their authors, mostly white employees of the East India Company, composed Indian characters and speech by orientalizing British cultural traditions and amalgamating English literary forms with Indian voices to produce a peculiar colonial idiom. They rewrote English poetry, filling it with Indian women who sing in heroic couplets and Brahmans who speak like Celtic bards. These authors sought to devise printed equivalents for the acoustics of oral and foreign voices (much as Gray did in his representation of Welsh bards). However, they also attended closely to the politics of impersonation and personae, using foreign content as a way to renovate conservative English literary forms.

These Anglo-Indian poems therefore are an important culmination of eighteenth-century poetry's impulse to listen outward from England for new inspiration and unusual speakers. This reading of Anglo-Indian poetry begins with the compositions of William Jones, a noted orientalist and legal scholar who took a position in 1784 on the Supreme Court in Calcutta. In his poetry, Jones portrays himself as an intermediary between Indian voices and English readers, and there is a strong similarity between his fictional Indian speakers and his function as a judge. The interrelationship of Jones's highly advanced linguistic skills and his Anglo-Indian poetic forms reveals how his colonial administration related to his experiments with English literary form.

The politics of these innovative poetic forms affected the impersonation of women's voices by male Anglo-Indian writers. I show that cross-gender impersonations of native Indian women created a complex sexual politics of imperial expansion, a structure that Gayatri Chakravorty Spivak discusses in her essay "Can the Subaltern Speak?" The chapter concludes by linking these gender impersonations with two revisions of Gray's "The Bard" which replace his Welsh speaker with Indian Brahmans. These rewritings of "The Bard" adapt the intricacies of Gray's poem to the specifics of Indian geography and cultural traditions, while simultaneously commenting on British colonialism in Asia. The impersonation of Indian voices and the creation of bardic Brahmans are examples of a "dislocated orientalism" that disembeds voices, shifting them between Asia and Europe to create new speaking subjects who reflect on colonialism. The multiplicity of these cultural appropriations and literary revisions force us to reassess the practices of orientalism and develop new ways to think about literature's role within it.

Voice and speaking personae thus become important in assessing what it meant to be British in the late eighteenth century. The complex jumble of racial and sexual politics at work in these impersonations shows that the addition of foreign voices motivated English poets to reconsider British cultural norms within the context of an expanding global worldview. Poetry, as Karen O'Brien argues, was not just an expression of a politics but an essential part of the "generation and elaboration" of thought about empire in the eighteenth century. She claims that when poetry ventriloquized native speakers and indigenous peoples it was an "uninformed ventriloquizing of an external point of view" that "never enabled genuine non-European participation in the debate about empire."[109] I disagree; I see the elaboration of foreign voices by British authors as the lucent backdrop upon which appropriations of colonial discourse were set to multiple ends that rarely can be classified as purely uninformed, repressive, or unimpeachably anticolonialist. In this way, I add to Suvir Kaul's idea that the eighteenth-century produced "poetry of contemporary globalization" that exhibits an "aggressive nationalism" which "desire[s] . . . a cultural power that would be more than literary."[110] Kaul has illustrated how poetic form can be both an instrument to manage the contradictions of an outward-looking and aggressively nationalistic poetry as well as a material record of the existence of those contradictions. All of the poems discussed here are examples of what he terms "anthems of empire," in that they offer an "ambivalent response" to the mercantile and colonial expansion of Britain and subject Englishness to comparative examination.[111] In my analysis of eighteenth-century poetry, following Kaul's international model, I discover a more dynamic sense of the colonizer that unflattens the operations of colonial power, showing that it included an uneven mixture of sympathy and collusion, evidence of which is fossilized in the period's literary forms and printed voices. Analyzing foreign speakers and subaltern voices raises pressing questions: Can European impersonations limn a subaltern subject, or are they always moments that extended imperialism? How deleterious is an anticolonial representation if it is ventriloquized? In what instances can ventriloquism and impersonation be seen as concordant with anticolonial representations?

The Coda concludes this line of inquiry by articulating a mode of archival reading that moves beyond appropriation and cooptation and that redescribes the link between colonial subjects and colonizing authors. I examine William Lisle Bowles's "Abba Thule's Lament for his Son Prince Lee Boo" (1794), a first-person monologue in the voice of a Pacific islander mourning the loss of his son, who had traveled with a British ship to England. Bowles's poem raises difficult questions about the role of authenticity and impersonation within postcolonial reading. I theorize an archive of the inauthentic that seeks to expand the colonial archive to include all of the impersonations, virtualizations, and appropriations of foreign speakers that circulated in the eighteenth-century British world. If we can strategically disable our desire to categorize texts according to their ability to reflect authentic, coherent cultural positions—colonizers, resistors, and so on—we might find additional vantages from which to hear the postcolonial lessons of eighteenth-century experiments with poetic voice.

CHAPTER 1

Thomas Gray, Virtual Authorship, and the Performed Voice

In the middle of a transition toward a fully developed literary marketplace from early modern notions of patronage and coterie circulation, eighteenth-century authors transformed and renegotiated their role in society. While the eighteenth century was not the first historical period to grapple with the effects of print on models of authorship—printing presses had existed in England since 1476—it was at this time that the widespread diffusion of printed texts seems to have necessitated a renewed examination of what it meant to be an author. Amongst this chaotic, rapidly changing social and economic situation, old literary questions were revisited: What constitutes an author's voice? Are authors and their voices the same? Do texts speak in voices? The answers to these questions about voice were twofold: first, the changing social dynamics between authors and readers that resulted from a growing literary marketplace altered authors' attitudes toward the virtual voices of the printed text; second, in response to these social and economic changes, authors experimented with different ways to represent oral voices on the printed page.

In the early eighteenth century, a confluence of factors spurred this reconsideration of the ideas of authorship, voice, and the print marketplace. As Paula McDowell has recently noted, the eighteenth century was a turning point in the construction of what we now call print culture.[1] This turning point was closely linked with the mid eighteenth-century revaluation of oral tradition, but it was also motivated by widespread economic shifts in print capitalism and changes in the nature of literacy and readership. Legislative circumstances, such as the lapse in 1695 of the Licensing Act, which had allowed preprint censorship of written works, and the abandonment of legal restrictions on the number of printing presses in England, led to increases in production of printed materials. More texts were being printed, exceeding an earlier high mark achieved during the 1640s during the political tumult of the English Civil War.[2] The print trade evolved into a marketplace industry, more motivated than ever before by competition among booksellers for the growing number of buyers. Increases in the forms of and venues for reading—journals and newspapers, pamphlets, posters, ballad broadsides; lending libraries, reading societies—meant that printed matter was more accessible than ever before. The spread of print drove social changes in the nature of reading; rather than focusing intensively on a few works, like the Bible, readers increasingly acquired and used a larger number of texts.[3]

One of the most powerful received narratives of literary criticism and cultural history is that with diffusion of print came a concomitant anxiety on the part of authors about exposure and alienation. Such a response suggests that authors closely identified with their printed productions. The withering of the amateur-patronage system and the rise of professional authorship established a new "ethos of productivity" motivated by the more rigid separation of authors and readers, making authors into producers and readers into consumers of commodified literature.[4] The result was the idea that printing a text always involves some level of technical alienation: sending a text out into the world as print means detaching it from its author.[5] Michael McKeon notes that printing is "an act of depersonalization that abstracts both author and reader from the concrete presence of face-to-face exchange."[6] Contra Derrida, he argues that eighteenth-century authors felt print to be a potentially depersonalizing act, unlike the more familiar intimacy of oral conversation and manuscript exchange. At the same time, print publication required not just the separation of the text from its author but also the circulation of oneself in the form of the text. A printed text was considered an extension of its author, whose person could be closely associated with the perceived qualities of the text. As Mark Rose elaborates, by the eighteenth century the literary work was "above all the objectification of personality. The commodity that changed hands when a bookseller purchased a manuscript or a reader purchased a book was thus personality no less than ink or paper."[7] The notion that print exposed authors, making them physically vulnerable, was a common fear, yet the impersonality of wide publication permitted authors to reach thousands of unknown readers in a way that is impossible for the localized techniques of spoken communication.

This potential contradiction affected the concept of poetic voice and textual persona that had thus far informed eighteenth-century texts. Before the advent of sound reproduction, writing—especially print—extended the human voice beyond the physical constraints of the body. In this way, print would seem to be another version of what Shaftesbury describes as one action of philosophy, to hold "us out a kind of *vocal* Looking-Glass, draw sound from our Breast, and instruct us to personate our-selves."[8] The poetic voice, then, is a kind of impersonation: the recreation of a virtual person in text, speaking to the reader. We might see Shaftesbury's *Soliloquy* not just as a philosophical argument but quite literally as advice to authors trying to survive and succeed in the world of modern media in which their personae can circulate widely.

In order to capture the immediacy associated with orality, authors realized that they needed to experiment with textuality. The effects of these innovations have been of exceptionally long duration. Despite the repeated (if varying) claims of New Criticism and post-structuralism that whatever we do as readers, we should *not* equate the author and the text, the controversies examined in this book were motivated by readers' expectations about the authenticity of the text and the link between an author and its speakers. Eighteenth-century readers, like modern ones, were apt to think of an author as all of the voices in a text. Yet, as print culture intensified during the eighteenth century, authors increasingly sought new ways to "personate" themselves in texts, with correspondingly innovative and catastrophic consequences.

In this chapter, I reexamine the career of Thomas Gray to explore these fraught issues of print circulation and poetic voice. Gray is typically seen as a gentleman-poet, a retiring scholar anxious to avoid the trials of the literary marketplace. His career has always been seen as pivoting around his enormously popular "Elegy Written in a Country Church-yard" (1751), which established him as the most widely respected poet of his era. Supposedly the antithesis of his contemporary Samuel Johnson, who famously quipped that "no man but a blockhead ever wrote, except for money," Gray has been portrayed as a relic of an earlier time, longing for a more intimate and friendly public sphere and anxious about printing his poetic works for payment.[9]

I argue that Gray, in addition to being this enticingly contradictory literary figure—a popular poet who nonetheless seems to have disdained publicity—was also the origin of an experimental tradition that sought to use elements and modes adapted from idealized eighteenth-century notions of oral performance as a way to reform the literary marketplace. This experiment operated in two interrelated ways. Gray approximated in his poetry some of the formal characteristics of oral culture in order to foster a sense of immediacy between himself and his readers. Yet, by inventing (and textualizing) a printed voice—an oral voice that enunciates (and is audible) as print—Gray simultaneously took advantage of the possibilities for a wider audience that the dissemination of printed texts offered him. Both "The Bard" and Gray's later imitations of Welsh and Scandinavian folk traditions from the 1760s use complex formal and editorial strategies to suggest the sense of vocal presence associated with oral performance. These literary techniques and editorial strategies constitute a poetics of printed voice.[10]

This experimental tradition is unlike the prolific, market-dominating masculine persona of an author like Johnson, yet it is no less deeply engaged with print. Gray's poetics of printed voice, rather than avoiding the literary marketplace, mark a concerted attempt to reformulate its operation. In place of a distanced, alienating model of authorship, based on the notion that texts circulate virtual versions of their authors, Gray attempted to substitute the immediacy of bardic performance as (paradoxically) channeled through the printed text, much as William Collins did in his Highlands Ode. Moving through Gray's career, from the "Elegy" to his imitations (from 1751 until the late 1760s) we can detect this evolving poetics. Gray's later poetry, often passed over by literary critics, was a direct response to the popularity of his "Elegy" and reveals a search for inventive notions of authorial personae and audience effect in an increasingly complicated printed world. The crucial difference between Gray and his early eighteenth-century predecessors like Alexander Pope and Jonathan Swift is that Gray explored how to adapt the idealized immediacy of oral voices in ways that they would have found vulgar. So, rather than turn away from the supposedly frightening popularity of the "Elegy," Gray's later poetry revisits and extends the textual mechanics of representing voice that the "Elegy" initially raises.

AUTHORING GRAY'S "ELEGY"

Three related poems illustrate the consequences of the shifts in modern printed authorship that motivated Gray's desire to reform the print marketplace: Lady Mary Wortley Montagu's and Lord Hervey's *Verses Address'd to the Imitator of the First Satire of the Second Book of Horace* (1733); Pope's *An Epistle from Mr. Pope, to Dr. Arbuthnot* (1735), which serves as a belated response to Montagu's poem; and Swift's *Verses on the Death of Dr. Swift, D.S.P.D.* (1738). All three of these poems explore the axis of body–voice–person in early-eighteenth-century poetry. Since at least two of these poems circulated in manuscript among smaller groups of friends and allies before they were made available in print, they show the degree to which print intensifies the dangers of disseminating oneself in the form of a text. For example, *Verses Address'd to the Imitator of . . . Horace* (1733), which directly attacks Pope and his writing, is generally attributed to Montagu and Hervey, a courtier and memoirist, although the *Verses* were published anonymously and authorship was identified only as "By a Lady."[11] This anonymity offered a safe haven to the poem's authors while mitigating the personal cost of their potential exposure to public critique.[12] Montagu and Hervey, motivated by their long-running feud with Pope, a former friend turned political opponent, consciously undermined the distinction between author and text to discredit Pope's literary reputation and to assault his body. As part of their verbal assault, Montagu insists that Pope's poetry resembles his body and its deformities. In Montagu's description of Pope, as Helen Deutsch argues, he "becomes a thing both written and written upon."[13] Pope was a hunchback, approximately four-and-a-half feet tall and by many accounts sexually impotent as a result of an illness he suffered as a child.[14] Montagu insists that no one could ever love such a physical freak:

> But how should'st thou by Beauty's Force be mov'd,
> No more for loving made, than to be lov'd?
> It was the Equity of Righteous Heav'n,
> That such as Soul to such a Form was giv'n
>
> (lines 48–52)

Pope and his texts are one and the same—the "Soul" given "Form"; the body made deformed. His verse cannot help but repeat those deformities, making it, like him, a "wretched little carcass" (70) and an "angry little Monster" (76). Readers can know that Pope's poetry is vulgar, Montagu implies, simply by looking at his person; alternately, his texts must be monstrous because they are the expressions of a contorted body. Montagu's dual focus on his body and the body of his texts exemplifies a cultural situation sensitive to writers' anxieties about print's ability to expose someone's body to literary and *literal* assault. Because his texts are like his body—monstrous and deformed—to assail his texts is to harm his body. Thus, Montagu crafted a poem that subverts the protections offered by earlier notions of poetic speaker and persona by insisting that in Pope's case printed text and human body are indistinguishable, regardless of who speaks in the poem.

Pope's responses to Montagu's assaults show that he, too, manipulated the continuum between his texts, his body, and his poetic voice. In the *Epistle to Arbuthnot*, he twists those deformities that Montagu satirizes into the embodiment of literary virtuosity. In response to his detractors, he asks rhetorically:

> Why did I write? What sin to me unknown
> Dipt me in ink, my parents or my own?
> As yet a child, nor yet a fool to fame,
> I lisp'd in numbers, for the numbers came.[15]

Pope disarms the attack upon his writing by dipping himself in ink, by making himself into the components of poetry: his blood is ink and his body the "lisp'd . . . numbers" he has spoken since childhood. The connection between the highly ordered couplets of Pope's poetry and his "indelibly marked" body, Deutsch asserts, is an expression of the "cultural imagination of authorship at a transitional moment" in the British "profession of letters."[16] If poetic voices and personae are virtual projections of an author, then Pope employed a strategy of bodily exposure in a cunning attempt to control the public representation of his personality as it circulated through polite culture in a textual form.[17] Pope's putting forward of his deformed body in his writing exemplifies the strategy, taken up by other poets during the eighteenth century, of manipulating the presentation of poetic voice and speaker for self-authorization and self-possession.

Swift adopted a similar approach in his *Verses on the Death of Dr. Swift*.[18] Like the *Epistle to Arbuthnot*, Swift's poem has an extensive autobiographical component. In the course of his poem, Swift makes himself dead, conducts a postmortem, and examines his life through the voices of other characters. The proliferation of voices in his poem is a proleptic attempt to control his literary reputation for posterity. At one point, objectifying himself, Swift imagines himself as a commodity in the bookshops of London, bound to be forgotten: "One Year is past; a different Scene; / No further mention of the Dean" (lines 245–46). In another episode, he voices his physicians as they conduct an autopsy on his body. After cutting him open, they pronounce satisfactorily that "all his Vital Parts were sound" (176). Swift's savage humor at the "sound" dead body is a comment on the alignment of the commodity and the author's person in the marketplace. If authors become their books, and voices are like their persons, then Swift's description of himself as a forgotten text or an autopsied body (with perfectly functioning organs) articulates a slight alteration to Pope's technique of exposing himself as a means of garnering the sympathy of his readers.

This manipulation is strongly evident in the lengthy final scene of the poem, when Swift asks his reader to

> Suppose me dead; and then suppose
> A Club assembled at the *Rose;*
> Where from Discourse of this and that,

I grow the subject of their Chat:
And, while they toss my Name about,
With Favour some, and some without;
One quite indiff'rent in the Cause,
My Character impartial draws:
(299–306)

What follows is an elaborate, flattering description of Swift as a politically independent, honorable man who "never Courted Men in Station" (325) and "bore continual Persecution" (400) from those more petty than he. This utterly self-aggrandizing voice is anything but impartial. It is Swift as he would like his readers to remember him. By making himself into many virtual voices, he creates a flatteringly multiperspectival poetic posterity that is difficult to dispute. These tactics allow Swift to speak as someone else, to adopt an "impartial" persona with whom to enumerate his enormous virtues. Print allows him to preserve this characterization and circulate it among an audience that does not know him but will, no doubt, readily pronounce their opinion of him once he is dead. By making himself dead, Swift beats them to the punch and takes up *all* the different voices, affirmative and negative, on his life before anyone else has the opportunity to do so. Swift knows that death, like being in print, means losing control of one's person; using structures of voice and persona, he regains some sense of self-possession. That he resorted to poetic self-murder and resurrection as an impartial voice demonstrates the measures needed to control one's reputation in a media world that circulates bodies in the form of texts.

These three poems share an interest in textuality's ability to project an author's presence. Voice, in this case, becomes shorthand for the intricate techniques by which authors make themselves virtual in a text. It also provides a type of prophylaxis against the very real effects that can rebound upon the body of authors because of their writing. Gray's "Elegy" is symptomatic of these shifting notions about poetic voice and authorial identity. Gray often felt the same anxieties as other writers did about print's ability to expose authors to unknowing and distant publics. Throughout his life, he carefully controlled what and when he published, because he understood print's ability to put his reputation at the disposal of others. He often imagined the literary marketplace as an assault; for instance, he refused an attempt by his publisher to print an engraving of his face on a collection of his poems, writing grimly that he would not "suffer my Head to be printed" as he thought it would be worse than the "Pillory."[19] At another point in his career, he expressed disapproval of readers who complained about his poetry but still "bought me . . . & put me in their pocket," referring to collections of his poems (*Corr.*, 2: 532). Like Swift, who worried that his verse, "when printed and published, is like a common Whore, whom any body may purchase for half a crown," Gray was concerned that printing his poetry meant that anyone had access to his body for the right amount of money.[20]

Gray resisted the potential for readers to buy or possess his person by making his poetry more impersonal as his career progressed. Before its publication in 1751, the "Elegy" went through a series of revisions. Initial drafts of the "Elegy" were shorter and had a single first-person speaker. While revising, Gray shifted his use of pronouns so that it became more difficult for crucial lines to be read as the voice of the poem's first-person speaker. He lengthened the poem substantially by including new characters (the "hoary-headed swain") and generic frames (the poem's final epitaph). The hoary-headed swain and the epitaph mark important turns in the development of the poem, because the potentially autobiographical first-person speaker is withdrawn. The multiplication of speakers occludes any sense that there is a single subjectivity behind the pronouncements of the poem which could be aligned with Gray, much as Swift did in writing his *Verses*.[21] The personal becomes more impersonal as other characters overwhelm the poem's first-person speaker.[22]

More recently, scholars have focused on what they perceive as the antagonism between oral and literate modes in the poem's revisions, the residues of which are evident in the poem. There is the famously "mute inglorious Milton," who was never able to speak, and the "unlettered muse," who presumably inspired the "rude forefathers" of the hamlet. Oral modes are accentuated by the inclusion of the hoary-headed swain, who tells tales about the rural village, rather than writing poems, like Gray. The epitaph is printed in italics, distinguishing it from the rest of the poem. Quite often during the early eighteenth century, italics were used to indicate speech, as readers of Daniel Defoe's novels will recall. However, in the "Elegy," italics indicate the shift from the orality of the speaker and the hoary-headed swain to the engraved epitaph on the tombstone. The shift in modes—from aural discourse to silent reading of written words—is marked by the shift to italic type. Expressing this media shift as a change in typeface is one experimental aspect manifested in the "Elegy."

For John Guillory, these characteristics indicate the poem's interest in the "cultural capital" of vernacular literacy, against both the knowledge of classical antiquity and the traditional oral storytelling that had dominated early modern culture. The "Elegy," in short, narrates what was changing in eighteenth-century British culture. In this reading, the poem is about what creates the conditions for speech, and it is therefore also an elegy for the intimate, face-to-face relationships of orality against the backdrop of a would-be Milton who has been made "mute" by rural poverty and illiteracy.[23] For other scholars, the real mourning of the "Elegy" is for the presumably noncommodified relations between singer and listener found in oral storytelling. Gray, wary of print publication, composed a poem that longs for a simpler cultural era.[24]

These analyses are helpful to the degree that they show Gray engaging with oral modes as a way to assess the consequences of print publication. But these portrayals of storytelling in the poem, rather than revealing Gray's disdain for print publication, in fact indicate the beginning of his career-long reconsideration of what it means to be a published author. He appeals to oral culture, not to eulogize it, but to discover how to make print imitate it. This might be demonstrated most clearly in Gray's reaction to the printing of the "Elegy." Gray sent the manuscript of the poem to Horace Walpole, who circulated it among select members of London society. But Walpole distributed it so widely that it was discovered and about to be published by the *Magazine of Magazines*, a new and relatively unknown journal. Gray was furious and quickly brought out an authorized edition of the poem with a more reputable publisher. Although published anonymously, the work was widely reprinted and attributed to him very soon thereafter. Following the successful reception, Gray thanked Walpole, joking that Walpole had acted as the poem's "father," with Robert Dodsley, his printer, serving as the "nurse" at the poem's birth. And, despite the rapidity of publication, Gray told Dodsley that he hoped his poem would have the "best Paper and Character" (*Corr.*, 2: 341; Feb. 11, 1751). The poet saw the "Elegy" as his infant—it was a poem that had come from his body. Like a parent, he followed its travels through the world, assiduously noting on a copy of the poem the different locations where it was subsequently reprinted.[25] Throughout his life, Gray was meticulous about how his works appeared in print. Understanding his poems to be extensions of his body led him to control precisely how that body was manifested. Yet, in this instance, Gray saw the parturition of his text as requiring the efforts of at least two other men, Dodsley and Walpole, giving the "Elegy" quite a queer birth. One interpretation of this situation may regard Gray as the mother of this poem and its voices; given recent scholarship on Gray, however, I am tempted to read it also as a metaphor for the collaborative nature of printed voice. That Gray included his printer as part of the poem's creation and Walpole as part of its pre- and post-print circulation shows his sensitivity to the many factors involved in bringing a text to public view. And, by figuring the birth of his printed voice as a collaboration among men, Gray ran counter to the typical alignment of the authentic singular self with poetic voice that would begin to prevail at the beginning of the nineteenth century.[26]

Gray's consideration of these aspects of publishing imply that he was not necessarily a retiring gentleman-poet uninterested in public presentation of his works. Such attention to the details of publication belies the general assumption (which, admittedly, he himself cultivated) that he was indifferent to the publication of his work. Uncomfortable with the virtual elements of modern authorship, Gray, rather than retreating from publication, engaged it on his own terms, by depersonalizing his poems and proliferating their speakers (and, as I have suggested, their authors and creators). Voice becomes a strategy for displacement and for self-containment. Therefore, the "mute inglorious Milton," the storytelling "hoary-headed swain," and the heroized village elders are not added to the final version of the "Elegy" to replicate some nostalgic oral past. These speakers—representatives of oral traditions—are an alternate future for print. Gray's revisions of the "Elegy" resulted from the attempt to manage his public exposure in print and led him to devise new models of the author-reader relationship that imitated and evoked the immediacy of storytelling and oral performance.

PERFORMING GRAY'S "ELEGY"

In a treatise from 1806 called *Chironomia,* which takes Gray's "Elegy" as a central example, the rhetorician Gilbert Austin presents a system of notation that he claims allows readers to "record and to communicate in writing . . . the various requisites for perfect rhetorical delivery."[27] Austin marked up the "Elegy" with notes that instruct readers how to modulate their voice, position their feet, and move their hands, arms, and head as they recite the poem. These notations are a version of the oral future of the printed "Elegy" that Gray himself might not have been able to imagine. An amateur chemist accustomed to publishing papers with the Royal Society of London, Austin used tables and diagrams to systematize the representation of spoken voices in a poem already filled with printed ones.[28] To twenty-first-century readers his textual annotations and emendations might look arcane and chaotic. Nonetheless, they raise important practical and epistemological questions about how best to represent the spoken voice on the printed page. Austin's version of the "Elegy" blooms with letters, numbers, italicized marks, lines and accents, above and below the text, particularly in the first three stanzas, in an attempt to convey the immediacy of oral performance (Fig. 3). Ironically, Austin's method increases the amount of printed text, requiring readers to refer to tables and diagrams to decipher his some-

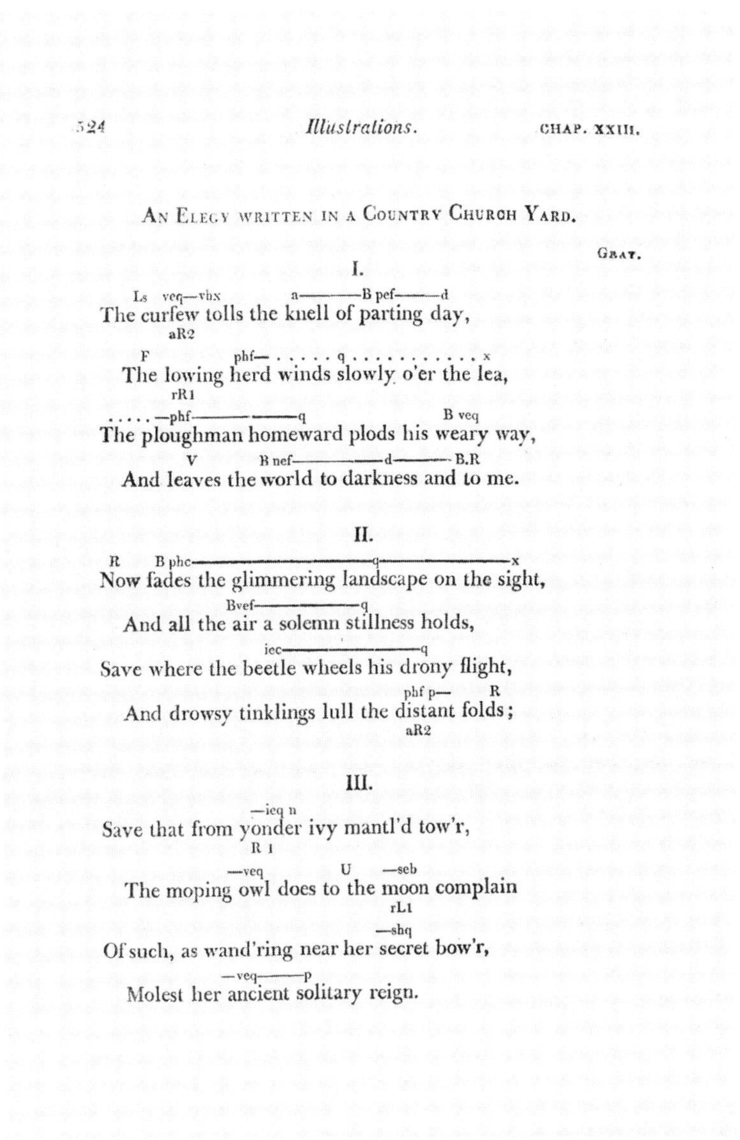

324 *Illustrations.* CHAP. XXIII.

AN ELEGY WRITTEN IN A COUNTRY CHURCH YARD.

GRAY.

I.

Ls veq—vbx a———B pef———d
The curfew tolls the knell of parting day,
aR2

F phf— . . . . . q x
The lowing herd winds slowly o'er the lea,
rR1

. . . . . —phf——— ———q B veq
The ploughman homeward plods his weary way,

V B nef———d——— B.R
And leaves the world to darkness and to me.

II.

R B phc———q———x
Now fades the glimmering landscape on the sight,

Bvef———q
And all the air a solemn stillness holds,

iec———q
Save where the beetle wheels his drony flight,

phf p— R
And drowsy tinklings lull the distant folds;
aR2

III.

—ieq n
Save that from yonder ivy mantl'd tow'r,
R 1

—veq U —seb
The moping owl does to the moon complain
rL1

—shq
Of such, as wand'ring near her secret bow'r,

—veq———p
Molest her ancient solitary reign.

Figure 3. Gilbert Austin's rhetorical notation of the first three stanzas of Gray's "Elegy Written in a Country Church-yard" (1806). Courtesy of the British Library Board (11805.i.18).

times counterintuitive system. The added detail overwhelms the poem, making it almost unreadable.

Austin encourages readers to convert his notations into an actual oral performance, matching the text with a gesturing body and a living voice. The notes for the stanzas shown here indicate that readers or performers should slowly step forward and then return to their original positions, all the while swinging their arms in front of them, pointing toward the horizon, before ultimately lowering their arms to their sides. The connection between the plot of Gray's poem and the action of the performance is explicit: as the sun "leaves the world to darkness and to me," reciters' hands fall to their sides, following the sun's descent. Simultaneously, performers turn their heads toward the audience, "listening" to the cowbells as the herd returns home.[29] Performers' voices and bodies imitate and enact the details of Gray's poem. Gestures dramatize and narrate the poem's setting and events. The goal of these actions, Austin claims, is to communicate emotions: "impassioned compositions delivered with proper feeling and expression open . . . to the view of the hearer the internal operations of the speaker's mind."[30] But which speaker? The oral performance could express the emotions of the oral performer. Or it could evoke the speakers in Gray's text—the first-person narrator and the hoary-headed swain—whose feelings can be definitively sensed only when the poem is dramatized aloud. Regardless, it is not clear whose mind speaks when the performer recites Gray's "Elegy" according to Austin's system. In his attempt to rationalize how printed texts can record and represent the physical actions of the body and the modulation of the voice, Austin offers few clues about the effect of performance upon the status of the printed text.[31]

Austin's approach is closely linked with the elocution movement, an enormously important cultural development in the eighteenth-century Anglophone world. For elocutionists, who, like Austin, adopted a scientized approach to oratory, rhetoric was a means of inciting and influencing the passions. In *The Art of Speaking* (1761), James Burgh declares that good oratory should be almost coercive in its power. "Like irresistible beauty," he claims, it should transport the speaker; "it *ravishes*, it *commands* the *admiration* of all, who are within its reach . . . . the hearer finds himself . . . *unable* to resist . . . . His *passions* are no longer his *own*. The *orator* has taken *possession* of them."[32] This breathless description makes oratory into a contest of wills, in which the speaker needs to invade and take control of the listener's body in a way that would seem to Pope or Gray a familiar danger. Thomas Sheridan, the most important elocutionist of the eighteenth century, agreed with Burgh, lamenting, "[O]ur greatest men have been trying to do that with the pen, which can only be performed by the tongue; to produce effects by the dead letter, which can never be produced but by the living voice, with its accompaniments."[33] Sheridan presumably fought the "dead letter" not just by improving public speaking but by preserving the unique character of spoken communication.[34] For Sheridan and Burgh, the goal of oratory was to excite the passions and reenergize the body through the living voice. Of course, like Austin, both of Burgh and Sheridan argued for the advantages of their own systems in printed treatises.

These rhetorical systems and oratorical philosophies led to practical methods of marking up the written and printed text so as to retrieve the "living" voice. Thomas Jefferson composed a copy of the Declaration of Independence that included accents (single and double quotation marks) that seem to indicate different reading speeds and the length of pauses after words.[35] Jefferson's friend Benjamin Franklin, in a letter to the dictionary-maker Noah Webster, proposed that printers reform their presentation of texts to make speaking them easier. In one example, he suggested that printers place question marks at the beginning rather than the end of sentences, so that readers could anticipate the need to inflect their reading voices.[36] The British rhetorician Joshua Steele developed a scheme for transcribing the prosody of a text; based on a musical scale, it attempts to answer how we speak texts' voices.[37] Steele used symbols to explain the different tones and gradations of voice, and his diagrams illustrate the system (Fig. 4). Consider his markings upon a well-known couplet from John Denham's 1642 poem *Cooper's Hill* (Fig. 5).

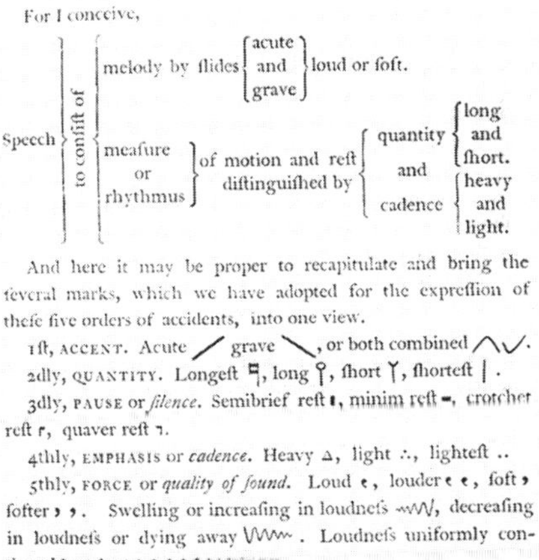

For I conceive,

Speech to confift of
- melody by flides acute and grave loud or foft.
- meafure or rhythmus of motion and reft diftinguifhed by quantity (long and fhort.) and cadence (heavy and light.)

And here it may be proper to recapitulate and bring the feveral marks, which we have adopted for the expreffion of thefe five orders of accidents, into one view.

1ft, ACCENT. Acute / grave \, or both combined ∧∨.

2dly, QUANTITY. Longeft, long, fhort, fhorteft.

3dly, PAUSE or *filence*. Semibrief reft, minim reft, crotchet reft, quaver reft.

4thly, EMPHASIS or *cadence*. Heavy △, light ∴, lighteft ..

5thly, FORCE or *quality of found*. Loud, louder, foft, fofter. Swelling or increafing in loudnefs, decreafing in loudnefs or dying away. Loudnefs uniformly continued.

Figure 4. The central elements of rhetorician Joshua Steele's notation system for the performed voice, from *An Essay Towards Establishing the Melody and Measure of Speech . . .* (1775). Courtesy of the British Library Board (RB.23.b.3187).

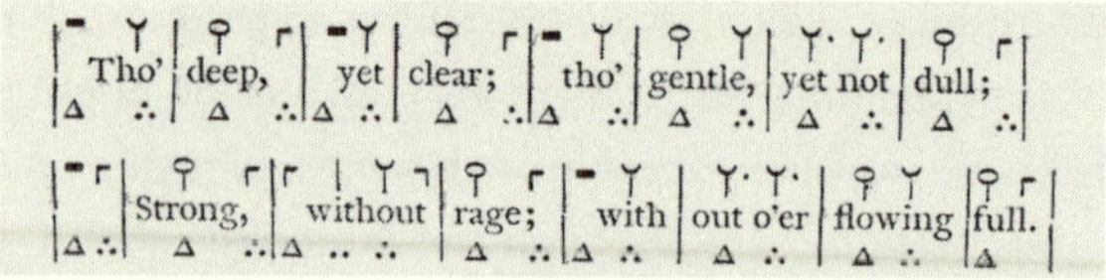

Tho' deep, yet clear; tho' gentle, yet not dull;
Strong, without rage; with out o'er flowing full.

Figure 5. Steele's notation of a couplet from John Denham's *Cooper's Hill* (1642). Courtesy of the British Library Board (RB.23.b.3187).

Of course, there are many ways to interpret these excerpts. One might see Steele's version as simply a reprinting of Denham's poem: a quotation. Another reading might interpret the markings as a poem that has been annotated with alien-looking runic symbols. Yet another interpretation might understand them as an inadvertent form of visual poetry, perhaps akin to George Herbert's pattern poem "Easter Wings" (1633). Regardless, while seeking to explain an animate aural text, Steele created his own densely visual one. His system possesses its own aesthetics of the printed voice, even though it claims only to explicate another's artistic object. Steele, Jefferson, and Austin, in their attempts to adapt a literate form for oral voices, created idiosyncratic, visually rich printed artifacts.

A related set of ways to edit speaking voices on the printed page is found in the investigations of modern anthropologists. Over the past thirty years, anthropologists have debated the best way to represent oral storytelling. They share with eighteenth-century rhetoricians the desire to create the correct editorial form with which to communicate the spoken word. After his studies of Zuni performances, Dennis Tedlock wrote, "[I]f the notation of the audible text of a storytelling event is to provide a *performable text,* it will have to follow a path between the conventions handed down in literate tradition and the purely hypothetical goal of total notation."[38] To interpret properly the traditional oral performances, Tedlock says, anthropologists must invent an "*open text,*" a text that "forces . . . the reading eye to consider whether the peculiarities of audible sentences and audible lines might be *good speaking* rather than *bad writing.*"[39] Tedlock proposes that texts create the "possibility of a further performance," achieved by a system that uses the variability and sophistication of typography as one way to encode an oral performance: "small or light type" for soft sounds, "large or bold type" for loud ones, and white space for silence.[40] Tedlock's "open text" is the literary and editorial equivalent of the spoken performance, and it is necessary, he argues, to record correctly the oral knowledge of traditional cultures.

As we read a "performable text," whether it is Austin's version of the Gray's "Elegy" or Tedlock's Zuni folk traditions, we are asked to determine if it is "good speaking." While Tedlock admits that completely notating a text is "hypothetical," he asserts that the goal of these systems is to return oral poetry to participation, since "an oral poetics that begins with living oral traditions is by its nature participatory."[41] The anthropologist Johannes Fabian likewise seeks to "document performances" in ways that allow them to be "re-oralized."[42] These documents would demand a "capacity to reenact or recreate the oral performance that is the source of the text."[43] The text itself would be like a set of signs, Fabian argues, that match with a "voice through which the text will take on a body—an audible body," because "oralization, that is, recourse to audible speech, actual or imagined, is an essential part of our ability to read texts."[44]

Tedlock and Fabian share an interest in capturing, recording textually, and reperforming the aural elements of performance in ways that are shockingly similar to the eighteenth-century experiments of Austin and Steele, which also sought to return texts to a spoken voice. Yet Tedlock and Fabian, like Austin and Steele, neglect to account for the ideological dimensions of literary forms. In attempting to understand the interaction between the oral and written texts, we must be careful not to fetishize performance, so that it seems rooted in an authenticity that precedes aesthetic or cultural forms. As Eileen Julien notes, it is necessary to reveal the ideological role of aesthetic decisions and the aesthetic aspects of ideology—that is, the cultural form that ideology takes. The attempt to encode and to re-oralize will always lead to a gap between the performance and the text. Julien suggests that, rather than trying to find the orality in a work as a way to bridge this gap, we turn our attention to the text's use of orality as a metaphor for its own form.[45] The necessary point of investigation is at the intersection of the formal and ideological—unraveling what Julien calls the "polyvalent symbol" of oral performance by exploring how it serves specific imaginative and aesthetic ends, in this case, of eighteenth-century poetry and its evolving representation of oral voices in the printed text.[46] The search for a visual form of the "living voice" has proven extraordinarily productive of new *literary* forms, even if the attempt to create a perfect printed equivalent for oral performance is by definition impossible.

IMPERSONATING THE BARD?

How did Thomas Gray use print to frame the speakers of his later poetry? After the "Elegy," Gray sharpened his appeals to oral voices to construct alternate models of the relationship between authors and readers. Like Austin, Steele, and modern anthropologists, Gray explored alternate ways of editing the oral voice. In his later poems, orality serves as both a metaphor and a concrete structuring mechanism for the poetic voice. But, rather than portraying a version of rural village storytelling, as he does in his "Elegy," Gray turned to a different kind of oral performance: that of medieval Welsh bards and of Scandinavian folktales.

Arguing that Gray intervened in the literary marketplace by appealing to an idealized oral performance might seem counterintuitive, since orality is often believed to be the antithesis of print. Recent critics have argued that Gray's interest in bards and oral cultures stemmed from his uneasiness with the professional authorship and public acclaim that accompanied the success of the "Elegy." Linda Zionkowski states that by embracing older models of authorship Gray was attempting to "recreate a pre-commercial past" as an alternative to the print marketplace.[47] Suvir Kaul describes Gray's attraction to Welsh and Scandinavian bards as an attempt to portray the "disenfranchised eighteenth-century poet ventriloquizing the voice of ancient cultural empowerment, finding in a feudal poetics a nostalgic celebration of bardic potency."[48] Imagining bards as secure, empowered, and respected poets supposedly eased the difficulty of negotiating between the desire for public literary authority and the aversion to market demands, concerns common to Gray's earlier poems, such as the "Sonnet on the Death of Mr. Richard West" (1742) and the "Elegy."

These accounts of Gray's relationship to oral culture do not explain why he, in allegedly trying to recreate a "feudal poetics" or revive a "pre-commercial past," repeatedly relied on commercial publication. Secure in a fellowship at Cambridge University, Gray did not publish for money. Uninterested in party politics and dismissive of courtly favors, he did not publish for patronage. If the goal of his later poetry was to escape the fetters of print by reverting to the inherently nonliterate relationship between performer and listener that made oral culture so attractive, why did Gray persist in publishing poetry at all after the "Elegy"?

I suggest that in his sweeping ode "The Bard" and in his later imitations of Welsh and Scandinavian oral poetry, such as "The Fatal Sisters" and "The Triumphs of Owen. A Fragment," Gray was extending the initial explorations of print-mediated orality which he made in the "Elegy" by positioning himself as an editor and translator of bardic voices. For "The Bard," he developed an array of typographical and literary techniques with which to make print seem to speak with the same passion and wildness that he saw in Welsh bardic singing.

He experimented with ways to textualize the face-to-face intimacy of an oral performance, setting it against the alienation of professional authorship for pay and the circulation of the self in the literary marketplace.

After the public reacted negatively to esoteric elements of "The Bard," Gray modified his approach to printed voice. Whereas the Welsh voices in "The Bard" are internally qualified by a verse narrator, the bardic voices of Gray's imitations are presented on their own, framed by a series of paratextual prefaces and annotations. These paratexts, by discriminating between Gray's editorial voice and the imitations' speakers, establish the opportunity—and the textual space—for bardic voices to appear without the kind of internal framing that exists in "The Bard."[49] With his imitations, Gray created a literary form that he believed allowed the reader to experience unadulterated bardic voices. Although most scholars view Gray's later poems as retreating into nostalgia for medieval modes of cultural authority or as simply appropriating the authenticity of marginalized figures, I suggest that he turned to oral cultures as a way to construct a poetic voice that would speak powerfully to particular audiences, as he felt bards once did, while simultaneously transcending the physical constraints of space and time in a way that can only be achieved through print.

"The Bard" revives a tale—suspected then and subsequently disproved—that the thirteenth-century English king Edward I executed all the bards while invading Wales. In Gray's poem, the last living Welsh bard alone confronts Edward's oncoming army. This poem, started in the early 1750s but not completed until 1757, signaled an important shift in Gray's career, and it encouraged his contemporary authors to attend to the ancient ballads, folk songs, and runic poetry of traditional Scottish, Welsh, and Irish cultures.[50] A short explanation of the poem he penned in one of his commonplace books makes clear that the poem experiments with representing bardic voice. Gray asserts that in the poem the bard calls out to Edward with a "voice more than human . . . and with prophetic spirit declares, that all his cruelty shall never extinguish the noble ardour of poetic genius in the island . . . and that men shall never be wanting . . . boldly [to] censure tyranny and oppression."[51] The description of the bard censuring tyranny in a superhuman voice constructs a complex political allegory that connects Welsh resistance to English incursion with the preservation of Britain's poetic genius. By resisting the English invaders, the Welsh bards are portrayed as defending their political independence and their indigenous culture, the two essential attributes, in Gray's opinion, of poetic vibrancy. The poem establishes a link between liberty and verse that is secured by the bard. But even as the bard calls out to condemn the English king, his speech is acknowledged to be futile.

By representing the final utterances and, ultimately, death of the last Welsh bard, Gray allegorizes, in a single tragic instant, the more gradual dissolution of the historical conditions that maintained bards as speakers firmly ensconced within the political structure.

Gray's ambivalent attitude toward the bards of this poem results from a desire for the public authority that he believed Welsh bards once possessed.[52] It is widely accepted that Gray identified with the last Welsh bard. This popular scholarly interpretation originates in a statement attributed to Norton Nicholls, who recalled Gray's saying, toward the end of his life, "I felt myself the Bard" while he was composing the poem.[53] Some scholars have read in this statement evidence of a liberating moment in Gray's authorial evolution—the successful discovery of character and persona.[54] Others have seen his identification with the Bard as the failure of his poetic voice after the "Elegy."[55] Still others have argued that Gray's fantasy was part of a larger tendency of eighteenth-century English authors to "impersonate" bards and thus appropriate their voices imperialistically without respecting their specific cultural significance.[56]

However, when placed within the context of mid-eighteenth-century experiments with the idealized oral performance, it becomes clear that for Gray the figure of the bard signified an immediacy that printed poetry should aspire to, not an authentic voice that could compensate for the collapse of his own. No instance better illustrates the realignment of author and reader that Gray hoped printed voice could accomplish than his description of his encounter with John Parry (1710?–1782), a Welsh musician who was popularly known as the "blind harper." At that time, Gray had lost interest in his draft of the "The Bard," but after hearing Parry play and sing, he felt inspired to complete the poem. Born in Wales, Parry was supported for the majority of his life by a prominent Welsh family, but he lived in London and performed what he called "Antient Welsh airs" throughout England, where he was received as living confirmation of the existence of Welsh oral traditions.[57] In 1757 Parry traveled to Cambridge, where Gray heard him. Gray reacted ecstatically to the performance, gushing in one letter that Parry "scratch'd out such ravishing blind Harmony, such tunes of a thousand year old with names enough to choak you, as have set all this learned body a'dancing" (*Corr.*, 2: 502).[58] Although Gray probably exaggerated when he described the songs as "thousand year old" tunes, he was clearly inspired by the way Parry's voice recalled historically distant Welsh art forms. He believed that through Parry's songs one could hear the past. Such a performance offered Gray an example of poetry that was embodied and immediate, and it suggested to him a model for his ideal reading audience. Parry satisfied his listeners by providing them with a conception of Welsh history while pleasing their senses. For Gray, this pleasure translated into renewed interest in "The Bard"; he comments approvingly in a letter that Parry's performance has set his poem—and its emergent poetics of printed voice—"in motion again" (*Corr.*, 2: 502).

Parry was not the only source for Gray's depiction of the Welsh bard, nor was Gray's imagination of this figure derived exclusively from Celtic sources. Gray claimed, for instance, that his models for the last bard also included Raphael's portrayal of God in *Vision of Ezekiel* (1518), and he later added that Parmigianino's fresco in Italy's Santa Maria della Stecatta of Moses breaking the tablets was even "nearer to [his] meaning" than Raphael's painting.[59] In both of these artworks Gray was attracted to the central figure's wild, uncouth looks—unruly hair, flowing beard—but one cannot discount their statuesque bodies, characteristic of Italian Renaissance painting. Perhaps most importantly, considering that Gray chose to compose "The Bard" as a modified Pindaric ode, both paintings represent biblical scenes of prophets. Abraham Cowley, who revived the Pindaric ode for English literature during the seventeenth century, suggested a connection between the style of the prophets ("especially of Isaiah") and Pindar when he argued that both "pass from one thing to another with almost *invisible connexions*, and are full of words and expressions of highest and boldest flights of *Poetry*."[60] Cowley's emphasis upon poetic flight accords with Raphael's depiction of God floating effortlessly among his heavenly host in *Vision of Ezekiel*, and Gray's interest in height and elevation, poetic and otherwise, is evident in his setting "The Bard" on Mount Snowdon, a dominant landmark and the highest point in Wales. Gray's imagination of the bardic figure, therefore, is not wholly Celtic in the way that has been often assumed. In fact, he created his own idiosyncratic image of the bard and affirmed Welsh oral culture by associating it with Greek poetry, the Bible, and Renaissance painting. Gray hoped to emphasize the kind of poetic effects, such as the elevated tone and flights, that Cowley described as occurring in Pindar, which Raphael depicted in his painting and which Gray felt while hearing Parry sing, as much as he hoped to capture the authenticity of cultural situatedness that, scholars argue, bards signified at this historical moment.

WILDNESS AND WELSH PROSODY

The authority and poetic elevation that Gray grants bardic performance has little similarity to "the *still small voice* of Poetry," which he had claimed years earlier was not meant to be "heard in a crowd." Gray's faith in poetry's ability to reach an audience was shaken in 1748 when Dodsley compiled and published *Collection of Poems. By Several Hands*, which included poems from Gray.[61] Although Gray had been writing verse for years, his verse had not been published before, and he professed himself to be "ashamed" to see his work in print (*Corr.*, 1: 295). His shame derived from the feeling that his poetic voice, like that of his contemporaries and unlike those of bards, was weak and inaudible. Gray's belief that printed publications might no longer reach their appropriate audience only exacerbated this sense of poetry's weakness.

This sense of shame and vulnerability is absent from "The Bard," particularly from the confident, exclamatory address of its first line: "'Ruin seize thee, ruthless King!'"[62] Although the poem opens with the Bard's voice in quotation marks, the identities of speaker and audience remain uncertain until the middle of the stanza. The speaker's anonymity makes it possible for his voice to invoke the collective power of "Cambria's curse," an effect which intensifies the stridency of the speech. From the outset the Bard's voice is prophetic, oracular, and accusatory, and Gray's description grants it a heightened poetic power not unlike the "highest and boldest" poetic flights that Cowley sees both in Pindar and the Bible. As the Bard's "sounds" spill down upon Edward they seem to take on a life of their own, confronting the English army and scattering "wild dismay" over Edward's "crest'd pride." And as the poem proceeds, the importance of bardic voice only becomes more pronounced. Except for a single, quick utterance from one English captain (who simply says "To Arms!" [14]) and the brief narration of the initial two stanzas and final two lines, the poem is cast in the voices of Welsh bards.

The collective presence implied by "Cambria's curse" takes on a new form near the middle of the poem. As in the "Elegy," the poem's voices multiply when the last living Welsh bard is joined by some of his executed companions, who have returned from the dead to avenge themselves upon their English oppressors. These ghostly bards' voices merge with that of the primary speaker, forming a supernatural choir whose intensified sound and dire predictions are described as "dreadful harmony":

'No more I weep. They do not sleep,
'On yonder cliffs, a griesly band,
'I see them sit, they linger yet,
'Avengers of their native land:
'With me in dreadful harmony they join
'And weave with bloody hands the tissue of thy line.'

(43–48)

Using slant rhyme and internal rhyme Gray reproduces the double cadence that he claimed was central to Welsh oral poetry.[63] This cadence—reflected in the combination of repeated sounds and caesurae in the lines "No more I weep. They do not sleep" (43) and "I see them sit, they linger yet" (45)—amplifies the bardic harmony referred to above. "Double cadence," Gray wrote in his commonplace book, arises from the "regular return of similar letters or syllables in the beginning or middle of a Verse," a technique he found "very pleasing" for the listener.[64] The natural melodies of oral poetry not only accentuate pleasure but also "assist the memory" by being both harmonious and strongly repeated throughout the composition, he recorded.[65] Although Gray relied on the systematic musicality and cultural function of Welsh verse, he also insisted that the Welsh had not reduced its "harmony" to a rule but had continued to "[practice] it wildly & without art."[66]

With his depiction of Welsh voices, Gray also traded on eighteenth-century perceptions that contrasted Welsh barbarism with English civility. The fantasy of a "wild Wales" endured into the nineteenth century and was confirmed by early travel writers like Thomas Pennant.[67] In a version of the climatological and topographical approaches that characterized so much thinking about race, ethnicity, and nation in the eighteenth century, the Welsh were seen as a product of the rough uncultivated terrain.[68] The Welsh language was dismissed as an obvious sign of the barbarity of the place; in his 1682 *Wallography*, a treatise on Wales, the English author William Richards describes Welsh speech as a "native *Gibberish*" that revealed the ignorance of the Welsh and the desolation of their culture.[69] This same feeling struck the anonymous author of *A Trip to North-Wales*, who claims that crossing into Wales was like reaching "*America*, or the most uninhabited parts of Arabia."[70] Gray hoped that the adaptation of Welsh verse would infuse "The Bard" with this atmosphere of wildness. Rather than seeing Welsh verse as culturally defunct gibberish, Gray discovered in its musical prosody and oral mnemonics a version of Parry's "thousand year old" tunes and an ability to recall history. "The Bard" has the capacity to arouse the reader's senses while tantalizing the imagination because Welsh prosody is both "very pleasing" and evocative of Welsh history. By simulating the resonance of Welsh oral poetry, Gray constructed a printed voice that transcends the limitations he believed made contemporary English verse unable to be heard and remembered.

QUOTATION MARKS

What follows the Bard's invocation of his deceased brethren is an elaborate history, imagined in the temporality of the poem as a prophecy, recounting the tragedies of England until the ascension of the Tudors, who are seen as restoring native British rule to the island. To the bardic chorus, Edward and his descendants represent illegitimate political power, unlike the "long-lost Arthur" (109) and the other "genuine kings" (110) of Britain's past. The chorus creates an opposition between Edward's genealogy ("line"), which they have cursed with their song, and the line of genuine monarchs that preceded Edward and that he violently usurped. The chorus celebrates these "genuine Kings" as "Britannia's Issue" (110), an image that reinforces their legitimacy over Edward's bloody line. In this sense, "The Bard" combats Edward, and the political and aesthetic contamination that he represents, not only with prophetic voice but with a poetic line that, like the bardic chorus, weaves the unfortunate fate of Edward and his descendants into a spoken curse. The form of the poem and its power to curse Edward are one and the same: the Bard's prophecy—itself interwoven through the use of alliteration—is in fact English history, which Gray and his readers already know has come to pass.

Gray's awareness of rhythm and meter and of their ability to aid memory and communicate to listeners and readers becomes explicitly thematized at those moments when he combines the poem's "double cadence" with the trope of weaving; the bards exclaim that they "weave with bloody hands the tissue of thy line" (48), and later that they "[w]eave the warp and weave the woof" (49) of their prophecy. These references to weaving, particularly weaving "lines," echo the alliteration and "double cadence" of the poem. The repetition of sounds interlaces individual lines, creating a verbal texture that is unified with the poem's subject matter—weaving occurs both in form and in content. It was Gray's research into Welsh prosody that led him to revive the use of alliteration, an unpopular literary device among eighteenth-century poets. Samuel Johnson declared that the use of alliteration in "The Bard" was "below the grandeur of a poem that endeavors at sublimity."[71] Johnson, whose skepticism about oral traditions is well known, overlooked the fact that Gray's metrical experiments were part of an effort to recall aural forms and to facilitate a sense of connection that was like the one between performer and listener. In a print culture that Gray perceived to be increasingly dominated by authors vulnerable to being misread, the intimacy made possible by textualizing a methodical yet presumably artless verse form structured through oral mnemonics must have seemed an exciting alternative to the alienation typical of printed poetry.

The similarity of bardic song, lineal genealogy, and the lines of the poem expresses the particular kind of power that Gray collects by recasting the events of English history as the not-yet-enacted elements of prophecy. The unusual temporality of "The Bard"—where English history is transformed retroactively into Welsh prophecy—grants the Bard a power that is accentuated by contemporary readers' collective acceptance of the history that he tells. In an odd way, then, Gray places the Bard in a position to recognize another "line": the line of poets that make up England's literary inheritance. The Bard states:

> 'A Voice, as of the Cherub-Choir,'
> 'Gales from blooming Eden bear;
> 'And distant warblings lessen on my ear,
> 'That lost in long futurity expire.
>
> (131–34)

The Bard's song in this passage prefigures the declining state of the English poetic tradition, which is depicted as lost, like a voice stretched to the greatest extent of its audibility. In a footnote to a later edition of this poem, Gray makes it clear that the cherubic voice that "gales" from "blooming Eden" is John Milton's, the "distant warblings" are the "long succession of poets" following him, and the "ear" that hears these voices belongs to the Bard.[72] Gray remarks that he did not intend his image of poetry's silence in "long futurity" to indicate that "[p]oetry in Britain was some time or other really to expire." He claims instead only to have meant that "it was lost from his [the Bard's] ear from the immense distance" (*Corr.*, 2: 504). "The Bard" thus attempts to spatialize temporality, much as is done in the "Ode on the Distant Prospect of Eton College" (1742). But, rather than looking into the past through memory, as in the Eton College Ode, the Bard listens to the future, finding that his hearing begins to fail after Milton's voice. This transforms prophecy from a vision to be seen into a song to be heard, emanating from the future back into the past, which the Welsh bards in turn re-vocalize to Edward and his English army (as well as to Gray's contemporary readers). Although Gray states that he did not want to suggest that English poetry was going to "expire," by positioning the Bard as an auditor of English authors' voices, he implicitly suggests that they are less audible—in other words, less memorable—than their predecessors, like Milton. The collective bards' prophecy thus comments on English poetry from a position outside of (and before) it.

The distinction between the relative audibility of English and Welsh and past and present voices is rendered even more precisely through the poem's formal properties. Rhetorical structure and typography differentiate the voices of "The Bard" and provide a guide, in tandem with point of view and stanza form, to their relative status and the relationships among them. Gray uses quotation marks to delineate the speakers of the poem—the verse narrator, the last Welsh bard, and the bardic chorus. He uses single quotation marks for the Bard's voice and double quotation marks for the chorus, adding a single inverted comma to indicate the presence of extra voices (compare Figs. 6 and 7). This typographical change signals not only a transition between voices but also an integration of human and ghostly voices and an intensification of the resulting song.

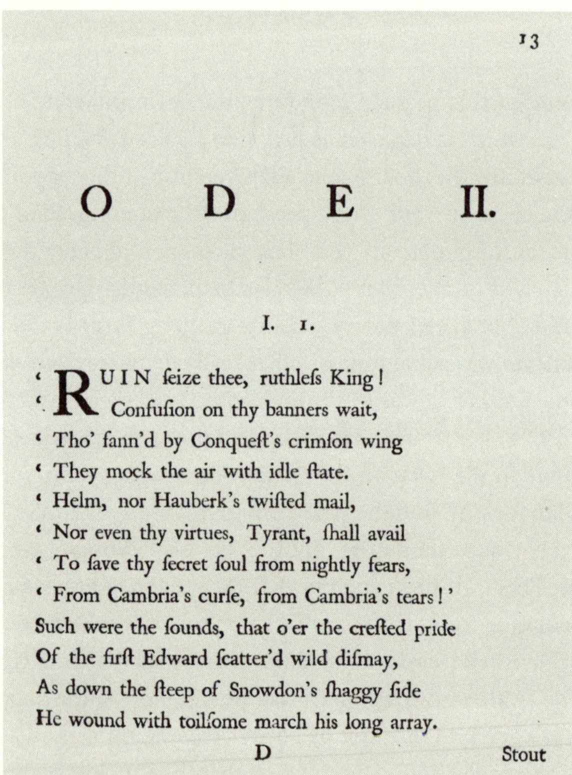

13

O D E II.

I. 1.

'RUIN ſeize thee, ruthleſs King!
' Confuſion on thy banners wait,
' Tho' fann'd by Conqueſt's crimſon wing
' They mock the air with idle ſtate.
' Helm, nor Hauberk's twiſted mail,
' Nor even thy virtues, Tyrant, ſhall avail
' To ſave thy ſecret ſoul from nightly fears,
' From Cambria's curſe, from Cambria's tears!'
Such were the ſounds, that o'er the creſted pride
Of the firſt Edward ſcatter'd wild diſmay,
As down the ſteep of Snowdon's ſhaggy ſide
He wound with toilſome march his long array.

D Stout

Figure 6. The first stanza of "The Bard" from 1757, when it was still titled simply "Ode II." The use of quotation marks ceases as the voice of the verse narrator appears. Courtesy of the Bodleian Library, University of Oxford (Don.d.3 [1], p. 13).

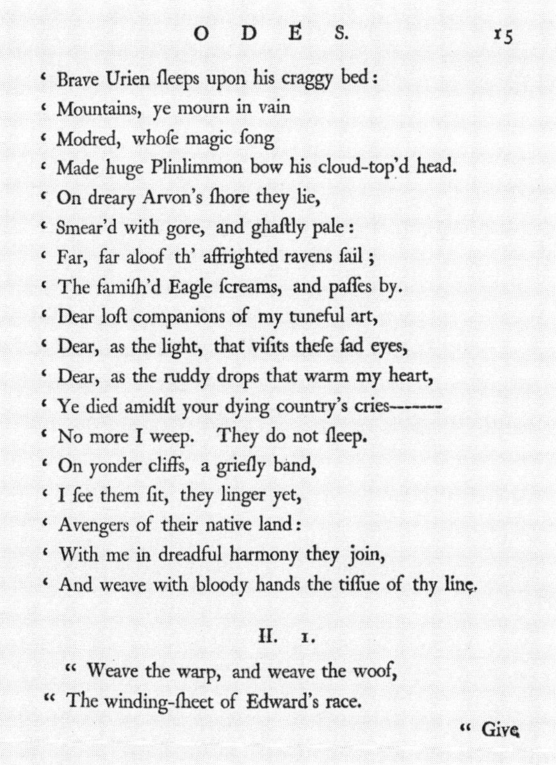
ODES. 15

' Brave Urien ſleeps upon his craggy bed:
' Mountains, ye mourn in vain
' Modred, whoſe magic ſong
' Made huge Plinlimmon bow his cloud-top'd head.
' On dreary Arvon's ſhore they lie,
' Smear'd with gore, and ghaſtly pale:
' Far, far aloof th' affrighted ravens ſail;
' The famiſh'd Eagle ſcreams, and paſſes by.
' Dear loſt companions of my tuneful art,
' Dear, as the light, that viſits theſe ſad eyes,
' Dear, as the ruddy drops that warm my heart,
' Ye died amidſt your dying country's cries-------
' No more I weep. They do not ſleep.
' On yonder cliffs, a grieſly band,
' I ſee them ſit, they linger yet,
' Avengers of their native land:
' With me in dreadful harmony they join,
' And weave with bloody hands the tiſſue of thy line.

II. 1.

" Weave the warp, and weave the woof,
" The winding-ſheet of Edward's race.

" Give

Figure 7. The end of stanza I.iii and the beginning of stanza II.i of "The Bard." Note that Gray shifts from single to double quotation marks as the single bard's voice is joined by those of his compatriots to form the poem's bardic chorus. Courtesy of the Bodleian Library, University of Oxford (Don.d.3 [1], p. 15).

The highly self-conscious use of typography adds a material dimension to the voices of the poem and amplifies the idea that quotation marks disembody speech by representing it on the printed page and thus distinguishing it from the rest of the text.[73] All voices in a printed text by definition are disembodied. Quotation differentiates the living bard's voice and the bardic chorus, whose utterances are doubly disembodied by being both cited and ghostly. But Gray employs quotation marks to suggest the material presence of the Bard's speech and the supernatural audibility of the choir. Since quotation marks were not mandatory for the duplication of someone else's spoken or scripted words until the end of the eighteenth century, Gray's use of varied quote marks is notable. As he composed his poem, there were no standard rules about the use of quote marks.[74] Before the eighteenth century, such marks were often used as a kind of pointer, alerting readers to important material. And, as in the case of Jefferson's Declaration of Independence, single or double quotes could be a written signal to inflect speech or alter the pace of an oral recitation. Their best-known modern function, as an indicator of proprietary material, connecting certain words to particular authors or speakers and thus establishing those words as property, was still being worked out by literary culture in the eighteenth century.[75]

These varying uses of quotation marks indicate what is at stake in the representations of voice found in "The Bard." It is not just the printed form of the text at issue but the social understanding and political relationships that the form implies. That the verse narrator's voice never appears in quotation, and thus in a sense remains unmarked—the basis from which the other voices of the poem should be distinguished—is crucially important to understanding Gray's poem. After the Bard delivers the lengthy invective against Edward, the poem's final two lines are pronounced by this unmarked speaker, who states: "He spoke, and headlong from the mountain's height / Deep in the roaring tide he plunged to endless night" (143–44).

Most critics have focused on the Bard's sudden suicide, but it is more significant that the poem concludes by reemphasizing what should already be obvious about the Bard: "He spoke." The poem is a speech act attempting to accomplish a political result. Furthermore, the poem ends not with the Bard's song but with the verse narrator's description of his death. The past tense of the verse narrator's voice differs from the present or future tenses of the bards' voices, showing that the verse narrator is reflecting on the Bard's actions after they have occurred. Gray considered a different ending for the poem that emphasized the cause of liberty, but ultimately he elected to place the verse narrator outside of the poem's dramatic action and distended temporality, permitting him to frame the Bard's enunciations in much the same way that the quotation marks do. Rather than impersonate or ventriloquize bardic speech, Gray qualifies these "wild" speakers, distancing them from their author yet simultaneously using them as a way to suggest the urgency of their voices, and thus the urgency of his poem.

Because print cannot take advantage of the obviously embodied, vocalized sounds of oral performance, eighteenth-century authors sought to devise techniques to simulate its presence. In reproducing the structures of Welsh prosody and experimenting with typography, Gray made poetic techniques, which are by definition disembodied, operate antithetically; that is, he made them evoke embodiment and immediacy. Quotation marks both disembody the speech of the poem's speakers while also offering the sense that ghosts really can return to life and haunt the English with their sound. This attitude toward the revitalization of voice would prove extremely persuasive for Scottish and Anglo-Indian authors, who later readapted Gray's experiment to their particular locations and politics. The ghostly voice would remain an effective means of political critique for the remainder of the eighteenth century.

(UN)EDITING THE BARDS

Few of Gray's contemporary readers appreciated his attempt to textualize bardic voices, largely because the unusual typographical techniques he used and the metrical schemes were associated with marginalized locales like Wales and with lower-class dialects.[76] Although Gray had hoped to make bardic voice present and audible to his readers, many of his contemporaries took issue with what they felt was the poem's obscurity, a difficulty that they often ascribed to Gray's inarticulateness or unintelligibility. Despite Gray's attempts to reproduce a plausible English version of Welsh orality, for most English readers the result sounded a bit too much like "native gibberish." On one occasion, after hearing Gray read his ode aloud, a member of the audience was reported to have leaned over to a companion and asked if Gray was speaking in English, complaining that he could not understand a single word.[77] Another reviewer dismissed the line "weave the warp and weave the woof" (in other words, Gray's approximation of Welsh metrics) as nothing more than "Spittle-fields poetry."[78] The Spitalfields area of London contained the majority of the English weaving industry and was densely populated with foreign immigrants, particularly Huguenots, most of whom spoke a type of French mixed with English phrases; as Maureen Waller writes, "in many of the streets of Spitalfields and Soho the immigrant population was so dense that it was rare to hear English spoken."[79] The jokes about Gray's obscurity and the references to "Spittle-fields poetry" show that some readers, rather than being pleased by the peculiar verbal texture and wild speakers of the poem, instead associated them with the foreignness of Wales, the vulgarity of working-class labor, and the unintelligibility of immigrants' French argot.

Gray reacted to these disparaging responses by questioning not his own articulateness or the form of his poetic voices but his readers' intellectual abilities. Before he had even completed his *Odes by Mr. Gray*, the collection in which "The Bard" first appeared, he confessed that it might exclude many readers:

> [T]here is no Woman, that can take pleasure in this kind of composition. if Parts only & imagination & Sensibility were required, one might (I doubt not) find them in that Sex full as easily as our own: but there is a certain measure of learning necessary, & long acquaintance with the good Writers, ancient & modern, wch by our injustice is denied to them. and without this they can only catch here & there a florid expression, or a musical rhyme, while the Whole appears to them a wild obscure unedifying jumble. (*Corr.*, 2: 478)

Gray was concerned that uneducated readers, whether men or women, would catch only a "florid expression" or a "musical rhyme"; that is, they would indulge in the immediate pleasures of orality and musicality without engaging the concomitant benefits of reason and learning. Interestingly, he expected that for educated readers Welsh metrics would impart a "wild spirit," but for uneducated readers, he feared that it simply would sound like a "wild obscure unedifying jumble."[80] The wildness cultivated in "The Bard" was thus apparently meant to be coupled with the learning that Gray so often found lacking among English readers. Those with what Gray perceived to be a deficient education might misread, or actually mishear, the printed voice he devised in "The Bard."

The motto that appears in Greek on the title page of Gray's *Odes*, which Gray later translated as "vocal to the intelligent alone," reinforces the sense that "The Bard" can only be understood by those readers who are well-versed in poetry and classical learning (*Corr.*, 2: 797).[81] He admitted after the publication of his odes that he was surprised how few intelligent readers there were in England, insisting nonetheless that his "ambition terminated by that small circle" (*Corr.*, 2: 797). However, upon hearing that a noted Italian critic had read and enjoyed his odes, he felt proud that "my voice has reach'd the ear and apprehension of a Stranger distinguish'd as one of the best Judges in Europe" (*Corr.*, 2: 797). The figuration of voice in these two instances—as intelligible only to a select few yet able to traverse geographic boundaries and reach a distant, unknown reader's "ear"—demonstrates Gray's belief that the printed voice in "The Bard" could transcend the physical constraints of space and time but also speak powerfully to particular readers, in much the same way that the bardic voice in Parry's songs affected Gray. It is a voice that mixes characteristics of both oral performance and printed dissemination, and the metaphors of audibility and intelligibility that Gray uses to describe this printed voice identify the type of audience and reaction that he imagined for his poems. The form of the poem finds its proper readers and discriminates among them.

Bruised by the popular responses to his *Odes*, Gray promised angrily that "the next thing I print shall be in Welch. that's all" (*Corr.*, 2: 524). Although Gray's statement was undoubtedly meant to show some studied nonchalance about his public failure, in the next few years he partly fulfilled this promise by beginning a series of loose translations of Norse and Welsh oral poetry which he called "imitations." Gray composed six imitations in total, though only three were published during his lifetime, in his 1768 *Poems by Mr. Gray*, which also included nearly all of his previously printed works.[82]

These imitations were initially inspired by research into ancient and medieval Celtic cultures that Gray undertook in 1759 at the British Museum. He intended them to appear in his widely anticipated but never completed *History of English Poetry*, as part of a record "as far back as can be traced" of the poetry of the "*Galic* (or Celtic) nations" (*Corr.*, 3: 1123). Toward that end, the imitations use many of the rhetorical features (such as alliteration) that Gray thought originated with Celtic culture and that he began to explore in "The Bard."[83] Creating these imitations was linguistically complex; Gray worked primarily from Latin translations, though he referred to transcriptions in the original language, whether Norse or Welsh, to decipher the metrical and aural qualities of the verse.[84] The fidelity of his technique varies widely. Sometimes he followed the Latin texts closely while at other times he departed from them or even added elements that do not appear in the originals or in the Latin. In calling these poems "imitations," Gray both unveils and obscures his role in their composition: imitation was widely understood to be the loosest form of translation, in which the author could both assert his or her presence and cancel it at the same time.[85]

Taken together, these imitations raise questions about what it means to be a printed author whose poems try to resemble the setting and conditions of oral poetry. They represent another step in the experiment with printed voice which Gray started in the "Elegy." In these imitations, he presents bardic voices on their own rather than mediated through a verse narrator. In part because of the confusion caused by "The Bard," Gray framed the speakers of his imitations through prefaces and annotations that help make their voices intelligible by providing the kind of information that, Gray complained, many of his readers lacked. One imitation, for instance, is preceded by a two-page preface and another by an introduction that explains the voices and historical events presented in the poem. An overall "Advertisement," which divides Gray's imitations from the other works in *Poems*, describes their evolution from Latin transcriptions into English texts. Gray also composed explanatory notes for the imitations, even if he claimed to have done so “out of spite.”[86] The mediation of bardic voices, rather than being internalized within the rhetorical structure of the poem, as it is in “The Bard,” migrates out into the paratextual material that surrounds the individual imitations. The added prefatory matter not only distinguishes Gray’s imitations from his other poems but it also separates the editorial voice of the paratexts, which can be identified as Gray, from the bardic voices of these imitations. The proliferation of paratexts, together with Gray’s assertion that the imitations represent “specimens” of other nations’ poetic heritage, craft a posture of disinterestedness and self-displacement.[87] The origin of these poems, Gray suggests, lies in another culture’s oral voices; his role as an editor and imitator is merely to present them to the reader.

Gray’s depiction of himself as an imitator of others’ initially oral compositions is intentionally simplified, of course, so as to convince the reader that they can actually hear bardic voices. He creates the opportunity for readers to imagine that they experience these voices coming through the text. For example, “The Fatal Sisters” recounts an Icelandic legend of twelve sisters (“twelve gigantic figures resembling women”) who sing while weaving human prophecies at their looms.[88] The collective voice of the twelve women is never interrupted within the poem. Instead, their voices are framed through a detailed preface that narrates how the poem ostensibly was disseminated by a curious “native” who eavesdropped on their song.[89] The poem turns dramatically in the penultimate stanza when the sisters address this male interlocutor. They sing:

> Mortal, thou that hear’st the tale,
> Learn the tenour of our song.
> Scotland, thro’ each winding vale
> Far and wide the notes prolong.[90]

It is through this listener that the sisters’ song is “heard, learned, and perpetuated . . . and passes into the historical and cultural vocabulary of all of Scotland.”[91] This type of mediation is supposedly an imaginative attempt on Gray’s part to contain the danger of powerful female voices, which are neutralized by the fact that the disseminator of their song is a man.

But the address to the male listener also fashions the poem’s prehistory in oral circulation. This self-reflexivity about oral dissemination does not appear in the Norse song or in the Latin transcription that Gray used to guide his imitation. The stanza is a versified instance of the scholarly tracing that Gray had hoped to accomplish in his aborted *History of English Poetry*. In actuality Gray did not so much search for the authentic origin of an oral tradition as he fabricated it. By lodging the oral legend's prehistory in an overhearing listener, he reduces, even obfuscates, his role in the composition of the poem. The extended transmission of which the sisters sing also distances him from his role as author. Most reviewers agreed, focusing upon the original documents and accepting Gray as merely a translator of them.[92] The mediation of a male interlocutor, whether a listening "native" or Gray himself, is absorbed as a facet of the sisters' prophecy. They predict not only the political and historical events that supply the content of the poem but also their song's diffusion among the future inhabitants of Scotland. Thematizing the poem's origin in oral tradition further legitimizes Gray's decision about how to present the sisters' voices as print, and his text becomes an extension of their command to disseminate their song "far and wide."

Authorship also emerges as an issue in "The Triumphs of Owen," which, complete with epic features such as epithets and kennings, presents the voice of a bard celebrating the achievements of Owen, a twelfth-century Welsh prince. Gray included a preface for this poem, although it is shorter and less detailed than that for "The Fatal Sisters." Even though he knew this fragment was commonly attributed to the Welsh bard Gwalchmai, its speaker remains unnamed, creating a sense of anonymous collective voice, through which, presumably, this tale had survived and been transmitted. The absence of bibliographical detail suggests that Gray removed any marker of individual authorship, an action that accords with his choice to compose imitations in the first place. In "The Triumphs of Owen," however, his consciousness about authorship and fragmentation has great significance, since this poem dramatizes its own uneasy transition from sung utterance to literate object. In the first line, its speaker states that "Owen's praise demands my song," but the title refers to it as a "fragment," thereby highlighting its current, literary incarnation and Gray's role as an editor rather than an author.[93]

Gray's figuration of himself as an editor and imitator of poems that ultimately originated in oral traditions is a crucial aspect of his printed voice after "The Bard." By reproducing bardic voices without any overt authorial mediation, Gray forcefully distances himself from the voices on the page. What Katie Trumpener has called the "impersonation" of bardic voice in eighteenth-century poetry becomes increasingly impersonal as Gray's experiment with printed voice shifts from the "The Bard" to the imitations. But Gray's goal is not to decontextualize or fragment oral traditions and then absorb their authentic voices as his own, as Trumpener and some others have claimed. In fact, Gray's printed voices answer the dilemma presented to early-eighteenth-century authors like

Pope and Swift by offering bardic voices that can *never* be confused with his own. His versions of medieval bardic voice are unencumbered by interlocutors and narrators, at least within the body of the poem, thereby more effectively conjuring their oral cultural context. Gray intended this context, recreated within the bounded space of the printed imitation, to replace the sense of disconnection that he felt existed between modern authors and their readers with the sense of connection that bards and their audiences enjoyed during oral performances. Their voices travel through the text to the reader's ears, much as Gray's voice traveled to the Italian critic that he believed to be one of the best judges in Europe.

In the evolution of Gray's printed poetic voice over his career we get an answer to the question of what might be the most efficacious literary form for preserving oral performances, an answer different from but related to those of eighteenth-century elocutionists and twentieth-century anthropologists. Although many scholars avoid Gray's later poetry and consider his imitations anomalous, we misunderstand his ambition as an author if we see his later poems as merely products of a sadly fading literary power or as evidence of a withdrawal from the literary marketplace into simple nostalgia for medieval bardic culture. The ambiguous authorial stance of the imitations and the complex editorial practices and textual forms that Gray created show that he continued to experiment with print and poetic voice until the end of his career, a fact that should alter our sense of him as an alienated writer whose growing skepticism of the marketplace eventually led him to disengage from it.

Instead, Gray's repeated and multifarious representations of bardic voices in print were an attempt to develop an alternative to the prevailing author-reader relationship that the print culture of mid-eighteenth-century Britain was creating. Performers like Parry, who in Gray's mind was a modern-day bard, exemplified to him the desirable relationship to audience. Parry's performance was communal, immediate, and embodied, and Gray hoped to approximate these characteristics in his printed texts as a way to counter his sense of being disconnected from his readers. While Gray's invocations of bardic figures had important political ramifications, for him these ramifications had as much to do with the perception that Celticism preserved political liberty, and thus guaranteed artistic vibrancy, as they did with the notion that he helped expand eighteenth-century British imperialism into a new colonial aesthetics. Gray's adoption of the bard does not necessarily imply thoughtless appropriation of a marginalized culture's more authentic voice or sense of place. His image of the bard originated not only in Celticism but also in Renaissance paintings and the Bible. A critical emphasis upon Gray's role in the appropriation of marginalized voices has obscured the fact that the printed voice Gray developed did not just borrow artistic techniques from other cultures but adapted them to new literary forms (like the revived Pindaric ode) and recontextualized them within the literary marketplace so as to simulate the immediacy that he increasingly felt print circulation was destroying.

This recontextualization depends upon Gray's exploration of the possibilities and advantages offered by the literate text and its printed dissemination. Kaul describes Gray's imitations as a "complex and overdetermined literary exercise" about the disenfranchised poet "ventriloquizing the voice of ancient cultural empowerment" and recreating a "feudal poetics." In this "literary exercise," bardic voice is staged and enacted in writing, in print, and in instances of reading. The self-consciousness of Gray's literary devices, such as the use of typography to distinguish among speakers in "The Bard" and the inclusion of paratexts to frame voices in his imitations, shows that the goal of his experiment was not to recreate an inherently oral "feudal poetics" or to revive a "precommercial past." Gray devised a poetry that combines characteristics of art forms from the oral tradition with print's ability to make present, delineate, and widely disseminate different voices. This poetry cultivates in its audience a relationship to reading texts that resembles listening to song and asserts that the intimacy of oral performance can be achieved by readers who are attuned, through education, to a text's aural possibilities. The composition of this audience excludes many readers, of course, and clashes with the notion that bardic culture is, by definition, accessible to everyone. Even so, the communality and collectivity of printed voice offer not an escape from the literary marketplace but a way to reform it. Gray's answer to the alienation that he encountered in the modern marketplace was to focus on a circumscribed, highly knowledgeable readership that would react to his printed works with the same sense of immediacy that he felt during Parry's performance at Cambridge. The knowing listener became Gray's model for the ideal reader.

Gray's experiment with printed voice in his later poems thus reveals a very different relationship to the literary marketplace and the capabilities of printed texts than that which is currently accepted in studies of Gray. Rather than retreating from poetry and escaping into fantasies of medieval culture, his later poetry reached out to the growing constituency of eighteenth-century readers, whom scholars have too often believed only offended or embarrassed him, in an attempt to demonstrate that texts could please their senses and offer them an experience of the past. Gray was more optimistic about print and the literary marketplace, that most modern of eighteenth-century institutions, than we have allowed him to be.

Furthermore, his carefully crafted attitude toward others' oral voices and the literate text proved to be extremely persuasive for later poets, who looked to "The Bard" (and to a lesser degree, his imitations) as a model for their own writing. Gray's attempts to reform the literary marketplace by engaging with representations of traditional oral voices motivated an important poetic tradition that lasted for the remainder of the eighteenth century. For Scottish authors, Gray's poetry helped establish the marketplace for the Ossian poems, and for Anglo-Indian poets of the 1770s and 1780s, Gray's representation of the bardic voice was an explicit template to be translated and adapted to the East as a way to comprehend colonialism. But it was Welsh authors, some of whom were Gray's contemporaries and correspondents, who were most directly affected by his strategies for editing bardic voices.

CHAPTER 2

Wales, Public Poetry, and the Politics of Collective Voice

In 1822, hundreds of participants gathered in London for an *eisteddfod*, the traditional Welsh music festival that had been restarted during the eighteenth century after long neglect.[1] The 1822 festival, held in a tavern called Freemason's Hall, had poetic recitations, competitions among musicians, and medals awarded for the best poems and essays. Participants could listen to Welsh national songs and instrumental music, including "singing with the Welsh harps after the manner of ancient Britons."[2] One correspondent enthused that these kinds of festivals were a new "dawning" for Wales that shed "light on the land."[3] Another reporter lauded the "festivity and good fellowship" he felt, approving of the "joy and enthusiasm with which all ranks participated in their national festival."[4] This national feeling and "good fellowship" was inspired by the perception that communal festivals revived traditional customs that had been gradually deteriorating over the preceding three centuries. The audience thus experienced a sense of bardic culture and could participate collectively in it. Some of the songs from the 1822 eisteddfod were arranged by the musician Edward Jones, who declared that Wales was a "land of song" and that Welsh music was the sound of "aboriginal Britons"[5]; those in attendance at the eisteddfod could imagine that they were listening to a distant, ancient Welsh past.

The revival of the eisteddfod was a significant part of the late-eighteenth- and early-nineteenth-century reconstruction of Welsh regional, national, and ethnic identity as both literally and figuratively an audible voice.[6] In the eighteenth century, as in the centuries that directly preceded it, Welsh cultural nationalists appealed to the past as a way to cultivate within their countrymen a sense of attachment to Welsh history and culture. In the early modern period, Philip Schwyzer argues, Wales was a "community of longing, united by a collective orientation toward its own vanished antiquity."[7] Eighteenth-century attitudes toward Welsh memory, while they engaged with this nostalgia for the past, considered "vanished antiquity" to be recoverable, believing that the past could be *heard*. Rather than being the sign of collective longing, the Welsh poetic voice could become the signal of and the mechanism for collective belonging. During a period when the British state was being simultaneously created and resisted, the oral past became a crucial element of resistant nationalisms, providing a sense of authentic culture that could counterbalance English cultural intrusions.[8] If Great Britain, and the modern European nation-state more generally, resulted in part from print's ability to inculcate a sense of belonging to an "imagined community" or a public sphere, then orality is often posed as the opposite of print nationalism; orality represents the residue of what is regional, authentic, and vestigial, a remnant of a time before the nation. In this interpretation, the oral past of British peoples, limited spatially in ways that print is not, is imagined as a cultural repository of local collectivities that do not align with the larger structures of an overarching British identity.[9]

The poetics of printed voice sought to adjudicate between these too rigid definitions of print as modern yet distancing and the oral as intimate yet local. Thomas Gray drew upon the authority of Welsh bardic voice to negotiate the publicity of the literary marketplace and the immediacy of spoken performance. This chapter explores how Gray's experiment with poetic voice was recruited by Welsh authors to make the oral past audible, after which it was used as a means of building a distinctive Welsh national cultural identity. Welsh writers' engagement with Gray challenges notions of English imperialism or British nationalism as being consistently set against resistant nationalisms of Wales, Scotland, and Ireland. Even as Welsh authors invoked their ostensibly authentic oral past, they adopted the experiments with Welsh bardic voices that originated in Gray, the most identifiable English poet of the era. The poetics of printed voice described here depend on English literary traditions as a means of fabricating these resistant nationalisms. Gray's original speech acts were struggled over, revised, and enacted in various ways by his Welsh contemporaries. All of those who engaged with Gray's imitations of Welsh voices sought out his experimental poetics and its (at times misunderstood) popular appeal. Gray's bardic curses and prophecies supply a ready-made model of authentic Welsh speech that could be used to oppose English domination. According to current scholarship, Welsh authors should have rejected Gray's models as inauthentic, as the impositions of an appropriating author. To understand this improbable combination of efforts and these unusual alliances and literary borrowings, we need a collaborative model of bardic nationalism in addition to our appropriative and nationalistic ones. This collaborative model was influenced by Gray's innovative literary forms and was turned to what appears at first glance to be antithetical political goals by enthusiasts of the eighteenth-century Welsh cultural revival.

BARDIC NATIONALISM RECONSIDERED

The annexation of Wales by the English monarchy, the subsequent abolition of its legal system, and the progressive anglicizing of Welsh life after the sixteenth century so atrophied the bardic system, Prys Morgan argues, that "the very lifeblood of the nation seemed to be ebbing away."[10] The renewed interest in native Welsh voices that began in the mid-eighteenth century was a response to this cultural bloodletting. If Gray attempted to reform the mechanics of the literary marketplace by appealing to the authority of the oral world of Wales, then Welsh festivals, singing competitions, and bardic-inspired poetry were contemporaneous efforts to make that world's voices audible. Katie Trumpener's *Bardic Nationalism* (1997) remains the most thorough description of eighteenth- and early-nineteenth-century British literary nationalisms.[11] While Trumpener focuses primarily on the Romantic novel in her study, her insights reconceive the formation of English literature, which she argues "constitutes itself . . . through the systematic imitation, appropriation, and political neutralization of antiquarian and nationalist literary developments in Scotland, Ireland, and Wales."[12] In her theory, English literature is a form of aesthetic imperialism. English poetry in particular, she claims, utilized systematic appropriation—stealing cultural resources from marginal peoples and places—as a way to invigorate its own flagging imagination. This methodical theft centered on the bard. During the eighteenth and nineteenth centuries, she argues, English authors "adopt the bard as a figure of cultural fragmentation and aesthetic autonomy."[13] They "impersonate the bardic voice and imitate bardic materials, without grasping their historical and cultural significance"; consequently, the "refunctioning of the bard merely displays the nominalism of imperialism in a new, aesthetic register."[14] She asserts that Gray's "The Bard" exemplifies the inauthentic use of others' cultural materials and that Welsh responses to Gray's poem were repudiations—attempts to revive authentic cultural materials and to reclaim them. By reviving their own culture and representing it in art, antiquarians and nationalists in Wales, Scotland, and Ireland opposed the deleterious effects of imposing English norms, claims Trumpener. For them, the bard was a figure of cultural situatedness and "a mouthpiece for a whole society" that otherwise might be lost.[15]

Bardic Nationalism produces a powerful generalization about the widespread tendency of peripheral British cultures to resist cultural imperialism. However, in her attempt to coordinate notions of appropriation and cultural change on the British Isles, Trumpener overlooks some important collaborations between these antiquarian artistic movements and English literary traditions. She provocatively suggests that the English "only have borrowed words," but what if we see *all* words as borrowed and exchanged?[16]

With this question in mind, I reexamine Gray's "The Bard" and consider one of its most intriguing responses, Evan Evans's "A Paraphrase of the 137th Psalm, Alluding to the Captivity and Treatment of the Welsh Bards by King Edward I" (c. 1757–64), which rewrites Gray's poem from a Welsh perspective, to pursue these linguistic politics of collaboration.[17] The intertextuality of Evans's poem, particularly its allusions to "The Bard," suggests that we reconsider what is going on when cultural revivals like those of eighteenth-century Wales borrow from the ostensibly alien traditions they are resisting to formulate their own nationalism. Far from dismissing and rejecting the poetic voices of Gray's "The Bard" and his folk imitations, Welsh poets insistently *continued* Gray's experiment with the printed representation of bardic voice. Rather than substituting their voices for Gray's last living Welsh bard, they aligned themselves with Gray's images, settings, and innovative poetic techniques to establish their own voices. Their revisions of Gray's poems show that Anglo-Welsh literary relationships in the late eighteenth and early nineteenth centuries were not simply appropriative or anti-imperialistic but also collaborative, in ways that crossed national and ethnic boundaries. Repositioning Welsh poets as in dialogue with their English appropriators enables us to reimagine the politics of eighteenth- and early-nineteenth-century literature and see that resistant literary nationalism emerges from an institutionalized system of cultural exchange and literary borrowing.

Because Evans was a pastor by profession but an antiquarian by passion, he corresponded, for a brief period of time in the 1760s, with Gray about Welsh poetry and, for a longer period, with Thomas Percy, the English ballad collector. Evans spent a large portion of his life traveling through Wales accumulating and translating ancient Welsh manuscripts in an attempt to preserve heroic traditions of the past. He was a member of the Cymmrodorion Society, a Welsh cultural society founded in 1751 in London, with participants in Wales, England,

and the American colonies.[18] Evans, who wrote in both Welsh and English, at times fashioned himself as a bard, under the names Ieuann Fardd and Ieuann Brydydd Hir. As part of his antiquarian interest, he repeatedly engaged with Welsh oral traditions, collecting what he called "specimens" of Welsh folklore. He was the period's foremost expert on these traditions, producing *Some Specimens of the Poetry of Antient Welsh Bards* (1764) while completing a "dissertation" in Latin on the bards of Wales.

His interest in preserving oral and manuscript traditions spilled into his poetry as well. "A Paraphrase of the 137th Psalm" takes up the same legend of the massacre of the Welsh bards that inspired Gray. Evans's "Paraphrase" is more than a retelling of the myth from a Welsh perspective, however; it elaborates the conceits and extends the voices that make up Gray's poem. Evans explicitly dramatizes the textual collaboration between himself and Gray, transforming their epistolary exchanges into a poem. And, in imitating Psalm 137, which details the refusal of the Jews to sing during the Babylonian captivity, Evans connects political protest with oral performance.[19] His poem's speaker, a Welshman imprisoned in England after the bards have been killed, is asked to sing a song. Instead, he states:

> And pity with just vengeance joined;
> Vengeance to injured Cambria [Wales] due,
> And pity, O ye Bards, to you.
> Silent, neglected, and unstrung,
> Our harps upon the willow hung.
>
> (lines 6–10)

Like the Babylonian Jews, the Welsh hang up their harps and call for retribution. His speaker insists that he would rather "let the tyrant strike me dead" than "raise a song / unmindful of my country's wrong" (49–51). The poem ends with this speaker's long lamentation about Wales that explicitly invokes Gray's poem for help:

> There oft at midnight's silent hour,
> Near yon ivy-mantled tower,
> By the glow-worm's twinkling fire,
> Tuning his romantic lyre,
> Gray's pale spectre seems to sing,
> "Ruin seize thee, ruthless King."
>
> (69–74)

Most noticeable about this conclusion is that Evans makes the first line of Gray's "The Bard" the last line of his poem. This results in two related effects. First, by emphasizing the fragmentation and ruin of the hallowed locations of bardic voice—such as Mona, an island off the coast of Wales and a traditional seat of the bards, and the Conway, a river running through what is present-day Snowdonia—bardic culture is portrayed as having been relegated to the past, much as Gray's poem allegorizes the dissolution of the bards in his poem's final suicide. Second, Evans's poem, and by extension Gray's text, which it cites, becomes the means by which bardic voices are recovered and made present again. Gray's printed voice supplies one venue within which the reclamation of Welsh bardic voices might come to pass. Even if the bards are dead and the Welsh will no longer sing, the voices originated in "The Bard" and recalled in Evans's "Paraphrase" continue a tradition that otherwise might be extinct. In this sense, Evans appeals to Gray's literary representations to reinforce the Welsh cultural revival that Gray is seen as having undertaken.

Furthermore, Evans did not just borrow Gray's image of the last living Welsh bard; he directly connected his poem with Gray's imitation of Welsh bardic voice. Gray's poem recalls the passion of "wild" Welsh prosody, a strange idiom that he translates into English. In lieu of a vibrant bardic culture, Evans relied on its representation and rearticulation by Gray. For Evans, it is Gray's "pale spectre" who speaks when actual bards cannot. Rather than "raise a song," Evans offers the curse of Gray's last Welsh bard as a substitute for silence. Evans's citation of Gray's language establishes a textual continuity in which, after reading the "Paraphrase," readers are immediately directed back to Gray's poem, returning them not just to a predecessor form but to a prehistory for which the "Paraphrase" is a bittersweet epilogue. The poems are like ruins, their voices channeling the Welsh bards. That Evans combined his own call for silent resistance—"Our harps upon the willow hung"—with the initial vocal curse of Gray's poem demonstrates that the speech acts of Gray's last Welsh bard reverberated and resonated through the Welsh cultural revival in part due to the capacities of quotation, literary collaboration, and printed circulation to enunciate an earlier poetic voice.

What are we to make of this moment of interconnection between English and Welsh traditions? The quite literal way that these two poems *speak* to (and of) each other is a version of the self-reflexive dialogue involved in Anglo-Welsh literary forms, which the intertextuality of the poems makes evident. Trumpener's model of bardic nationalism seems unable to account for this collaboration. For Trumpener and other commentators, "The Bard" exemplifies an English literary aesthetic that appropriated Welsh traditions, turning them into English inspiration. Trumpener claims that Evans's "Paraphrase" shows that bardic nationalism developed in resistance to English appropriation, by refusing the "arrogant assumption of the English that other cultures are there to be absorbed into their own."[20] Evans's poem, she continues, was part of an effort by Welsh authors to emphasize the "cultural rootedness of bardic poetry and its status as historical testimony."[21] Shawna Lichtenwalner acknowledges that Gray's poem was taken up enthusiastically by Welsh authors, but she argues that this adoption "undermine[d]" Welsh cultural identity because "The Bard" presents an image of a "doomed race" that existed only in the past, not in the present, thereby damaging attempts "to create a living cultural heritage."[22]

My position is closer to that of Sarah Prescott, who argues that Evans's poem suggests the "dual processes of reciprocal influence and antagonistic distrust that . . . typify Anglo-Welsh relationships." Yet she wonders if "the original act of cultural obliteration is strangely reenacted" in Evans citing Gray's poem.[23] Rather than being imperiled, I think Welsh nationalism is strengthened by the reference to Gray's "pale spectre." Evans adopts Gray's bardic speaker and cites his exact written language as evidence for Welsh bardic traditions. Poems like "The Bard" and the "Paraphrase" recapitulate the practices that created them. That they thematize cross-cultural exchange *as* intertextuality is made most strongly apparent by Evans's exact quotation of an English author whom he would be expected to reject and by his invocation of English forms that some have considered to be inauthentic. It is telling, for example, that Gray evokes Welsh oral prosody in his poems and Evans does not. One explanation may be that Evans, as an antiquarian who spoke and wrote Welsh and adopted a bardic name, did not need to imitate Welsh orality in an English medium. But the more striking explanation is that the authenticity ascribed to Evans's poem results as much from his quotation of Gray as it does from his identity as a Welsh author or his repetition of Welsh oral forms. The "Paraphrase" is not concerned with retrieving bardic voice from English authors. In fact, Evans used Gray's Welsh bardic voice to legitimize his own. In this sense, Evans did not undermine Welsh cultural development by quoting Gray; he accelerated it by making the poetics of printed voice collaborative and reciprocal.

Evans's "Paraphrase" suggests a cultural nationalism based on adaptation and cultural translation as much as textual authenticity and purity of national origin or ethnic belonging. Some of his successors agreed that "The Bard" provided important opportunities for extending Welsh bardic voices. In 1798, a bardic festival on Primrose Hill in London awarded a prize for the best translation into Welsh of Gray's ode.[24] In 1822, the same year as the bardic congress at Freemason's Hall in London, W. Owen Pughe published his Welsh translation of "The Bard," which he titled in Welsh "Y Bardd," the existence of which one reviewer called "peculiarly gratifying" because of the "historical events on which [Gray's poem] is founded."[25] The review lauds Pughe for having "transfused into his version the wild abruptness of the original" while maintaining the "native energy and beauty of diction" of Gray's poem. That the reviewer lauds Pughe's ability to capture the "wild abruptness" and "native energy" of Gray's poem shows the extent to which Gray's bardic voices become an asset for defining Welsh culture. "Transfusion" functioned as a synonym for "linguistic translation" in the eighteenth century, but I think here it also connotes the more modern medical sense of transfer of blood.[26] Early attempts at medical transfusion introduced alien blood through the mouth. In the late fifteenth century, for example, a dying Pope Innocent VIII is supposed to have swallowed the blood of three young boys as a curative. This technique, obviously unsuccessful, was motivated by the late medieval association of circulation with ingestion.[27] The metaphor of transfusion captures Pughe's fascination with injecting the wildness and energy of "The Bard" into the Welsh language, the presumed origin of that wildness. By appearing in the Welsh language—a return to its phantom cultural origins—Gray's poem invigorates the voices of the culture from which it came. Setting the first sentences of Gray's poem side-by-side with Pughe's translation shows the degree to which Pughe preserved the innovative form of "The Bard." The oracular, accusatory voice of Gray's last Welsh bard is translated into Welsh, but with the crucial features of Gray's poem—the quotation marks, the exclamation points—adopted precisely. Pughe rewrote the opening line of Gray's poem ("'Ruin seize thee, ruthless king!'") in Welsh as "'Rheibied tranc ti, vrenin trwch!'" (Fig. 8).

Sensitive to the formal "wildness" (described in Chapter 1) of "The Bard," Pughe transfers not just the language but also the typographical innovations of Gray's imitation of Welsh oral voices. The transfusion of energy comes in part from the translation of poetic structure, giving a sense of body and blood to the text and ink of the poem. Writing becomes an arterial pursuit that is life sustaining, and the Renaissance association of blood and mouth makes transfusion into an early metaphor for what we now might call cross-cultural poetics, in which Welsh culture was revitalized by its *contact* with other cultures, not its rejection of them. The politically active reiterations of the last Welsh bard's startling curse do not replace or obliterate the silent harps of Evans's "Paraphrase" or the energetic infusions of Pughe's translation; imitation becomes reinvigora-

Y BARDD.

I. 1.

' RHEIBIED tranc ti, vrenin trwch!
' Càn drwst cei wae o dristwch;
' Trwy gad cei vrad àr dy vri,
' O gwydd, o gawdd banieri,
' Er i orvod, rudd yrva,
' Heiliaw hawl ei hwyl i dra.
' I ti ni ddora er tawr
' Gyvgaened wèn na phènawr,

Figure 8. Part of the first stanza of W. Owen Pughe's "Y Bardd" (1822), his Welsh translation of Thomas Gray's "The Bard" (1757). Throughout the poem, Pughe kept Gray's typographical presentation of different voices. Courtesy of the British Library Board (872.i.41[2]).

tion as the Welsh cultural revival is made more vital by these poems' citation of Gray's bardic voices and the translation of his poetic forms. By disseminating their own adaptations of Gray's voices, Welsh authors devised significant vehicles by which to enact politically that which they wrote about. Gray is presented both as an important origin and an authenticating figure for the national history that Welsh authors hoped to intensify with their own writing and performances. That this history is ostensibly one of the English invading Wales does not change the fact that for them an English author had become the best-known critic of this history and one of the most successful exponents of a resistant Welsh national identity.

THE ABORIGINAL AESTHETICS OF IOLO MORGANWG

Evans's "Paraphrase," Pughe's "Y Bardd," and the bardic festivals demonstrate that public performances and collaborations with English literary traditions were sources of experimentation for late-eighteenth- and early-nineteenth-century

Welsh literature. A different approach to the authenticity of Welsh oral voices was devised by the author and political radical, Edward Williams, better known by his Welsh bardic name, Iolo Morganwg.[28] Morganwg established a system of bardic performance by amalgamating cultural materials. These materials, Morganwg claimed, were aboriginal: he believed that the Welsh were the aborigines, the original people of the world. As evidence, he offered that the Welsh called themselves "*Cymry*; the strictly literal meaning of which is *Aborigines*."[29] They were the "ancients," he writes, and had "been distinguished by that appellation in all ages . . . as if they considered themselves the Aborigines of the world."[30] Their language reflects this status; it is an "*aboriginal*, or *primitive* language," which indicates "something very remarkable" for the Welsh people, that "remotest antiquity" is their "far nobler origin" (*Poems*, 2: 8); far nobler, that is, than the one typically ascribed to them by English authors, whom Morganwg felt were dismissive of Wales and its culture.

We typically think of aborigines as unfamiliar with the processes of modernization, making them important impediments to the globalization of commerce. Morganwg, however, thought of the Welsh aborigine as primitive yet sophisticated, updating the Enlightenment's notion of the noble savage. His work portrays ancient Wales as a golden age of mountains and streams, its indigenous culture alive with the sounds of peaceful learned bards. But his aesthetics depends on a type of racism that distinguishes Welsh aboriginals from the "state of nature" popularized by Rousseau or the primitivist paradises that appeared in travel narratives of Tahiti and other Pacific islands.[31] For example, when he disapproved of his Welsh contemporaries—something that seems to have happened frequently—Morganwg compared them to Africans. Closely identifying with southern Wales, Morganwg slandered the performances of northern Welsh authors in bardic competitions by claiming that they were "formed on Hottentotic principles," referring to the name used for black South Africans. He complained of one Welsh-language publication that it was "nothing but rank Hottentotic" and lamented of a young Welsh bardic performer that his language was "in a Hottentotic degree barbarous."[32] He lambasted London, where he had failed to make a literary reputation during the 1790s, as enamored with the "Hottentotic arts," referring perhaps to the popularity of exotic poetic voices from Africa, India, and the Pacific being published at the time (*Poems*, 2: 38).

The word "Hottentot" was invented in the seventeenth century, as Linda Merians points out, by Europeans who wanted a "politically useful" way to describe southern Africans. She suggests that because the English constructed themselves as the "world's most superior society" they found it "equally necessary to imagine humanity's worst."[33] This attitude informs Morganwg's use of the term to discriminate among Welsh cultural nationalists. Hottentots served as the antithesis of sophisticated English culture, and Morganwg adapted this racial charge to distinguish Welsh aboriginality from fashionable but benighted exoticism. For him, the racial content of "Hottentotic" provided a means of controlling the aesthetics of Welsh cultural nationalism: that which did not fit Morganwg's publicly performed version of aboriginality was made foreign and thus a betrayal of Welsh history. He advocated for his own home-grown primitivism, rejecting equally exotic, but degraded, overseas voices.

In his person and his public performances, Morganwg sought to personify this home-grown primitivism. In *Poems Lyrical and Pastoral,* he names himself a "BARD OF BRITAIN'S ISLE . . . reviv'd in yon supernal clime" and claims that he has been "finally restored" to his "true character and ultimate station, as originally destined by the CREATOR" (2: 207). In an article for the *Gentleman's Magazine* in 1789, he styles himself the only remaining descendant of a long line of "Ancient British Bards," making him the embodiment of the last Welsh bard of Gray's poem, despite his complaints that Gray's poem was "truly ridiculous to an Ancient British Mythologist . . . with its *savage Scandinavian Mythology*."[34] As Cathyrn Charnell-White describes it, Morganwg presented himself as "a piece of living archaeology," as the manifestation of the vocal landscape divinely ordained by God to take a special station in world history.[35]

In Charnell-White's sense, Morganwg hoped to make the ground and stones of Wales speak through him. He was the conduit by which the pure Welsh past could become audible, a past unadulterated by foreign customs and myths. During the 1780s, he literalized this role by organizing the *gorsedd*; this Welsh word he translated variously as "convention," "national convention," "bardic convention," and "voice convention."[36] These multiple translations reveal the degree to which vocal performance, history, and cultural nationalism were aligned in his thinking, much as they were for other Welsh writers. The gorsedd was a poetry festival that Morganwg claimed was based on ancient druidic rituals he had rediscovered in the course of his research on Welsh history. In actuality, he invented the majority of the festival himself; he attributed it to a Welsh oral past as a means of legitimizing his gatherings.[37] As with many other literary forgers of the eighteenth-century, like Thomas Chatterton, Morganwg went to great lengths to authenticate his work. He devised elaborate costumes for his bardic performances and planned assemblies at inspiring natural locations throughout England and Wales. He developed complex, arcane rituals for participants to follow and even composed a bardic alphabet and writing system that he asserted was based on ancient runes. Morganwg initiated followers, the Lichfield poet Anna Seward perhaps among them, and enveloped Welsh bardism in a pseudo-governmentality, complete with bardic certifications that included three levels of competence (ovates, bards, and Druids).[38] His efforts were remarkably convincing; scholars did not notice his inventions until the early twentieth century. By then, many of the traditions he created had been absorbed into the National Eisteddfod that still occurs every year.

Morganwg went to such great lengths because he felt that the public performance of poetry was an essential part of speaking in the "Welsh manner" or the "old national Manner," which was communal and tied to its aboriginal roots.[39] This "old national Manner" is a kind of aboriginal aesthetics, ostensibly reconstructed Welsh oral traditions that make the voices of the past audible again. One of the first meetings of this new bardic festival was a small gathering on Primrose Hill in 1792 attended by a few guerilla bards in which the performers spoke poems out loud. Dressed in multicolored robes with symbolic props, such as sheathed swords, and standing on stones placed in a circle, they recited Welsh history. (Morganwg believed that any "regular Welsh bard can in a few minutes" give a better history than "all the cobweb'd rolls of antiquity."[40]) Morganwg's gorsedd requires publicly demonstrating the events of Welsh history. It also emphasizes the alignment of aboriginality with collective belonging and the public performance of communal voice, which Morganwg diagramed in a hand-drawn plan for the poetry gathering (see Fig. 9).[41] It shows a circle of stones, with a few of the stones moved outward from the circle to make an opening. One edge of the opening points toward the "Summer Solstice," the other toward the "Winter Solstice," and the opening faces the "Equinox." Participants are meant to stand "unshod and uncovered" beside the stones on the periphery of the circle directing their attention to the "Presiding bard," who stands on the central stone ("Presidial Stone" or "Mean Gorsedd").

Morganwg's bardic gatherings were a means of perpetuating and reinstitutionalizing Welsh bardism. A handwritten note from the 1790s, written by Morganwg, calls the performers from the Primrose Hill gathering to perform on the "Long Field" behind the British Museum. He summoned them there to "produce poems and orations on given subjects," threatening that anyone who did not attend would "renounce his claim to Title and character of Bard" and all the rights and responsibilities that came with it.[42] This indicates that Morganwg was not just the inventor but also the organizer and proponent of his created traditions. He hoped through his revival of performances to retrieve the spirit of "ancient versification" and renew its aboriginality as a modern cultural insti-

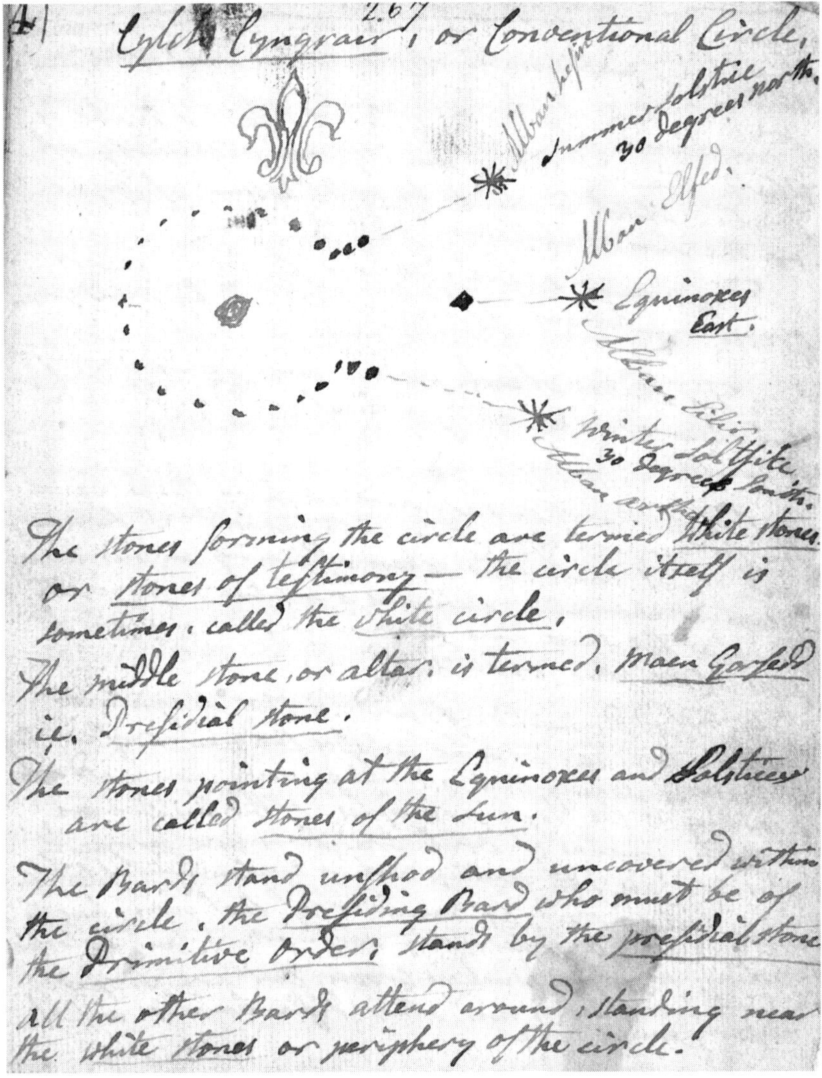

Figure 9. Iolo Morganwg's plan from 1792 for a *gorsedd* circle. By permission of Llyfrgell Genedlaethol Cymru / The National Library of Wales.

tution.[43] He wanted to endow a bardic school of poetry for "very ingenious young men of a poetic turn," who would "hold frequent meetings in the ancient manner" to bring British bardism back from "oblivion."[44] In utilizing the mythology of circularity, collectivity, and aboriginality, and choosing locations like Primrose Hill and the British Museum, Morganwg pieced together a tradition that drew from both ancient customs and self-created rituals. More dramatically than other literary forgers, Morganwg constructed textual practices, public performances, and archaeological artifacts, linking them with scholarly and natural surroundings, to supplement and undergird the ostensibly autochthonous traditions of his bardic performances. This notion of rootedness and primacy was meant to display the deep cultural memory of Wales. By mixing elements of actual Welsh traditions with images of ancient oral festivals, Morganwg created voices whose origins preceded not just English but every literary tradition. Yet, while Morganwg may have rejected what he perceived as adulterated beliefs in favor of something historically pure, his aboriginal aesthetics are in fact derived from popular recreations of idealized oral traditions. One of his sources may have been William Collins's "Ode to a Friend" (also known as "An Ode on the Popular Superstitions of the Highlands of Scotland, Considered as the Subject of Poetry"), a stanza of which Morganwg copied into one of his notebooks. Other passages came from Thomas Hanmer's *Chronicles,* the Book of Exodus (28:31), and radical "freethinker" John Toland's *Miscellaneous Works.*[45] Morganwg mixed these traditions and passages with elements of radical philosophy and pagan religions, like Hinduism's notion of metempsychosis (the transmigration of souls), to construct his own idiosyncratic institutional form of Welsh bardic performance.

One of the explicit tasks of his poetry was to fashion the metaphors and literary forms for institutionalized bardic performance by invoking communal voices and composing in collective pronouns. The opening stanza of Morganwg's "A Song, usually Sung by the Society of Ancient Britons in London, At the Admission of Members" encourages participants:

> . . . to the harp's harmonious voice,
> Attune our choral strain.
> Around the bowl, a mirthful throng
> Of BRITONS bold and free,
> We swell the trills of native song,
> All join'd in jocund glee.
>
> (*Poems,* 2: 92)

The insistence on joining in a "native song" is repeated later when Morganwg boasts, "We Britain's nervous tongue retain / in songs of high renown . . . a language still our own" (*Poems,* 2: 92, 95). Of course, boasting of possessing "a language still our own" appears odd in an English-language poem, making it an announcement that at once engages and perhaps undermines its political assertions. Still, the song's chorus affirms the attachments of the "mirthful throng":

> *New brothers, come, we'll hold them dear*
> *Sons of our Parent Land!*
> *Raise high the shouts of joy sincere!*
> *They join our social band.*
>
> (*Poems*, 2: 94)

In these instances, the exclamatory techniques and tones seek to create communities on the printed page: a "mirthful throng" and "social band" of vocal singers. The music of the harp is attuned to the choral strain, reinforcing one another and establishing a public that, by their voices, announces that they are "bold and free." At times these communities seem almost to be physically touching—participants made tangible to one another—as the voices suggest that "*New brothers, come*" so that "*we'll hold them dear.*"[46]

The act of singing together becomes a way of asserting the nativism of the Welsh revival that Morganwg would meticulously detail in the lyrics, settings, and accoutrements of his public performances. As the title of the song suggests, being inducted into the Society of Ancient Britons—or gathering for the gorsedd—is not just to be admitted as an antiquarian but to contribute to Welsh memories, which are also enactments of its specific politics. This politics is evident throughout Morganwg's *Poems*, including his facetious rendition of "God Save the King," which asks, "Sons of BRITANNIA's Land, / Let us a loyal band, / Together cling" (*Poems*, 2: 134). As with his "Song" of the Society of Ancient Britons, this song interprets Britannia narrowly to mean Wales, supposedly the oldest inhabited part of the island. Collective pronouns are the mechanism by which a community of readers is invoked in text and in performance. This community is exclusive and limited in scope, perpetuating a vocabulary of social memory ostensibly drawn from ancient customs. As scholarly societies came into being and rejuvenated the performance of bardic poetry, poetic voice became an active part of a social agenda to preserve these memories and customs. Morganwg's song, therefore, was a public proclamation of this agenda and a means of enacting it. The use of first person plural pronouns not only establishes an audience and collectivity for the poems but provides a mechanism for their commanding call to action.

Morganwg was not the only poet who signaled his desire for a circumscribed community of listeners by the use of both specific details and collective pronouns.

"The Heroes of Cymru," a poem by John Parry (1776–1851), ends with a cheer to Welsh warriors who

By gentler passions now are led,
And haste to throng the magic ground,
Where the Music's charms and song abound,
To cheer the social train.
(*Cambro-Briton*, 2: 89–90)

An anonymous author used similar tactics when writing a poem in the persona of a Welsh bard singing lovingly to his native land:

CYMRU! As my days decline,
May such favour'd lot be mine,
Near some lonely mountain stream
Thus to chaunt my bardic theme,
Thus my social harp to ply,
Thus to live, and thus to die!
(*Cambro-Briton*, 2: 188)

The social aspect of bardic voice invoked by late-eighteenth- and early-nineteenth-century Welsh authors arranges public speech as memory. The memories in Parry's "The Heroes of Cymru" are grounded in a place where song "charms" and "cheer[s]" the "social train" of its audience. This sense of song as something that may unite readers is apparent as well in the apostrophe to "CYRMU!" (Wales) as the locale within which to chant a "bardic theme" and "ply" a "social harp." The image of living and dying in Cymru gives a sense of how the metaphorics of voice are turned toward the goal of achieving a distinct Welsh identity that is founded on the retrieval of the audible past.

These poems, along with Morganwg's, radically expanded the range of Welsh bardism, recreating it as a comprehensive system in which he was one of its most exuberant examples. He invented new traditions while simultaneously revivifying the present. He recognized the advancements that a complex bardic system could offer to poetry, and transferred these innovations from the page to the public performance and back again. The printed voices of Gray's bards were refashioned into expressions of Morganwg's publicity. Despite the fictional origins of his bardic system and his distrust of English authors, Morganwg's institutionalization of Welsh oral performance popularized poetic forms that had thus far existed largely on the printed page.

LISTENING TO THE WELSH PAST

The creation of communities that were held together in part by vocal performances at public gatherings continued well into the nineteenth century. Felicia Hemans's poem "The Meeting of the Bards, Written for an Eisteddvod, or Meeting of Welsh Bards, Held in London, 22 May 1822," which was read aloud to the bardic festival attendants,[47] summons the voices of the Welsh past, binding the audience together as a community. The imagery and metaphors of voice found in the poem anticipate this sense of communal belonging. The landscape depicted in the poem reverberates with moans and songs: the ground is "heaving to the blast" of the "blue resounding firmament" beside the "roar" of water that is "deeply mingling" with the noise of the wind.[48] This audible landscape is a record of Welsh speech, in that it vocalizes "proud answers to her children's voice" (line 38) in a nation-forming call-and-response:

> . . . though our paths be changed, still warm and free,
> Land of the bard, our spirit flees to thee!
> To thee our thoughts, our hopes, our hearts belong,
> Our dreams are haunted by thy voice of song!
>
> (53–56)

Since, for Hemans, Wales was a text that spoke, she utilized the same first person plural as Morganwg's "Song" and his public performances did. Her poem celebrates a combined listening and enunciation that portrays the past as manifest in haunting and ghostly voices. "The voices of the dead may speak freely now only through the bodies of the living," claims Joseph Roach in his study of circum-Atlantic performance, *Cities of the Dead* (1996). He argues that memory is preserved through performance, which seeks to make the remote and ineffable present again through ritual and which transmits the knowledge that contains a community's social identity.[49] Hemans attempted to establish a similar continuum between her texts and the oral voices that haunted them, transforming culture into an enduring apparition. She convened a Welsh community around these nationalistic voices and their phantasmal forms, a community much like the ones that gathered around Morganwg's bardic circles or that attended the eisteddfod of 1822 and heard her poem read aloud.

Hemans's verse appeals both to structures of vocal performance and to a deeply sedimented history and a collective memory that inform those structures. This appeal is a crucial part of Hemans's engagement with the traditions of the dramatic monologue and of public performance.[50] For my purposes, it is more significant to recognize how her attempt to reinfuse wildness and vigor into Welsh poetic voices and to create viable publics around Welsh memories depended on the techniques of address that would eventually evolve into the dramatic monologue later in her career. This notion of address, apostrophe, and the listening publics that they imply—so significant to Morganwg (and to James Macpherson's Ossian poems discussed in Chapter 3)—was harnessed by Hemans as a means of extending the "dawning" of Wales with its "festivity and good fellowship" that many felt during the eisteddfod at Freemason's Hall in 1822.

At the time of the 1822 bardic meeting in London when her poem had its inaugural reading, Hemans was already a successful writer. Discouraged by her male contemporaries—Lord Byron wished that she would "knit blue stockings instead of wearing them"—she was consigned to being a "poetess" of "hearth and home."[51] But even if she was dismissed as domestic by many readers, she was lauded by Welsh writers and antiquarians as a champion of Welsh culture. Hemans's poetic career, as Tricia Lootens has noted, was "devoted to the construction of national identity."[52] This national identity, however, could be unclear. Hemans was born in Liverpool, but she moved to Wales as a young child, where she adopted a Welsh identity.[53] She was an honorary member of the antiquarian Cymmrodorion Society due to her "zeal in the cause of Welsh Literature."[54] Her poetry of Wales was not nearly as successful among readers as her explanations of *English* nationalism found in poems like "The Name of England" or "England's Dead."[55]

Hemans's engagement with Welsh culture dates from her earliest poetry, necessitating that we read her not only through theories of nationalism and gender relations but also in ethnic and regional contexts. An 1808 poem, "Genius," portrays a Welsh Ossian ("Cambrian Ossian") who hears "airy music murmur'd in his ear" while he wanders through the countryside.[56] Even as the poem complains of Wales that its "sweetest bards are dead / And fairies from the lovely vales are fled," it admits, addressing Wales, "in thy songs the musing mind may trace / The vestige of thy former, simple race." "Genius" elaborates multiple circuits of listening and speaking for the reader, each of which is meant to recapture the vestigial: Hemans's poem is presented as the song of an ancient bard being heard by a Cambrian Ossian; this Cambrian Ossian is described in turn as an "ear" for the poem's speaker, who will learn "the soft bewitching art" of performance and deliver it to Hemans's readers.[57] The reference to a Cambrian Ossian seeks to establish for Wales the community of readers that arose with the popularity (and controversy) of Macpherson's Ossian poems. And the multiple interlocking layers of mediation in "Genius" recall the structure of William Collins's ode on Scottish superstitions discussed in my Introduction. However, unlike the distant Scottish interlocutor of Collins's poem, the Welsh bard of Hemans's poem transcends the boundaries of time, permitting the poet to listen in on the past and align her "genius" with it. This poem is part of Hemans's juvenilia, but it already shows enormous sophistication in its treatment of orality in print. "Genius" suggests that the voices of Welsh culture are, quite literally, in the air. The melancholy of loss (the "sweetest bards are dead") matches the nostalgia of its speaker, who is enabled by the power of printed poetry to recover this ancient music. Listening becomes a refuge for rituals that no longer can be seen or experienced firsthand. The "genius" of the poem is its optimism that it can recreate in print the attitudes of ancient Wales from Welsh sonic remains.

This notion of a distinctive Welsh aurality rooted in the landscape but unmoored from time is developed further in Hemans's later poem "The Rock of Cader Idris" (1822). Cader Idris, a mountain in northern Wales, has mythological significance; legend proclaims that whoever stays overnight on its slopes will become either insane or poetically gifted (proposing, of course, the identity of these two conditions).[58] Hemans's poem figures ancient traditions as a form of "deep music" and ghostly haunting: "phantoms" and spirits populate the mountaintop and around it "for ever deep music is swelling" (lines 2–3). These apparitions are vocal—the voices of bards, of the wind, of the mountain itself—so that the overpowering inspiration of Cader Idris is an ability to hear deeply into Welsh culture.

> Things glorious, unearthly, pass'd floating before me,
> And my heart almost fainted with rapture and awe.
> I view'd dread beings around us that hover,
> Though veil'd by the mists of morality's breath;
>
> (11–14)

These apparitions roll and sweep across the mountaintop, imbuing the speaker with the spirit of the past in the form of a "flame all immortal, a voice and a power!" (28). Hemans reworked the imagery of the Pentecost, in which tongues of flame descended to give the Apostles the ability to speak Christ's ministry, into an image wherein to be given a voice is also to be given a power to speak the culture which is still audible atop this Welsh spiritual monument. "Genius" and "The Rock of Cader Idris" offer a theory of Welsh cultural continuity as voice and sound: a "deep music" that is sung through generations, suffusing the country's atmosphere and terrain. Such continuity is evident because of Hemans's poetry; deep music exists not just atop Cader Idris but also in "The Rock of Cader Idris." By this logic, the vestigial voice can be revived and made readable if authors use specific types of cultural and textual mediation, techniques that have been developed by English poetry since the 1750s.

In addition to "The Rock of Cader Idris," Hemans's lyrics in the 1822 volume *A Selection of Welsh Melodies* also thematize the ability of poetry to take what is almost ineffable, "unearthly," and aural, and give it material shape. This collection includes "imaginative recreations of Welsh history and loose translations of medieval poetry" in the form of songs, soliloquies, and dramatic addresses by poets, mythological heroes, and political figures, such as Owain Glyndwr, the fourteenth-century Welsh rebel who, for a brief time, expelled the English from Wales.[59] These poems were published with Welsh music composed by John Parry. Parry combined Hemans's words with his musical arrangements, noting that the appropriate mode of singing was based on the "manner of the Ancient Britons." According to Hemans and Parry, this ancient manner involved improvisation, variation, and often the rotation of speakers and singers within a communal chorus.[60] Even though subsequent editions of these poems were stripped of their explicit music, the atmospherics of oral culture abound—epic singing and heroic warriors courageous in battle, excessive in celebration, and unafraid of death—making these poems an example of what Hemans calls in "Cader Idris" the "deep music" of ancient Wales. Their monologues and soliloquies operate in communal voices and work in collective pronouns. Readers, modeled as listeners, are encouraged to imagine themselves as participants in the poem, facing down advancing English armies, listening to Welsh heroes, or cheering the Druids' attempts to repulse the Romans with their song. The *Welsh Melodies* are preoccupied with creating models of continuity and cultural memory, as Lichtenwalner notes; Hemans imagined such continuity as ancient music and past voices that could be retrieved and heard in the present.[61] The public effects of Hemans's poems show that representing autochthonous speech that preserves oral traditions formed an important link between the eighteenth-century experiments with printed voice and the early Welsh-inspired poetry of Hemans.

In the "Lament of Llywarch Hen" and "Taliesin's Prophecy," for example, Hemans recalls two well-known Welsh poets who pine for an earlier time when the "bright hours return, and the blue sky is ringing / with song," an era that had faded with the passing of Welsh autonomy ("Lament," lines 1–2). The speakers of these two poems drift oddly between third- and first-person address. "Taliesin's Prophecy" begins: "A voice from time departed floats among thy hills, O Cambria! Thus thy prophet bard, thy Taliesin sung!" (1–2); yet the poem continues in the voice of Taliesin, who delivers his prophecy, as if his floating voice has been made manifest by the poem. This dramatic structure mimics Gray's "The Bard" in its use of external narrators—"Thus thy prophet . . . sung"—to frame these first-person enunciations.

Other Hemans poems give an immediate, specific sense of the audience being addressed that recalls Gray's 1760s imitations. In "Howel's Song," a soliloquy of a fourteenth-century bard, Howel urges his steed on, declaring that "the maid I love," who is dying, "looks o'er the fairy world below, / And listens to the sound!" (7–8). Much as with Parry's evocations of Cymru as "magic ground," in this poem Hemans has the maid looking down and listening to the ground, and what lies below it. In "Prince Madoc's Farewell," Madoc bids farewell to Wales before leaving for America. Madoc was a legendary Welsh navigator said to have discovered the North American continent in the sixth century. (Some nineteenth-century Welsh scholars argued that Native Americans were actually the descendants of these Welsh explorers.) Hemans turned this mythological figure into a powerful orator meditating on his homeland and its music. Madoc asks:

> Why rise on my thoughts, ye free songs of the land
> Where the harp's lofty soul on each wild wind is borne?
> Be hush'd, be forgotten! For ne'er shall the hand
> Of minstrel with melody greet my return.
> ——No! no!——Let your echoes still float on the breeze,
> And my heart shall be strong for the conquest of the seas!
>
> (7–12)

As Madoc pays homage to Wales he addresses the "free songs of the land" and mentions the "harp's lofty soul." Wales itself seems to be a listener. Simultaneously, Welsh songs become apparitional echoes that "float on the breeze," following him and sustaining him as he sails away from his homeland.

In the "The Dying Bard's Prophecy," the ability to speak or be silent is politicized, much as it was in Evans's "Paraphrase." Another retelling of Gray's last Welsh bard, Hemans's dying bard exclaims, "Saxon, think not *all* is won," referring to the effects of his death (16). "Think'st thou," the bard asks with his last breaths, "because the song hath ceased, / The soul of song is flown?" (21–22). The answer is an emphatic "No!"

No! by our wrongs, and by our blood,
We leave it pure and free;
Though hush'd awhile, that sounding flood
Shall roll in joy through ages yet to be."

(25–28)

This song, the dying bard claims, will be left "upon our children's breath" so that "Our voice in theirs through time shall swell" (35). Here, Hemans enlarges the conceit—evident even in her early poem "Genius"—that traditions are voices that can be heard and perpetuated in the present by speech acts and that their perpetuation is itself an important nationalistic triumph.

The importance of Welsh public voices becomes even more apparent in the "Druid Chorus on the Landing of the Romans." In this poem, Hemans presents readers with the collective voices of Welsh Druids, reacting to the Roman invasion of Britain by Julius Caesar. Only the poem's title indicates who speaks the poem's violent prophecies. Such open perspective and point of view make readers at once both members of the chorus, singing out in anger, and Roman listeners, who are hearing an angry song. Of course, the fantasy of this poem is that speaking may possess physical power equivalent to the sword. In a series of questions and answers, the Druids articulate and enact these fantastical powers, hissing:

Know ye Mona's awful spells?
  She the rolling orbs can stay!
She the mighty gravel compels
  Back to yield its fetter'd prey!
Fear ye not the lightning-stroke?
  Mark ye not the fiery sky?
Hence!—around our central oak
  Gods are gathering—Romans,
   fly!

(9–17)

The speakers of this poem are a communal "we" invoking the past, speaking for a homeland, weaving a curse. The Druids function as a group, undifferentiated, singing the same vocal curse that made Gray's "The Bard" seem so wild to its readers. The "Druid Chorus" is also a moment of Welsh wish fulfillment. They hope with their song to repel the Romans, an outcome their military power cannot deliver. (This wish fails, of course, since the Romans, like the Anglo-Saxons, the Vikings, and the French after them, did not "fly.")

The impulse for political fantasy only intensifies in Hemans's "Chant of the Bards before their Massacre by Edward I." This poem recalls the legend of Edward's massacre of the Welsh bards retold by Gray, Evans, and Pughe. The substantial innovation of Hemans's version of the legend is that she offers her readers only the bardic chorus, who begin immediately by addressing their English captors:

> Raise ye the sword! let the death-stroke be given;
> Oh! swift may it fall as the lightning of heaven!
> So shall our spirits be free as our strains—
> The children of song may not languish in chains!
> . . . .
> Rest, ye brave dead! midst the halls of your sires,
> Oh! who would not slumber when freedom expires?
> Lonely and voiceless your halls must remain,
> The children of song may not breathe in the chain!
> (1–4, 9–12)

The imperative address and the dramatic exclamations ("Oh!") give some sense of this poem's "chant." Unbounded by any identifying features besides the title, the poem seeks to create something akin to a collective monologue, a group of speakers that achieve one powerful, prophetic voice. The poems in Hemans's *Welsh Melodies* tend toward this type of collective speech. They personify, modernize, and politicize Welsh historical figures and events to provoke a cultural nationalism, but in this poem, they also invoke the bards as an undifferentiated group who incite their English invaders. The bards' deaths, oddly, mark both the cessation and the perpetuation of this song: the "halls of . . . sires" are made "[l]onely and voiceless," and yet the bards' musical strains, like their spirits, are made "free" (9, 11). In this sense, the "Chant" recapitulates many of the techniques seen elsewhere in Hemans's Welsh poetry, in which physically absent voices produce a progeny of apparitional ones. These are the "children of song" who will not breathe in chains but will still survive in the ghostly singers and printed voices of Hemans's verse.

All of these poems from her *Welsh Melodies* display some of the essential characteristics that eventually would develop into the more fully evolved dramatic addresses of her better-known poems, published in *Records of Woman*, such as "Properzia Rossi" (1828). Recent scholarship has begun to refocus on these dramatic voices in Hemans's poetry.[62] In their form, we might think of the poems from *Welsh Melodies* as transitional to Hemans's better-known dramatic monologues from the 1820s and '30s. But her melodies also reveal an earlier preoccupation with using individual monologues and collective speakers to articulate the political and cultural ends of Welsh nationalism. At times, these speakers hope to bring into existence the history they foretell, in much the same way that the prophecy of Gray's last Welsh bard tells a story of cultural dissolution and revival that had already come to pass. Similarly, the grammatical and formal features of Hemans's soliloquies, chants, and songs reinforce the impression that Welsh history is an audible past, whose political implications can be reanimated in the present through printed poetry and public performance. And, much like Evans's "Paraphrase," Hemans's poetic lamentations of the fading Welsh voices are a means of restoring them, of arguing that the voices have transcended into more agile, apparitional forms, forms connected with yet informing Hemans's solid verse. By dramatizing this imaginative history, Hemans created communities of Welsh authors and readers who may have conceived of themselves as the addressees of those speeches and voices. She and her contemporaries are the "children of song" who replaced the absent bards by reviving their traditions and memories. Their attempts to resurrect dead voices and recall the "deep music" of Welsh culture demonstrate how important dramatic address was to rooting the collectivities of Welsh nationalism within Britain and yet outside of its orbit.

DEAD VOICES REANIMATED

By experimenting with collectivity, community, and explicit cultural remembrance, Hemans seems to have believed that dead voices could be brought to life again, recruited into assisting the nation. The politics of doing so are evident in the controversial topics and speakers she chose. The past is necessary for Welsh poetry, because it is the repository from which the poetry draws its cultural authority; and in her poetry, Hemans makes the past available by imagining that it can be heard.[63] These Welsh authors perceived themselves as uniquely attuned to these voices, but they also engaged with images and concepts created by English authors to create this sense of aural acuity. That they drew from English literature at all demonstrates that, for Welsh writers, national belonging could be considered a set of textual effects and literary collaborations, rather than an attribute of birth or a product of geographical location.

Making ancient Welsh voices audible necessitated the invention of new relationships to textuality predicated on formal innovation, not on ethnic belonging. In these experiments, the text becomes the way to hear the past speak, and reading texts aloud becomes a way to revive the ancient voices and to effect the politics of cultural revival. Gray, Evans, Morganwg, and Hemans all strove to create texts that seemed to be animate, alive. This striving occurred in different forms: Gray's modified Pindaric ode, with imitations of Welsh prosody and sophisticated typography; Evans's retranslation of biblical psalms; Morganwg's public performances; Hemans's deep listening into an audible cultural history. What joins each of them, however, is their attempt to mediate to readers something like the passionate oral performance and the context of a lost Welsh past and to apply them toward the construction of a Welsh national identity. Their experiments with printed voice and oral performance were critical because nationalism depends on what Schwyzer calls "a form of legitimized necromancy."[64] This necromancy, as Michael Taussig argues, is a "magical harnessing of the dead" to create a vehicle by which to invest abstract entities with being, resurrecting those who have died for one final national service.[65] Voices of the past—massacred bards, defeated soldiers, forefathers and nation-founders—are brought back to life in poems and books to speak again. Rhys Jones, in the preface to his 1773 publication *Gorchestion Beirrd Cymru*, an edition of ancient and medieval Welsh poets such as Aneurin and Taliesin, expressed his belief that the revival of the Welsh language through publications like his would allow the dead to speak again. "I see the great love that gentry and commonalty have for the British tongue [Welsh]," Jones enthuses, "and for the works of the old bards too; and thus we shall soon see the Muse (in a very short time one hopes) bursting forth from the graves of the skilled bards in unalloyed splendor."[66] His fantasy of overturned graves might seem more fitting for a gothic tale, yet, for Jones, perpetuating the Welsh language and ancient bardic voices made the dead walk and talk again. The dead are revivified as printed texts; they are imagined to be escaping from the ground to remind the Welsh of a past that is both their inheritance and their political future.

Such a fantasy epitomizes the optimism of late-eighteenth-century Welsh authors about the powers of the poetic text. The resurrection of dead voices through inert text creates an almost alchemical reaction in which inanimate things somehow combine and imaginatively come to life. When texts reproduce voices, Jones suggests, graves can speak. The perceived authority of these voices helped compensate for the relative feeling of powerlessness often shared by the colonized peoples of the British Empire, whether in Wales, Scotland, and India, or even in Africa and the Caribbean. In this way, Gray's "The Bard" set in motion a new paradigm for cultural nationalism, one that was forged by a set of innovative literary techniques for constructing and conferring voice. Gray, still considered to be the most esoteric, retreating British poet of the eighteenth century, paradoxically composed a poem that functioned as a primary articulation of these literary techniques and imaginative possibilities. The children of his song—Evans, Pughe, Hemans, and even at times Morganwg—looked to "The Bard" as a model from which they spoke their own nationalistic concerns. His techniques were recast by Welsh respondents for the ensuing seventy years. In the process of creating their own poetic voices, they further explored the possibilities and the limits of what a text could be imagined to accomplish.

Resurrected voices are not real, of course. Jones's daydream of bards once again walking among the green hills of Wales while singing epic songs would not come to pass, as even he no doubt understood. The ghosts heard by Welsh authors are a metaphor that explained their experiment with new forms of printed voice and new types of nationalism that they helped to promote. Still, ancient Welsh voices, dead but made alive through the powers of textuality, reinjected the promise of passion and the hope for the continuation of ostensibly lost traditions. The authors voiced all of the parts, using the text as a way to negotiate between their image of the past and the new future they wished to create. Yet, even while literary experimentalism led to new attitudes, new forms, and new national hope, the voices of the dead had a way of continually constraining the conversation.

CHAPTER 3

Scotland and the Invention of Voice

Perhaps the most controversial English language text of the eighteenth century was James Macpherson's *Fragments of Ancient Poetry, Collected in the Highlands of Scotland, and Translated from the Galic or Erse Language* (1760). Replete with warriors and ghosts, desolate landscapes and chivalrous romance, these fragments of poetry were considered by some to be an invaluable cultural artifact illuminating the past and by others to be a cunning forgery. Macpherson's collection purported to translate the work of Ossian, a semimythical third-century Scottish bard in the mold of Homer, who preserved his culture's traditions in song. The epic storytelling of Macpherson's *Fragments*, and of his subsequent expansions of the Ossian myth in *Fingal* (1762) and *Temora* (1763), foreground high-stakes issues about the authenticity of oral voices and performance as a means of cultural continuity. As with the Anglo-Welsh authors discussed in the previous chapter, Macpherson positioned himself as merely a translator of a much older song that had been preserved for centuries in oral storytelling. Thomas Gray's complicated depiction of Welsh bardism had caused serious consideration of orality among London's intellectual elite, so when Macpherson's *Fragments* appeared three years later, readers responded with intense curiosity. The most profound claim of Macpherson's collection—that it was the "genuine remains of ancient Scottish poetry"—attracted passionate adherents and provoked debate about the cultural functions of orality.[1] Gray himself declared that he was in "extasie" after reading the poems, characterizing Macpherson as a thrilling "demon" of poetry, and he was not alone in his admiration.[2] The fragments spread widely across Europe and America, gaining diverse readers, ranging from admiring tourists in Scotland to notable authors and prominent national figures (such as Johann Wolfgang von Goethe, Thomas Jefferson, and Napoleon Bonaparte). Readers were drawn to Macpherson's depiction of ancient Scotland as both civilized and exotic. For nationalistic Scots, Ossian provided a tantalizing image of an advanced culture comparable to and contemporaneous with those of classical Greece and Rome. For many English authors, Ossian served as an example of native British creativity that superseded the neoclassicism of the early eighteenth century.[3] Not everyone was so complimentary, however, and the fervor of Macpherson's admirers was matched by that of his detractors. Many critics suggested that Macpherson had invented Ossian and had forged the poems to succeed in a literary marketplace that had largely ignored his earlier publications.[4] Samuel Johnson unequivocally asserted that the poems could not be genuine because they were "too long to have been remembered" by an ancient people who had not developed writing and therefore must have been uncivilized.[5]

The controversies over the legitimacy of Macpherson's Ossian poems have tended to obscure the role that Macpherson played in eighteenth-century British poetry and in the emergence of modern poetic voice. Macpherson's Ossian is more than an example of native creativity or Scottish nationalism. The Ossian poems are the best-known instance of a wider tendency, shared by many mid- and late-eighteenth-century authors, to make oral traditions—considered politically and geographically marginal to civilized Britain—central to the period's most innovative poetic experiments. Macpherson expertly positioned his text along an oral-literate continuum. While Macpherson claimed that he merely uncovered and translated the spoken traditions of Scotland, examining the Ossian poems as a printed object reveals that he actually reconstructed oral traditions by using literary devices such as personification, mode of address, archaic language, obsolete diction, and diacritical indicators like quotations marks. The narrative style of Macpherson's Ossian poems imitates the characteristics of oral discourse, particularly in its use of repetition and tense shifts, to create what I call "restored voices," moments when the text approximates the experience of aural reception. Macpherson emulated bardic speech and the intimacy of the bards' implied audiences as a means of creating a participatory mode of reading in which readers could imagine themselves as auditors. Some connection among authors, readers, and texts—which we might label "voice"—is arguably part of any reading experience; yet the species of readerly intimacy constructed in Macpherson's poems is predicated on reproducing the passion and intensity that eighteenth-century scholars believed existed between oral performers and their listeners.[6] In lieu of the corporeality of actual speakers functioning in a living oral tradition, Macpherson's works offer a set of conventions that materially structure the representation of voice on the page so as to enact these idealized expectations of performed poetry.

In summoning the spirit of bardic voice, Macpherson extended the new conceptualization of printed voice first developed in the poetry of William Collins and Gray. Beginning with the *Fragments*, Macpherson established a system to represent the oral voices of traditional storytelling as literature. He further developed new metaphors of how texts can act on readers. Rather than suggesting that through texts readers could *see* an ancient Scotland, he inculcated the sense that through texts they could *hear* it. This notion of hearing the sounds of the past, so important to the national cultural revival going on in Wales, was central as well to the eighteenth-century understanding of Ossian. The Ossian poems, in using such innovative literary and typographical techniques to portray traditional customs, proved to be a crucial turning point in the emergence of modern British poetic voice.

Macpherson's poems are not oral performances, or even transcriptions of oral performances, in the way we might think of the *Iliad* or the medieval Welsh storytelling collection the *Mabinogion*. He developed an intricate mixture of well-understood literary devices to produce new readerly effects. The benefits of his attempt to approximate oral discourse were *literary*, felt most earnestly through the strange and confusing printed artifacts that he composed. With the Ossian poems, Macpherson complicated the Enlightenment debate about poetry as a means of cultural preservation and forced eighteenth-century readers to contend with differing claims about the materiality of oral traditions. He likewise provided an alternate understanding of the reciprocal relationship between orality and literacy, in which verbal content migrates back and forth between media.[7] Early modern scholars thought of the oral and the spoken as ephemeral. Macpherson's work reminds us that the oral can be material, although its materiality is different from that of writing and print, and therefore more difficult for modern users, educated in book cultures, to comprehend. Macpherson thematizes a cultural situation in which performed poetry and song are communal memory. Yet, because he presented oral poetry as a "total technology" for preserving cultural communication, the *practices* of his texts heralded fresh attitudes and techniques with which to invent a sense of the oral on the page. Within the Ossian poems, the aura of the oral world is (re-)made by print.[8]

PRIMITIVE PASSIONS, POETRY ADDICTION, HISTORY

Scotland played an essential role in this refunctioned oral world. By the time Macpherson published his poems, there had already been a long artistic and critical history of associating Scotland with orality, examples of which include Elizabeth Wardlaw's forged ballad, "Hardyknute" (1719) and Allan Ramsay's 1724 collection of Scots songs, *The Tea-Table Miscellany*. For English authors like Collins, Scotland was a reservoir of novel artistic techniques for those willing to seek them out. Such enthusiasm for Scottish culture was natural, Penny Fielding argues, because orality served as a "site of contested authenticity and a figure of national origin" that survived in an English-dominated Britain.[9] Indeed, Leith Davis and Maureen McLane have claimed that Scotland (and Scottish poetry in particular) was the context in which emerged a "new, multi-valent literary orality" that challenged the "political and aesthetic presumptions [of] the . . . English language and the homogeneity of the British nation."[10] Scotland was not the only locale involved with the creation of a "literary orality," but its songs and ballads were essential (especially after the 1707 Act of Union) to preserving Scottish culture and to popularizing the century's poetic experiments with printed voice and oral performance.[11]

Macpherson, a native Gaelic speaker, probably came into contact with these songs and ballads in both oral and printed forms. As an adult, he traveled through the Highlands, collecting manuscripts and interviewing other Gaelic speakers, so he claimed. After publishing the *Fragments*, he went back to the Highlands to conduct more research, returning to Edinburgh with material for later expansions of the Ossian myth into *Fingal* and *Temora*. These new collections depict a Scottish past abounding with supernatural voices, honorable warfare, and a sentimental warrior-king, Fingal, whose heroic accomplishments were recorded and memorialized by his son, Ossian, ostensibly their original bardic performer. It is impossible to confirm the veracity of Macpherson's claim that his Ossian poems originated in Scotland's oral traditions, but there is ample evidence for the continued existence of these traditions during the eighteenth century.[12] Although the epic storytelling associated with Scottish heroic poetry had all but ceased, the Gaelic ballads which provided much of the source material Macpherson reworked into some of the characters and plots of Ossian had endured for over seven hundred years by the time he arrived for his proto-anthropological Highlands trip.[13] By claiming that the *Fragments* (and all the Ossian poems more generally) were "genuine remains," Macpherson invested these folk traditions with the sense that they are an authentic historical record of ancient Scottish customs and practices.

Samuel Johnson famously discounted these claims of authenticity in *A Journey to the Western Islands of Scotland* (1773). He doubted that lengthy oral poetry existed at all, and he rejected the idea that oral traditions could remain coherent over time.[14] To Johnson, supporters of Macpherson were deluded, ignorant, or superstitious; he noted sourly, "[H]e that goes into the Highlands with a mind naturally acquiescent, and a credulity eager for wonders, may come back with an opinion [about Ossian] very different from mine."[15] Johnson's reaction shows that the debate about Ossian was not just cultural and political, but also aesthetic. Those feelings of credulity, primitivism, and wonder that troubled Johnson were precisely the characteristics that Macpherson hoped to cultivate in his poetry. What for Johnson was the most dubious element of the poems was for Macpherson and his numerous admirers a crucial aesthetic feature and pleasure. Macpherson's contemporary, Jerome Stone, argued in 1756 that, because the Highlands' peasants were "far removed from what may be call'd the modern Taste of Life," they retained the "custom of singing the praises of their ancient Heroes," songs "daring and incorrect, passionate and bold."[16] Stone asserted that the performances of these peasants were "hardly to be equalled among the chief productions of the most cultivated nations."[17] Hugh Blair, an influential critic, university lecturer, and ally of Macpherson, perceived a similar antithesis between the primitive past and the civilized present, as well as between culturally peripheral locales like the Highlands and the more influential English south. Blair insisted that, in its "ancient state," language was "more favorable to poetry and oratory"; and he lamented that in "modern times" it had become "more correct" and more "accurate" but also "less striking and animated."[18] The Ossian poems were a central example of language and customs in this "ancient state," when men were "much under the dominion of imagination and passion."[19] For Blair, the Highlands exemplified a location out of step with modern time and thus a repository of artistic vibrancy. Highlanders' natural propensity for imagination and passion, he believed, created a style of expression more potent than the tepid poeticizing of civilized culture.

In fact, Blair found Highlanders so interested in poetry that he described them as "addicted" to it.[20] The early-nineteenth-century Scottish author John Sinclair likewise asserted that the Celts were "addicted to Poetry"; he observed that they needed to remember everything important to them, since they lacked writing, and oral poetry made this possible.[21] John Smith, in a two-volume collection of "Gaelic antiquities" from 1787, warranted that Highlanders were "addicted to song" and spent "most of their leisure hours" singing and listening.[22] He compared Highlanders to Native American orators and Persian poets.[23]

This appeal to a concept of worldwide orality, in which the comparisons among Scottish bards, Scandinavian muses, American Indian chiefs, and Persian poets, all of them passionate about poetic performance, established what we would now think of as a comparative ethnology that seemed to buttress them against the advancements of anglicized print culture. For these Scottish thinkers, the comparison of Ossian to foreign poetries and the insistence on the Highlands' poetry addiction generated a new history and an alternate logic for linking community and performed memory.

Macpherson's poems engage and solidify these fantasies of a Scottish predisposition toward the communal performance of poetry. And, by assuring readers that Ossianic voices originated in a context like the ones that Stone, Blair, Sinclair, and Smith described, they reflected an imaginative past that had never been corrupted by rational thought. The climax of *Fingal*, for example, explicitly portrays singing as the formation of history: during the feasting that follows Fingal's final victory, the speaker recounts, "we sat, we feasted, we sung."[24] "A hundred voices at once arose," he states, "a hundred harps were strung; they sung of other times, and the mighty chiefs of former years."[25] Collective singing is figured as an act of remembrance and bardic voice functions as a custodian of traditions. Ian Haywood sees the innovation of the Ossian poems as being their ability to reproduce what readers could imagine is a credible version of oral culture. Macpherson establishes this credibility by aligning his poems with these songs "of other times," repeatedly dramatizing their status as spoken chronicles.[26] Thus, the turn to the oral past as a gesture toward authenticity proves to be at work in Macpherson's Ossian as well. Singing preserves the past because it performs what Ossian collected in his memory and passes it on to future generations. Ossian *is* history, Macpherson suggests; historical events and their commemoration by a bard are indistinguishable, and the audience is connected to this history because of its participation in the performance.

Macpherson legitimized these memories, however, by using avowedly literate techniques and attitudes. The historicity of the Ossian poems is a result of style and printed presentation as much as an authentic attempt to approximate orality. His bardic speakers are presented using archaic language and obsolete diction. In *Fingal*, for instance, an intricate courtship scene is recounted in obviously outdated English:

> From the hill I return, O Morna, from the hill of the dark-brown hinds. There I have slain with my bended yew. There with my long bounding dogs of the

> chace.—I have slain one stately deer for thee.—High was his branchy head; and fleet his feet of wind.
>
> DUCHOMAR! calm the maid replied, I love thee not, thou gloomy man.—Hard is thy heart of rock, and dark thy terrible brow. But Cathbat, thou son of Torman, thou are the love of Morna.[27]

Using "thee," "thou," and "thy" pointedly recalls the speech patterns of medieval and Renaissance English. By the end of the seventeenth century, such patterns were rare and largely confined to ornate literary discourse.[28] In addition, this passage, like many others, is in metrical prose. Together with self-consciously epic epithets—such as the reference to hunting dogs as "dogs of the chace" or bows and arrows as "my bended yew"—Macpherson's cadenced writing and uncommon lexicon imparts some sense of Ossian's alien history and hints at an origin in public performance. All of these elements of Macpherson's style are meant to appear as the linguistic manifestation of legitimate historical distance.

Macpherson coupled archaic diction with equally outmoded syntax that inverted the rules of contemporary English to reinforce the sense of antiquity he associated with his speakers. He used inverted phrasing to compose one scene from *Temora,* which describes the vastness of Fingal's army in a lengthy dramatic monologue, like those found in the *Iliad:*

> Do the chiefs of Erin stand . . . silent as the grove of evening? Stand they, like a silent wood, and Fingal on the coast? Fingal, who is terrible in battle, the king of streamy Morven.—Hast thou seen the warrior, said Cairbar with a sigh? Are his heroes many on the coast? Lifts he the spear of battle? Or comes the king in peace?"[29]

Stilted phrases like "Do the chiefs of Erin stand," "Stand they," and "Lifts he" were obsolete in the eighteenth century, and they strengthened the sense that *Temora* must be old. In this way, Macpherson created what Andrew Elfenbein has described as a moment of stylized grammatical usage.[30] In this stylization, Macpherson satisfied the expectation for otherness by creating archaic English equivalents for the speech that readers imagined might once have existed in ancient Scotland. The diction and grammar capture what Macpherson hoped to inculcate in his readers—an ancient culture of performance made available more in the style of the work and the events of its plot than in the authenticity of its documents or the accuracy of his fieldwork. Authenticity in Macpherson's poetry thus presents a dual problem. For Johnson, who demanded manuscripts to certify that Macpherson's poems were, in fact, translations, the authenticity of poetic voice was undercut by the lack of documentation. Macpherson, however, attempted to transcend this distinction by materializing oral voices *through* printed documents, arguing for their authenticity by the style in which they are presented. Macpherson did not explore new and innovative literary techniques simply for the sake of experimentation; rather, he invented these printed voices as a way to reclaim the heroic, passionate style of Scotland's past, and he linked this style with performed poetry. The credibility of this depiction of collective singing and communal memory depends on these literary techniques that construct it.

AMBIGUOUS SPEECH

To portray Ossianic voices as the revivification of the past, Macpherson detached voice from its usual association with human speech. He mixed quotation marks, points of view, and discursive modes. The proliferation of speakers and voices in the Ossian poems makes apparent that Macpherson sought to do more with his textualized voices than simply translate ancient Scottish poetry into English and into print, as he initially claimed.[31]

It is often overlooked in criticism of the Ossian poems that the term "voice" encompasses more than collective history or oral performance; it designates more than oral tradition in the process of creation or verbal narration modulated by a singing bard. Not just a function of social memory, voice also appears to be a defining characteristic of the geography and a property of inanimate objects. In Macpherson's fourth fragment, for instance, one speaker asks, "[W]hose voice is that, loud as the wind, but pleasant as the harp . . . ?" (*Fragments*, 19). Later, another speaker claims that a voice is "like the streams of the hill" (38). These two references demonstrate the close relationship between human voices and natural processes, where the former become coherent only by referring to the latter. The speaker of Fragment III sets the scene by stating that "no voice is heard except the blustering winds" (16). In another fragment, the speaker mourns a friend who has drowned by wondering "if we might have heard, with thee, the voice of the deep" (16) and states, "[T]here, was the clashing of swords; there, was the voice of steel" (29). Significantly, in these instances inanimate objects and natural processes are personified: they are given voice in a way that relates them to the articulate human speakers found throughout the poems.

Voice is even associated with ghosts. This link dramatizes the difficulties and the possibilities involved in creating printed texts that try to establish more intimate connections to readers. In making voice independent of human bodies and detaching it from its common alliance with verbal articulation, Macpherson enlarged the range of objects that could possess voice and thus redefined it. In the process, he imagined new possibilities for what it could do. These possibilities are revealed most fully by the confusion about who is speaking that pervades the Ossian poems, especially the *Fragments*. Speakers often ask, "What voice is that?" or "Whose voice is that?" The Preface to the *Fragments* hints that a single bardic speaker organizes the various voices of the poems, and *Fingal* and *Temora* extend this idea by more obviously figuring Ossian as the primary speaker. But these questions reveal that voice exists in a perpetual state of transformation and uncertainty.

The purposeful absence of typographical marks and the rapid shifts in temporality and point of view reinforce the uncertainty about who is speaking. This confusion, which is particularly salient in Fragment I, demonstrates the importance of printed form and rhetorical devices for Macpherson's depiction of oral performance. The fragment is presented visually as a dialogue between two lovers, Shilric and Vinvela, but they seem not to be in each other's presence when they first speak. Vinvela describes Shilric in the third person, as if he is not there, so she cannot directly address him. She begins by stating, "My love is a son of the hill. He pursues the flying deer." Even though Shilric repeats many of Vinvela's images, the separation between the two lovers is confirmed when he replies, "What voice is that I hear? that voice like the summer-wind." That voice is Vinvela's from the stanza-paragraph before; like the summer wind, it traverses the physical distance that separates her from Shilric and the graphic space that distinguishes each voice in this dialogue (Fig. 10).

A change occurs toward the middle of the fragment when Shilric, away at war and concerned about its dangers, asks Vinvela to remember him if he dies. She responds to his request as if she has heard his statement, suggesting that some kind of direct discourse has commenced between them. Voice is particularly acrobatic here. The distance between the speakers that was formalized by their initial third-person address is overcome with a shift in point of view. Macpherson reunites the two speakers across the physical distance that is implied by the white space that blocks off their individual enunciations. A narrative for this first fragment is created from these graphical cues and variations in mode of address: at their widest narrative separation, Shilric's and Vinvela's voices likewise could be said to be at their most grammatically distant—that is, in the third person—while a sense of immediacy is made evident at the end of the dialogue by the transition from third-person to second-person address, as when, in response to Shilric's request to remember him, Vinvela says "Yes!—I will remember *thee*" (11, emphasis mine).

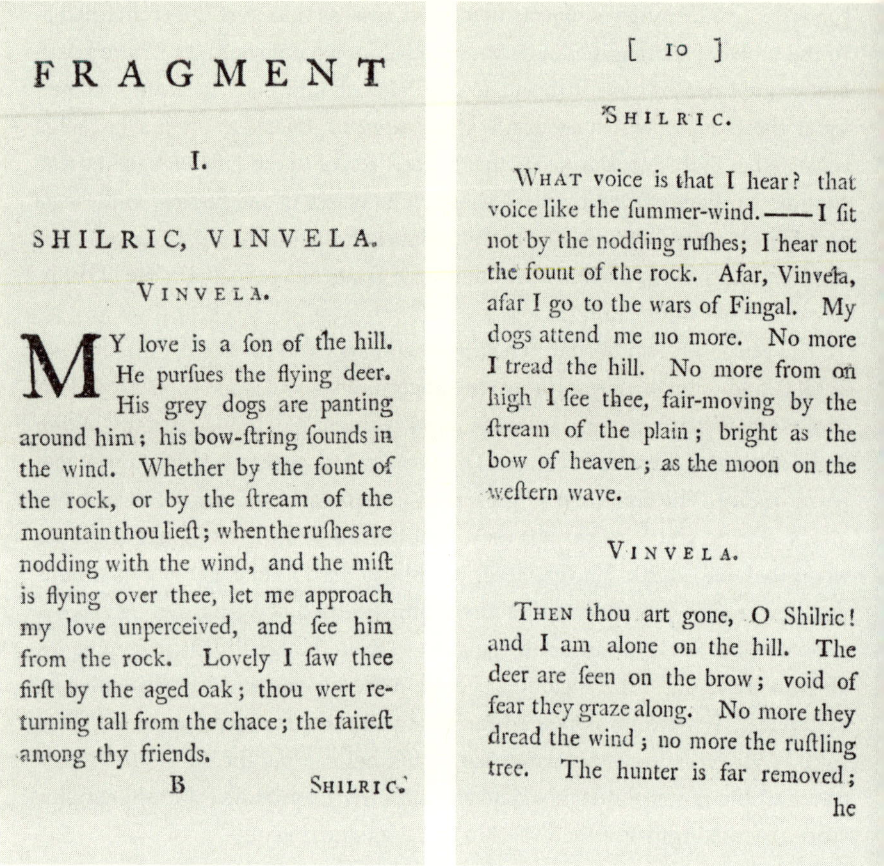

FRAGMENT

I.

SHILRIC, VINVELA.

VINVELA.

MY love is a ſon of the hill. He purſues the flying deer. His grey dogs are panting around him; his bow-ſtring ſounds in the wind. Whether by the fount of the rock, or by the ſtream of the mountain thou lieſt; when the ruſhes are nodding with the wind, and the miſt is flying over thee, let me approach my love unperceived, and ſee him from the rock. Lovely I ſaw thee firſt by the aged oak; thou wert returning tall from the chace; the faireſt among thy friends.

B SHILRIC.

[10]

SHILRIC.

WHAT voice is that I hear? that voice like the ſummer-wind.——I ſit not by the nodding ruſhes; I hear not the fount of the rock. Afar, Vinvela, afar I go to the wars of Fingal. My dogs attend me no more. No more I tread the hill. No more from on high I ſee thee, fair-moving by the ſtream of the plain; bright as the bow of heaven; as the moon on the weſtern wave.

VINVELA.

THEN thou art gone, O Shilric! and I am alone on the hill. The deer are ſeen on the brow; void of fear they graze along. No more they dread the wind; no more the ruſtling tree. The hunter is far removed; he

Figure 10. The opening two pages of Fragment I of Macpherson's *Fragments of Ancient Poetry* as they appeared in its first edition (1760). Courtesy of the Trustees of the National Library of Scotland.

The shifting of speakers' positions and modes of address becomes more pronounced in those fragments that include the voices of the dead, which are numerous in the *Fragments*. Eighteenth-century Anglo-Welsh poets used dead voices to create connections throughout Welsh culture. The dead legitimized a national revival that appropriated English literary traditions to give it shape. As in the Anglo-Welsh examples, dead voices appear frequently in Macpherson's Ossian poems, linking the antiquity of Ossian to contemporary British cultural norms. The distinction between the living and the dead, however, is significantly eroded in the *Fragments*, since the landscape and the social order are populated by the spirits of those who have died. These ghosts are an important part of Macpherson's conceptualization of literary voice, because they occupy a liminal point between literacy and orality. Their voices are unmoored from the constraints of human corporeality, allowing them to circulate in inventive ways (much as print extends the possibilities of distribution in ways speech and handwriting cannot). The confusion about who is speaking and how one is meant to read these ghostly voices is an explicit effect of the *Fragments*' form, and readers' delight or consternation arises in part from puzzling over these moments. The second fragment, which continues the narrative of Shilric and Vinvela, provides an excellent instance of this dynamic:

> BUT is it she that there appears, like a beam of light on the heath? bright as the moon in autumn, as the sun in the summer storm?—She speaks: but how weak her voice! like the breeze in the reeds of the pool. Hark!
>
> RETURNEST thou safe from the war? Where are thy friends, my love? I heard of thy death on the hill; I heard and mourned thee, Shilric!
>
> YES, my fair, I return; but I alone of my race. Thou shalt see them no more: their graves I raised on the plain. But why art thou on the desert hill? why on the heath, alone?
>
> ALONE I am, O Shilric! alone in the winter-house. With grief for thee I expired. Shilric, I am pale in the tomb.
>
> SHE fleets, she sails away; as grey mist before the wind!—and wilt thou not stay, my love?
>
> (*Fragments*, 14–15)

This fragment is difficult to follow due to its depiction of voices. The majority of the fragment appears in Shilric's voice. He has returned from abroad only to learn that Vinvela has committed suicide after mistakenly believing that he was dead. While he mourns this tragedy, the spirit of Vinvela appears to him, interrupting his thoughtful first-person reminiscence. Unlike the first fragment, here Macpherson supplies few signs that specify who is speaking or that identify the transition between different voices—there are no character titles in this fragment and there is no standard punctuation, such as quotation marks, to differentiate one individual's speech from another's or from the narration. How are readers supposed to know which voices are external and which are internal? How can they distinguish verbal conversation from characters' interior thoughts? Readers must infer these details from the content, syntax, modes of address, and the use of names. The lack of diacritical marks is a deliberate strategy to amplify the sense of ephemerality surrounding Vinvela's voice: the absence of printed conventions reinforces Vinvela's uncertain corporeality. When she disappears, Shilric returns to his monologue, referring to Vinvela again in the third person, demonstrating that her spirit has left and their direct conversation has ceased. His question "wilt thou not stay, my love?" seems addressed to her absence. Or her voice may simply be a hallucination produced by Shilric's grief, Macpherson's way of indicating the disconnection between her voice and her body. In all of these scenarios, identifying and comprehending these spectral voices requires a high degree of literacy and the ability to attend closely to the form of the text.

By reserving indicators of reported speech, Macpherson encourages readers to decide whether Vinvela's voice is "real" or not. Susan Manning argues that the "literary ghost is an interpreter" who acts as a "go-between from one culture to another . . . an ambassador from the edge of cultural memory."[32] The power of ghosts is that they are liminal: they can cross borders, especially social borders and cultural divides.[33] Macpherson extended and built on the trope of the ghost as vehicle for boundary crossing, making the apparitional speaker a thought-experiment about the phenomenological state of voice. Voice is one of our strongest indicators of human subjectivity; in the act of speaking, we are assumed to assert our personhood, which is why politics is often described as involving the *vox populi* and why modern political disenfranchisement is so often associated with being silenced. If, as Steven Connor argues, voice has the dual purpose of producing articulate sound and producing "myself, as a self-producing being," then the ghosts of Macpherson's Ossian test this border, questioning exactly what "self" is produced by the articulate voice.[34] Further complicating the connection between self and voice is the fact that Macpherson's ghosts speak with their loved ones alongside talking swords and screaming winds. In this sense, poetic voice is a written self and the imaginative processes by which that self comes into being; yet it is also an oral specter, that which remains outside and beyond the written self and the Enlightenment subject, as intangible as Vinvela's ghostly light.

The humans in *Fragments* therefore can be thought of as being constituted primarily by their voices, by the conditions of utterance. Their voices are not entirely divorced from their bodies, and their corporeality is registered most vigorously at those moments when they provide accounts of physical separation, mourning, or loss, all of which are tied to the disposition of bodies. Ghosts like Vinvela, who drift into and out of the narrative, reveal most clearly the motive behind tethering humans to their voices, and then testing the strength of that connection. These apparitions are literary voice in its most rarefied and purified form, because they transcend the restrictions of human corporeality. For Macpherson, these ghosts were so attractive (and are thus so pervasive in his text) because they are not limited by the body or by the seeming impermanence of oral dissemination: they range across physical states and temporal boundaries. The mobility of these ghostly voices and their survival after death identifies one of the advantages of print publication. In a sense, Macpherson did not just recreate oral culture but invented a printed voice that first reenacts and then surpasses bardic voice by deemphasizing the significance of living bodies (while indicating the tenuousness of his texts' connection with actual bards). Creating poetic voice is an act of impersonation, of fabricating persons, potentially without end. It creates written subjects but also forges their lives in a way that is repeated in the spectral presences of the poems and the poems' uncertain and contested origins.

WRITING, RE-PERFORMANCE, AND RESTORED VOICES

Macpherson's printed voices were inspired by bardic performance and the immediacy of a listening audience, but they do not depend on actual singers or auditors. And, by filling his history of Ossian with the ghosts of heroes and the songs of bards, Macpherson carefully excluded the role of writing from the ideology of his poems and maintained the consistency of Ossian's oral traditional setting.[35] But a close inspection of Macpherson's poems reveals that the construction of Ossian's oral voice required writing, if not within the imaginative logic of the poems, then at least within their printed manifestation. His ghosts are the figure for the possibilities and the limitations of transposing orality into a printed environment. Even as Macpherson wanted his readers to focus on the Ossian poems' origin in oral traditions, he employed a wide range of written and printed techniques to create this effect. This is especially clear in Fragment VI, in which the present tense of Ossian's song brushes up against its thematization of memory. This fragment begins with a request by an interlocutor, who is referred to as the "son of Alpin," for Ossian to tell a tale:

> SON of noble Fingal, Oscian, Prince of Men! what tears run down the cheeks of age? What shades thy mighty soul?
>
> MEMORY, son of Alpin, memory wounds the aged. Of former times are my thoughts; my thoughts are of the noble Fingal. The race of the king return into my mind, and wound me with remembrance.

> ONE day, returned from the sport of the mountains from pursuing the sons of the hill, we covered this heath with our youth.
>
> (*Fragments*, 26)

As with many of the Ossian poems, here the transition between voices and tenses is abrupt. But unlike the dialogues between Shilric and Vinvela, the Son of Alpin's appeal to Ossian fosters a sense of a present performance within which a tale from Ossian's memory is embedded. The explicit invocation of a listening audience is a consistent feature of the Gaelic ballad tradition, and Macpherson signaled this convention in the way he composed and related the printed voices of this fragment.[36] When Ossian begins to remember ("ONE day"), which is also when he begins to perform, the fragment shifts into the past tense.

While Ossian's stories concern his memories and thus appear in the past tense, the voices of his story's characters often appear in the present tense. These tense shifts presumably denote the way he recalls and performs the voices from the past, acting them out for his listeners. Fragment VII, which recounts the death of Ossian's son Oscur, begins, like Fragment VI, with an invocation of memory, and changes quickly into the past tense to signify the beginning of Ossian's reminiscence. But the present tense returns again when the fragment introduces the voices of other characters, such as Oscur and his friend Dermid, and the daughter of their enemy Dargo, whom they both love. When Dermid learns that Dargo's daughter is infatuated with Oscur and not him, he asks Oscur to kill him and end his misery. The return of present-tense narration in the poem at this moment offers the feeling of immediate action and encourages readers to become absorbed in the plot, as if it were happening rather than being remembered.

> SON of Oscian, said Dermid, I love; O Oscur, I love this maid. But her soul cleaveth unto thee; and nothing can heal Dermid. Here, pierce this bosom, Oscur; relieve me, my friend, with thy sword.
>
> MY sword son of Morny, shall never be stained with the blood of Dermid.
>
> WHO then is worthy to slay me, O Oscur, son of Oscian? Let not my life pass away unknown. Let none but Oscur slay me. Send me with honour to the grave, and let my death be renowned.
>
> (*Fragments*, 33)

This passage illustrates what many scholars have noted is an affinity between the Ossian poems and actual techniques of oral performance: the use of epithets, the repetition of phrases, and what Joseph Roach has described as "re-performance," a process whereby culture is perpetuated through pairing "a collective memory with the enactments that embody it through performance."[37]

According to Roach, re-performance operates through "surrogation," the idea that culture has no beginning or end but simply reproduces itself by filling vacancies as they appear.[38] Surrogation's continuous temporality of endless substitution is, for Roach, a constitutive characteristic of oral traditions. But in the seventh fragment, written techniques, and the temporality that they denote, are another critical part of invoking Ossian's re-performance of bardic voice. Ossian, in the present of the poem, turns to the past tense to tell the historical events surrounding his son's death. The interjection of "said Dermid" conveys the sense that Ossian is "restoring" the characters' voices through his song; it delineates Ossian's position in regard to other speakers and clarifies whose words he speaks when they are not his own. It cues Dermid's words as reported speech for an audience who presumably has not heard what Dermid said or witnessed his actions.

These indicators of reported speech gradually diminish, however, as the fragment highlights the interactions of characters. The shift into the present tense reanimates these characters' voices for Ossian's listeners and accentuates the sense of dramatic action. The jarring shifts between past and present become more pronounced as the fragment switches quickly between the voices of the characters and the voice of their performer and narrator, Ossian, who frames their speech: "And fallest thou, son of Morny; fallest thou by Oscur's hand! Dermid invincible in war, thus do I see thee fall!—He went, and returned to the maid whom he loved; returned but she perceived his grief" (34). Only a single dash divides the present-tense description of Oscur murdering Dermid from the reminiscent narration of Ossian. In this complicated framing of voice, Ossian sings to an audience and in the process re-performs Oscur calling out to Dermid. The past and present mingle ambiguously at such moments, pronouns become elusive and perplexing, and writing's ability to manifest or withhold tense changes, speakers' identities, and framing gestures is an essential part of representing how voice functions in these poems and how readers experience it. Changes in temporality and the presence (or absence) of speech markers such as "said Dermid" encourage readers to read Macpherson's poems in the way that auditors would supposedly listen to Ossian's storytelling. This framing structure insists that readers understand that they are removed from the oral telling described in the poems while nonetheless being addressed as a participating public. It allows Macpherson both to reassert and to revoke the distance—

temporal and spatial—involved in the act of writing these poems and in the act of reading them.

Macpherson refined this structure in later volumes of the Ossian poems. In *Temora*, for example, Ossian recounts Fingal's revenge for his son's death. Quickly shifting between the past and present tense disorients readers by forcing them to consider simultaneously two different temporal moments—the past of Fingal's actions and the present of Ossian's tale: "Fingal heard the sound; and took his father's spear. His steps are before us on the heath. He spoke the words of woe. I hear the noise of war. Young Oscar is alone. Rise, sons of Morven; join the hero's sword."[39] By shifting between tenses, Ossian seems to experience these events (again) and recollect them for his listeners. The simultaneity of telling and retelling, of the original event and its remembrance by a bard, make the plot described in this passage seem present and distant all at once. Fingal's actions are narrated in the past tense—he "heard the son" and "took his father's spear"—but the speaker also slips into the present tense, raising the figure of Fingal as if from the dead for his audience—"His steps are before us on the heath"—and enjoining his listeners to see him, hear him, and rise to help him. It is unclear whether "us" refers to the implied auditors of Ossian's performance, to Fingal's loyal warriors, among them Ossian, who participated in the battle with their king, or to readers who are supposed to imagine the scene of carnage the text describes. Nonetheless, the imperative mood addresses readers as if they were present at the site of the battle while Ossian implores them to action. The grammar of the passage makes readers into present(-tense) witnesses of Ossian's performance. Swaying back and forth between tenses, these sentences reposition readers as listeners, as those "sons of Morven" who should respond to Ossian's act of oral telling.

What is evident in these examples of carefully cultivated ambiguity concerning speaker, voice, temporality, and point of view is that Macpherson drew from both mimetic and diegetic practices to generate his idealized sense of oral performance. Reported speech, third-person narration, and direct address each corresponds to a different degree of intimacy within a framing narrative in which a storyteller performs and in the process re-produces the voices of his characters. This mixed mode of writing tends toward immediacy—readers are offered the fiction that they are present at the scene of action, as they would be in an oral performance. What seems so experimental, and sometimes simply confusing, about Macpherson's work is not just the intermixture of these tenses and time frames within the same text but the way in which he slips quickly from one into others with little warning. This feeling of surprise and of improvisation may be one of the effects provoked by Macpherson's sense of virtualized immediate performance. As we are subsumed into the story of Shilric and Vinvela or Dermid and Oscur, the intermediary apparatus of narration and designation of speaker is peeled away, presenting characters' voices without framing. This movement from direct address to recollection and from reminiscence to reported speech collapses the difference between speakers, making how we know who is speaking ever more difficult to ascertain; but it also gets closer to the passion and immediacy that many—such as Macpherson, Blair, and Stone—believed was the experience of ancient Scottish poetry.

INTIMATE HAILING

Macpherson's Ossian poems invent an oral style for a printed text, using rhetorical techniques to impart to readers a sense of performance and to distinguish among different types of intimacy for them. In these poems, therefore, bardic voices are unveiled as a literary technique in themselves, akin to personifying the north wind or the ocean's depths. Voice is embedded within the literary, creating a connection to readers like the sense of communal belonging that attends embodied oral communication. Macpherson thus figured his poems as an extended instance of readerly interpellation, simultaneously addressing readers and conjuring them as an imagined audience of proximate auditors. This figuration, and the innovative printed techniques that promulgate it, are an illusion intended to offset print's potential for solitariness and alienation. By striving to recreate in print the immediacy of ancient oral voices, Macpherson sought to construct a participatory mode of reading that establishes a close connection between the speakers of his poems and their readerly audience.

The impassioned reactions to the Ossian poems by readers confirm the success of Macpherson's experiment. Blair fondly calls them "the poetry of the heart" and describes Macpherson as having "an exquisite sensibility of heart."[40] The playwright Frances Sheridan, wife of the elocutionist Thomas Sheridan, claimed that people's reactions to Ossian fixed their "standard of feeling." Ossian, she remarked, was "like a thermometer by which [one] could judge the warmth of everybody's heart."[41] Werther, Goethe's hero of sensibility, reads Ossian and promptly pronounces that Ossian has "ousted" Homer from his heart.[42] The emphasis on the "heart" as the location of feeling and sentiment appears in many readers' responses.[43] As these reactions demonstrate, Ossian elicited sentimentalized effects from contemporary readers, who imagined that they were hearing bardic voices and absorbing them into their bodies. These readers with rejuvenated hearts express the immediate connection they feel between their interiorized sentiments and the history recounted by the texts. Their bodily reactions to Macpherson's textualized voices in turn authorize the feelings provoked by those voices. Macpherson's poems propose the satisfying delusion that, by reading, one can hear Ossian speaking and can feel the emotions that a listener in the exotic world of ancient Scotland would have felt upon hearing his voice burst into song. So, while the debate continues to this day about the claim that the Ossian poems are "genuine remains of ancient Scottish poetry," Macpherson seems to have instilled a sense of intimacy and passionate expression that eighteenth-century authors and readers perceived to be characteristic of traditional art forms and the experience of oral performance.

These reactions evince what Helen Vendler has called an "intimacy effect." Poetry, she argues—lyric poetry, in particular—presents "tones of voice" that represent "by analogy" relationships among "invisible listeners," that is, relationships among readers distant from the author and from one another but who nonetheless imagine themselves to be listening in on the same speaker's voice.[44] Macpherson's work shows the degree to which eighteenth-century poets sought a new ethics of intimacy in the wake of print culture and the alienation it created among readers. Macpherson attempted to design a text that would overcome the distance of printed poetry and connect to his readers through the perceived immediacy of voice. I call this kind of immediacy "intimate hailing."

What is the difference between the intimacy of communal oral performance—an intimate space or event—and the intimacy of personal contact, the kind we typically reserve for sexual or familial relationships?[45] In the humanities many theories about intimacy have grown out of studies of politics and the public sphere. Print has played a significant role in these discussions, most notably with the idea of a nation as an "imagined community" that functions through shared reading experiences, or the connection that Michael Warner calls "stranger relationality," which distinguishes public belonging from the "copresence" of an immediately available communal performance.[46] This active participation creates a version of what Lauren Berlant has defined as an "intimate public," by which strangers "share a worldview and emotional knowledge that they have derived from a broadly common historical experience."[47] Since, as Adela Pinch puts it, feelings and emotions were described by late-eighteenth-century authors as "transpersonal, as autonomous entities that do not always belong to individuals," they were also fundamentally "social stories" about communal membership.[48] Pinch details how feelings were viewed as originating in individual experience, while being impersonal, conventional, and collective. In her calculation, feelings are influenced by their public performance as much as they are an authentic upwelling of interior identities; the personal idiosyncrasies of emotions were helplessly intertwined with their wider political importance.[49]

Macpherson's Ossian poems are a paradigmatic example of applying print to an idealized version of oral performance to construct an intimate public in which passion can be felt among strangers at a distance. Since this intimacy is textual, and thus virtual, one need not be in the physical presence of others, because that presence is implied in the experience of shared reading (those same elements that were essential for the construction of the public sphere and the nation). The intimate hailing that Macpherson achieved in his poetry was created when he adopted the tactics of public belonging and transpersonal feeling, adapting them to the modes of intersubjective connection and making them the basis of a common historical experience. In this way, Macpherson's invocation of a participatory mode of reading aligns with the role of printed voice in cultural nationalism. In crafting a text that solicits active participation from its readers, creating a sense of virtual co-presence and common sentimentality, such as we witness in the description of Oscur's death in *Temora* ("rise . . . join," Ossian screams), Macpherson borrowed techniques that had been honed in the public sphere and in the incremental changes in how eighteenth-century subjects structured intimate emotional relationships with others.

The appeal to the communal tradition of intimate public performances is an alternative to other postures of eighteenth-century poetry, such as the antihistorical "literary loneliness" described by John Sitter or the "habits of solitude and Anchoritism" found in the mid-eighteenth-century poetry of enthusiasm described by Shaun Irlam.[50] The intimacy expressed in Macpherson's Ossian poems was not inspired by the avoidance of historical topics or the adaptation of religious passion to poetic epiphany. Rather, it originated in the ability of oral performance to evoke a model of collectivity and a passionate enunciation that counters the deprivations of rational language, civilization, and solitary reading. The invisible ties among readers and intimate publics that Macpherson's poetry creates and that authors like Blair championed were intended to mitigate this solitariness, which isolates readers. The Ossian poems reveal an aspiration to use oral performance—and its sense of immediate passionate affects—as a model for intimacy that can be felt and shared despite the fact that readers operate silently and in isolation.[51]

Thus, it is the feeling of a close connection among readers that turns them into the intimate publics hailed into being by Macpherson's enunciations. The intimate publics created by Macpherson's Ossian poems possess a different form of group feeling and public belonging, constituted not so much by the emotions that readers believe to be uniquely their own but rather by the feelings that they imagine to be shared with others. To the extent that feelings and emotions are perceived to be extravagant and contagious, circulating among individuals as much as produced by them, they resemble the forms in which they are made. Some eighteenth-century visual illustrations of Ossian performing help to explain the contradictory manner by which literary form can evoke a sense of virtual, communal auditory participation. The title page of *Fingal*, for example, shows Ossian in a rugged mountainous setting surrounded by attentive listeners (Figs. 11 and 12). Ossian is dressed in loose, almost Roman robes.

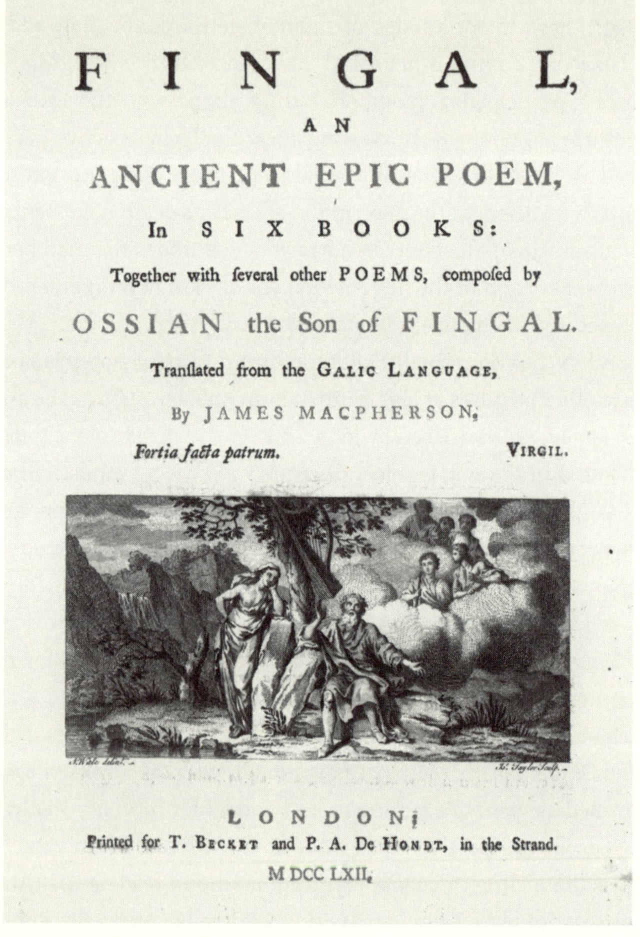

FINGAL,

AN

ANCIENT EPIC POEM,

In SIX BOOKS:

Together with ſeveral other POEMS, compoſed by

OSSIAN the Son of FINGAL.

Tranſlated from the GALIC LANGUAGE,

By JAMES MACPHERSON.

Fortia facta patrum. VIRGIL.

LONDON:

Printed for T. BECKET and P. A. DE HONDT, in the Strand.

MDCC LXII.

Figure 11. Title page of James Macpherson's *Fingal, An Ancient Epic Poem . . .* (1762), engraved by Isaac Taylor. Courtesy of the Trustees of the National Library of Scotland.

Figure 12. Detail of the title page of Macpherson's *Fingal.* Note the orientation of the figures, toward Ossian, showing readers what it *looks* like to listen. Courtesy of the Trustees of the National Library of Scotland.

He is bearded and blind, features that recall Homer and that had become associated with British bards by the mid-eighteenth century. His arms are in motion and his mouth is opened wide, presumably singing or chanting exactly those poems that are collected in the volume. The figures in his listening audience peer over his shoulder or leisurely rest on rock outcroppings. The key aspect of this image is the placement of the audience members behind Ossian; while listening to him, they are also facing the reader. And while Ossian cannot see the audience, the reader can, a visual cue that suggests that the picture functions as a model for what it means to be an auditor hearing Ossian perform. The openness of the composition allows the viewer to enter the space, to join the audience, and be part of the narrative.

A similar attention to audience is visible in Alexander Runciman's sketch for *The Blind Ossian Singing and Accompanying Himself on the Harp* (1772); it shows Ossian singing to a crowd of listeners (Fig. 13).[52] After the publication of Macpherson's *Fragments,* Ossian became a popular decorative subject in eighteenth-century Scottish homes. This sketch, for a wall-sized mural painted in Penicuik House in Scotland, portrays Ossian as an active performer—bearded, heavily muscled, playing a gigantic harp. It emphasizes the ongoing action of performance, as Ossian is shown drawing his fingers across the harp strings. Eyes closed, with a contemplative look, he seems as if he is about to break into song. As in the *Fingal* illustration, this sketch reveals the function of

Figure 13. Alexander Runciman, sketch for a mural, *The Blind Ossian Singing and Accompanying Himself on the Harp* (1772). Courtesy of the Scottish National Gallery.

audience. The auditors listen attentively to his song. A number of figures are folding their hands or cocking their heads, looking as though they are following along rapturously. This is a visual presentation of the kind of passionate listening that Macpherson wanted to suggest to his readers.

The peculiar composition of the figures in both of these illustrations suggests the importance of the ghostly in the construction of intimate listening. The majority of the listeners on the title page of *Fingal* seem enshrouded in mist, recalling the spectral figures prevalent throughout the Ossian poems. Unmoored from the earth, they seem to float, as if apparitions like Vinvela. And the unfilled outlines of dogs at the center of Runciman's sketch seem consistent with Macpherson's description of the "dogs of the chace" repeatedly invoked in *Fingal* and other Ossian poems. They may be the characters of the Ossian poems, imaginatively brought to life from the dead by Ossian's singing, conjured by the engraver for readers to see, yet they are also portrayed as Ossian's audience, placed in such a way that they become a proxy for listening in on Macpherson's poems.

In these illustrations, the participatory mode of reading which Macpherson promoted to readers overlaps with the characters and figures of his poems, so that readers are given a sense not only that they may experience the heroic culture of Scotland but that these figures serve as models for their own participation. Readers become like the characters they read. These images supplement and give shape to the literary techniques with which Macpherson constructed this experience, encouraging readers to imagine themselves as listeners, not just as users of a silent printed book. These listening figures are the visual instantiation of the intimate public that Macpherson sought to create between texts and readers.

OSSIAN'S AFTERLIFE

A text's intimate hailing is the way it represents the intersubjective relations of author and readers. This intimacy is a series of relations that are evoked by Macpherson's metaphorization of oral voicing. Authors like Macpherson who felt the expansion of print culture as a type of alienation and cause of solitariness responded to these effects by trying to change the way print worked upon its readers. Some readers responded in kind, reworking the Ossian poems through new imaginings of their intimate publics, as found in a number of reprintings and rewritings of the Ossian poems, especially by women. One collection from 1789, put together by Mary Potter, reproduces the Ossian poems in italic type to resemble handwriting, lending an intimate and personal aspect to the printing (Fig. 14).[53] The heavy gothic type Potter used for the character titles in "Vinvela and Shilric" accentuates the delicacy of this virtual handwriting. Meredith McGill claims that handwriting can be a figure for printedness, rather than something explicitly opposed to the impersonality of print.[54] In this instance, the intimation of handwriting is meant to personalize the poem; it makes this printed text seem more unique and idiosyncratic, with a "typographical elegance" and a "style entirely new," as the collection's title page claims. Potter's choice of typeface was attuned to early modern theories that saw handwriting as a more immediate form of transmission than print because it directly engaged with the body of the writer. This contradictory performance—in which print masquerades as another medium—mimics the similar processes at work in Macpherson's poems, which evoke communal performance and transpersonal feeling. Potter's typographical experiments are a memorial to Ossian's voice as well as an attempt to modernize it.

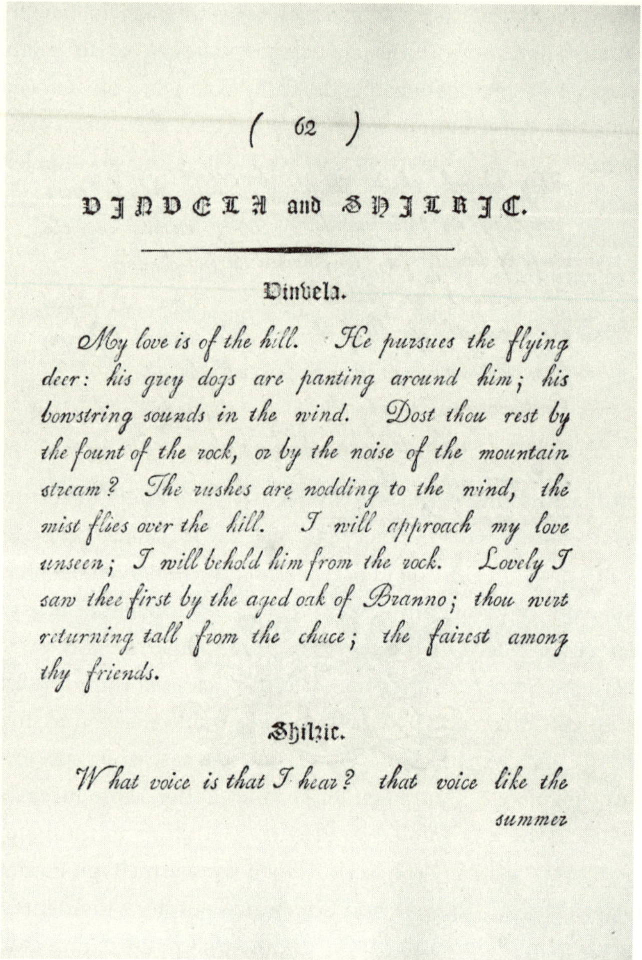

(62)

VINVELA and SHILRIC.

Vinvela.

My love is of the hill. He pursues the flying deer: his grey dogs are panting around him; his bowstring sounds in the wind. Dost thou rest by the fount of the rock, or by the noise of the mountain stream? The rushes are nodding to the wind, the mist flies over the hill. I will approach my love unseen; I will behold him from the rock. Lovely I saw thee first by the aged oak of Branno; thou wert returning tall from the chace; the fairest among thy friends.

Shilric.

What voice is that I hear? that voice like the summer

Figure 14. The opening of Macpherson's first fragment, "Vinvela and Shilric," as reprinted in Mary Potter's *The Poetry of Nature . . .* (1789). Courtesy of the Trustees of the National Library of Scotland.

While Potter extends Macpherson's typographical experiments as a form of homage, the author Catherine Talbot conceived a version of Macpherson's intimate publics composed primarily of women. Talbot, a member of the Bluestocking Circle, produced three imitations of the Ossian poems from the perspective of his female speakers. First published in a collection of "essays," Talbot's poems are "directed to women and their concerns about ethics, economy, manners, and learning."[55] The representations of gender in Ossian's ancient Scotland and in the eighteenth-century world of Macpherson's poetry overlap in Talbot's rewriting. These imitations work as a sequence of dialogues on the subject of female vocal performance. The first opens by asking, "Why dost Thou not visit my Hall, Daughter of the gentle Smile"—ostensibly the voice of Ossian—yet concludes with its female speaker, Therina, wondering, "Will no Voice reply to my Song? I too have a Harp" (139). The latter question is taken up and answered by Talbot's poems, in an eighteenth-century version of call-and-response. Talbot cleverly conflated Macpherson and Ossian, replying to Ossian while imagining her poems in dialogue with Macpherson. She did this by taking up the voices of his poetry's female characters, establishing herself as that "daughter of song" who replies to Ossian and thus counteracts the male bardic voice with her imitations.

One of Talbot's goals was to insert Christian elements into Macpherson's pagan mythological poetry. By speaking back to Macpherson's Ossian, Talbot's poems volunteer an alternate bardic voice premised on Christian female chastity, as opposed to the heroic warrior culture of Ossian. Female Christian fellowship is more durable and lasting, Talbot argues, than the martial accomplishments recounted in Ossian's storytelling. Worrying about Ossian's salvation, Talbot's speaker declares: "Bright was thy Genius, Ossian! But Darkness was in thy Heart: It shrank from the Light of Heaven" (142). Ossian is chastised for ignoring the "true" singing that is God; "The lonely Dweller of the Rock, sang, in vain, to thy deafened Ear" (142). Ossian's deafness—metaphorically paired with his oft-represented blindness—leads Talbot to conclude that Ossian is a sad, isolated figure, a singular voice unaware of the Christian brotherhood that surrounds him. Concerned for his eternal soul, Talbot's female speakers implore Ossian to remember that he has a "Kindred higher in Heaven" (142) and to join the community of Christianity. Of course, this would be historically impossible, and thus the conclusion of Talbot's third imitation is characteristically dramatic and final: "Harp of Ossian be still," the daughter of song states (142). Silencing Ossian was a means of criticizing Macpherson for focusing on pagan mythologies rather than current Christian issues: "While thou sattest gloomy on the Storm-beaten Hill," declares Talbot, "still Destruction spread[s]: still human Pride rises with the Tygers of the Desart, and makes its horrid Boast!" (143). As JoEllen DeLucia notes, for many women writers—and Talbot in particular—the Ossian poems were ripe for rewriting; these female characters become a version of female authorship and propound an "Ossianic women's history."[56] The poems presented an opportunity "to track the development of manners and the role of women in civil society," in much the same way that the Ossianic world was indebted to the mid-eighteenth-century aesthetic categories of the Enlightenment.[57]

The plea for a Christianized Ossian demonstrates that Talbot perceived a different interpretation of the cultural significance of Macpherson's poems. By imitating Macpherson's female voices in a way that interrogates the content of the Ossian poems, she adapted the conceits of his invented oral traditions to expand what she presumed were its religious and historical limits. The regendering of bardic voice occurs by rewriting what is presumed to be a masculine warrior culture, expanding upon what were already feminized elements of the Ossian poems. Pinch argues that by the end of the eighteenth century, poetry possessed a "special relationship to the cultural prestige of feminine feeling."[58] In the reprinting by Potter and the rewritings by Talbot, this special relationship is routed through the sentimentality of a male bardic voice. Much like the revisions of Gray by Welsh authors discussed in Chapter 2, such sentimentality is set to new, even contradictory ends by women. For Macpherson's imitators, therefore, oral voices are more than relics of past traditions; they emanate into the present, via textuality, and revive a civic intercourse modeled on the bond thought to exist between oral performers and their listening audience. The reprintings and rewritings of the Ossian poems, as exemplified in Potter and Talbot, demonstrate how the literary devices of Macpherson's poems could be used to construct new social intimacies and readerships. The aura of authenticity that Macpherson invented in his texts could in turn be revised by female authors looking back to bardic culture as a model with which to reconceive the gender and religious politics of the mid-eighteenth-century world. In each of these examples, the voices of the Ossian poems prove to be avenues by which new publics could be described and brought into being.

Thus, the cultural notions and literary devices typically seen as nostalgic for an oral world before print were in fact the ways these eighteenth-century authors registered a new kind of presence in texts and crafted a more intimate relationship with their readers. The popularity of Macpherson's poems stemmed in part from the heroic manners and pleasing sentimentality described in them, from the sense that they were sophisticated remnants of an indigenous Scottish culture, and from the feeling of national pride sparked by their assertion of a cultural tradition worthy of Homer. However, the central reason that Ossian still entrances us is that Macpherson's texts permit readers to indulge in the fantasy that we are inheritors of heroic Scottish values, which in turn can be modified by different audiences with alternate politics in mind. His texts recreate the intimate intercourse of an imaginary ancient past that is reclaimed and made present again through reading. Print culture, as scholars have observed, provokes a shift in understanding about the difference between the past and the present by its ability to preserve and codify accounts of historical events.[59] Yet, Macpherson's printed forms reject this shift by a deliberate, even inevitable, interpenetration of the past and the present. The Ossian poems establish continuities with the past that elide the feeling of rupture that occurred in Scottish culture with imposition of anglicizing norms subsequent to the defeat of Jacobite forces at Culloden in 1746. Macpherson's poems draw readers in by offering the possibility of reading differently, that is, of reading the sounds of Ossian as ancient listeners might have heard them, and then of relating the communal feelings and emotions that result to the contemporary world around them.

CHAPTER 4

Impersonating Native Voices in Anglo-Indian Poetry

In addition to hiring tax collectors, surveyors, and merchants, the East India Company—that "great Machine!" of sprawling commerce, as one admirer described it—also employed imaginative authors and scholars, to advance British interests.[1] If the conquest of India was a "conquest of knowledge," as Bernard Cohn suggests, then writers and scholars were as important to it as generals and cannons, ships and sepoys. These skilled workers created the flow of information that was crucial to making the machinery of the colonial project work. Anglo-Indian poetry composed by white authors—some emigrants to India from Britain, others born in Asia—had a small but significant role in this machinery. Poetry was an instrument for mediating Indian knowledge to English readers. This knowledge, particularly of Sanskrit oral traditions, was portrayed as exotic, as about a distant place and from an ancient past. These Indian traditions were highly valued because they were thought to be made up of authentic voices from the other side of the globe, at the edges of the British imagination. British orientalists saw themselves as preserving and codifying traditions that otherwise might go unnoticed or disappear entirely.[2] That Anglo-Indian poetry drew upon these presumably authentic voices made it orientalist in its attitudes, as has been explained by Edward Said and subsequently elaborated upon by a generation of scholars.[3] The texts of these colonizing authors established the discursive forms and epistemologies that created orientalism and turned Indian forms of knowledge into European objects.[4] Because the British appealed to native traditions for the purpose of expanding their colony and governing their subjects, rationalization of Eastern knowledge, aided by writing and disseminated through print, was an important element of their imperial ambitions.[5]

As part of this "conquest of knowledge," Anglo-Indian authors composed poems in which they impersonated Indian speakers. They created these speakers by orientalizing British cultural traditions and amalgamating English literary forms with Indian voices to create a peculiar colonial idiom. They rewrote English poetry, filling it with Indian women singing in heroic couplets and Brahmans speaking like Celtic bards. These poems personified Indian subjects, obsessively exploring their subjectivity and sentimentalizing their characters. In such poems, Hindu speakers are depicted as passionate enunciators or dying prophets. Anglo-Indian poetry presents a collision of British and Indian perspectives as a two-part dialogue or contest of voices: a fictional Eastern speaker whose language is created and reported from the perspective of a Western one, while simultaneously clarifying British expectations and fears about colonial rule. In this poetry, authors imagine what their colonial subjects might say if they were made to speak intelligibly in English. These experiments with Indian voices thus mark a culmination of eighteenth-century poetry's impulse to listen for new modes of inspiration and unusual speakers.

The impact of this listening was pronounced. The expansion of the British imagination and the extraction of exotic Asian traditions propelled what Michael Franklin calls a late-eighteenth-century "Indomania" that made Eastern knowledge "safe," "domesticated," and fashionable.[6] But Anglo-Indian poems are not always safe, sometimes featuring such violent and controversial topics as wife burning and famine. They are extremely difficult in form and content, creating highly complex cultural amalgamations by combining European genres like the Pindaric ode and pastoral eclogue with Indian scenes and mythology, and by replacing British speakers, such as the figure of the Celtic bard, with Indian ones. Even while British authors of colonial India strove to make their topics intelligible to English readers, who were largely ignorant of Indian affairs, they still presented sophisticated and bracing portraits from the perspective of an alien culture. In fact, their impersonation of Indian speakers shows that British authors transformed themselves into asymmetrical versions of their colonial subjects. Eighteenth-century Anglo-Indian poetry thus served as a means of surveillance, created a cross-cultural poetics, and spoke for a politics of imperial occupation. It extended overseas the experiment in mediating the sound of oral forms onto the printed page.

There are some important differences, however, in the political and cultural consequences of these experiments with printed voice. While the Welsh and

Scottish authors of their respective cultural revivals viewed themselves as recalling oral voices from the past to reanimate indigenous national identities, Anglo-Indian authors borrowed from those cultural revivals in Britain to represent ethnically and racially alien traditions. They shared literary techniques—and in some cases, crucial elements of the exact same poems—to impersonate their speakers and evoke their voices. Interest in the printed acoustics of poetic voice was less pronounced among these authors, because they transposed British poetic innovations to Asia to explore the multifaceted politics of European colonialism. However, the way in which oral voices are evoked remains a significant element of Anglo-Indian impersonations; their authors often recalled techniques already employed by their Welsh and Scottish counterparts. This transplantation of literary techniques and cultural attitudes was intentional: Anglo-Indian authors connected their concerns about empire to simultaneous debates about nation formation (and its resistance) in Britain. They linked the written imitation of oral performance and the reevaluation of the Celtic bard with the impersonation of colonial subjects. The different adaptations of imitated sounds and bardic speakers by Anglo-Indian authors reveal their varied reactions to the colonial project. Examining this poetry allows us to reassess the practices of orientalism by emphasizing the dispersals and collisions involved in cultural exchange, as well as the contingency of the forms that make those exchanges possible. It offers us another way to expand on scholars' attempts to read eighteenth-century British poetry internationally and to think about literary form as a vessel for the macropolitics of British colonialism in Asia.[7]

These English poetic voices were reshaped by their contact with Indian culture. Anglo-Indian poetry was both a vehicle for the advancement of colonial politics and a record of its consequences. Three questions, therefore, guide this investigation: What formal effects resulted from the adoption of Indian speaking positions by British poets? How did these authors integrate Indian voices into their poetry, and how did late-eighteenth-century poetry change as a result? Poets were attracted to the idealized oral performance of ancient Wales and Scotland. Adopting those passionate voices required that authors invent poetic practices that broke with those of their neoclassical predecessors. Late-eighteenth-century Anglo-Indian authors built on these new techniques in speaker, address, and typography—all of which enabled print to evoke oral voices in innovative ways—when they enlisted native Indian voices to personalize the effect of Britain's colonial expansion. At the same time, they reworked familiar (even conservative) poetic genres and forms, especially pastoral, hymns, odes, and heroic couplets. At first glance, the use of conventional forms seems incongruous with the new imaginations that India is supposed to have supplied English writers. The use of these retrograde literary forms leads Nigel Leask to conclude that the encounter between orientalist authors and indigenous Indian poetry had little effect on the form of British writing.[8] Yet, as Mary Ellis Gibson notes, eighteenth-century Anglo-Indian poetry was written in a "thoroughly multilingual space" and often was produced through a "process of reiteration, revision, and citation" that created colonial texts intelligible to multiple audiences.[9] If we broaden our understanding of poetical style and form used by these writers, the influence of Asian poetry and fictional Asian speakers comes into sharper focus. Fictional foreign voices renovated conservative literary forms. Rewriting earlier poems and merging familiar forms and genres with Indian speakers and topics circulated Britishness through India and made the familiar forms feel new again.

The multidirectionality of Anglo-Indian poetry's cultural appropriations and literary revisions coincides with our ongoing reconsiderations of orientalism, of the literary forms of colonial discourse, and the methods of postcolonial criticism. These poems explore the social and psychic significance of British governance of parts of India. They offer inconsistent and at times hypocritical answers about what it meant to be British and about the significance of the still growing British Empire in India. Some celebrate dominion; others do not, instead presenting radically different visions of colonialism that warn of its dangers. In these poems, Britain is thought in turns to be emboldened and corrupted, strengthened and undermined by its imperial project.[10] The sometimes confusing transcultural voices of Anglo-Indian poetry are not easily categorized as indigenous or anglicized, resistant or interventionist. Evoking Indian voices was one of the ways that British authors could "speak back" about empire from a perspective subordinated within those very colonial structures that many of these authors helped to create.[11]

This chapter begins by focusing on the compositions of William Jones, a noted orientalist and legal scholar who cast himself as an intermediary between Indian voices and English readers. There is a striking similarity among his authorial persona, his fictional Indian speakers, and his work as a linguist and judge. The interrelation of Jones's advanced linguistic study and his Anglo-Indian poetic translations illustrates how colonial administration and imaginative writing exacerbated the British dominion of India but also renovated English literary forms. The politics that accrued around these revised forms can be seen by examining the impersonation of women's voices by male Anglo-Indian writers, a moment that Gayatri Chakravorty Spivak has discussed in her essay

"Can the Subaltern Speak?" These cross-gender impersonations of native Indian women created a complex sexual politics of imperial expansion. Similar kinds of impersonation appear in two revisions of Thomas Gray's "The Bard" (1757), which replaced his Welsh speaker with Indian Brahmans. These imitations of "The Bard" adjust the intricacies of Gray's poem to the specifics of Indian geography and cultural traditions while simultaneously assessing colonialism in Asia. The impersonation of Indian women's voices and the creation of bardic Brahman voices involve what I call a "dislocated orientalism," a phenomenon that operated by disembedding voices from their original context and shuttling them back and forth between Asia and Europe to create a new kind of poetics which modulates global and local elements of empire.

WILLIAM JONES AND THE FOUNTAINHEAD OF VERSE

The 1770s and 1780s, when the majority of the poems discussed in this chapter were written, constituted one of the most tumultuous periods in British colonialism. During this time, the British lost their thirteen American colonies and radically changed their dominion in India. With military successes in the 1750s, the East India Company, which had until then focused primarily on trade, began to take on the administrative functions of government. Although its possessions in 1783 included only northern provinces (such as Bengal), the city of Bombay, and territories in the south, and though the number of company employees in India was small—perhaps below three hundred—the British colony there was expanding as the East India Company acquired territory and subjugated local rulers.[12] As part of its governmental role, and in concert with the British Parliament, the East India Company established courts of law, settled disputes, and began collecting tributary revenues (*diwani*) from the inhabitants of its provinces.[13] This shift from a commercial to a governmental attitude necessitated the creation of intellectual institutions and imaginations with which to legitimize this new dispensation. During this period, Warren Hastings, an experienced former East India Company employee appointed as first governor-general in India in 1772, helped found the Asiatick Society of Bengal. This society, modeled on the Royal Society, was devoted to all aspects of scholarly research on the Indian subcontinent. It compiled a comprehensive, systematic vision of Asia, and it included some of the luminaries of Bengal's British administrative class, who delivered papers and published findings on topics ranging from astronomy to zoology.[14] In their attention to scientific exploration, they did not neglect political expediency; a copy of their publication, the *Transactions of the Asiatick Society*, was presented to King George III at the royal court by an employee of the East India Company.[15] In addition to the Asiatick Society, Hastings also patronized individual authors, such as Nathaniel Brassey Halhed, who in 1776 produced a translation of Hindu laws, and Charles Wilkins, who in 1785 produced the first English translation of the Hindu scriptural epic, the *Bhagavad Gita*. These writers benefited from Calcutta's incipient English publishing industry, and their scholarly productions were seen as having important mutual benefits for the colony, extending and refining Britain's influence while uncovering a reservoir of traditions from which new kinds of English writing and knowledge could be produced.[16] This writing was seen as a way to popularize Indian culture in Europe and to influence British public opinion positively about the East India Company, which was always toggling between admiration and suspicion.[17]

William Jones was one of Hastings's close friends and beneficiaries. A brilliant linguist—he read many languages—Jones spent much of his life promoting his belief that Eastern voices could rejuvenate European art. He arrived in Calcutta in 1784 as a member of the newly established Supreme Court in Bengal. The position he created for himself—as a cultural mediator, an avid orientalist, and a colonial administrator—is comparable to the intricate literary revisions that resulted from his mixing of Eastern and Western cultural forms.[18] He had been interested in Eastern poetry since attending Oxford University; after receiving his degree, he published a collection of Arabic and Persian translations, titled *Poems, Consisting Chiefly of Translations from the Asiatick Languages* (1772). Later, while serving as a justice in Bengal, Jones learned Sanskrit, which he called "sweet as nectar," eventually becoming a fluent speaker, reader, and writer of the language.[19] Although he initially learned Sanskrit to administer better justice to the natives of India, who traced their laws back to ancient religious codes, he eventually became an admirer of its antiquity, translating its prose, poetry, and drama into English.[20] Jones even composed poetry in Sanskrit, which apparently was accomplished enough that his teacher made copies so that his own son could memorize and recite it.[21]

The foreignness of Indian culture was crucial to Jones's poetic inspiration, and he sought to harness its exoticism. In his "Essay on the Poetry of Eastern Nations" (1772), Jones claims that European poetry had "subsisted too long on the perpetual repetition of the same images, and incessant allusions to the same fables."[22] India, Jones felt, was a "fountain head" from which almost limitless inspiration could be derived.[23] This new fount, he thought, could overcome the staleness of neoclassicism that wearyingly traced itself back to and repeated the cultural forms of Greece and Rome. He added Arabic and Indian poets to the typical model of literary influence propounded by Alexander Pope, in poems like *An Essay on Criticism* (1711), that asserted Homer and the Greeks as the beginning of all literature. Jones saw Indian knowledge as a valuable resource—like cotton or silk—that could provide Europe with something it lacked. As a resource, it was meant to be extracted. Jones commented positively about working in the "mine of Indian literature"; while preparing to return to England in 1793—a trip cut short by his death—he packed manuscripts, books, and other printed matter of Eastern works, a collection he wrote was meant to "introduce books, which Europe never saw before."[24] In his aesthetic geography, India was an origin, a chronological precursor to Greece and Rome in the westward progression of the arts (*translatio studii*) that was such a powerful cultural myth for eighteenth-century authors. Jones believed that in India he had discovered something anterior to European culture, and he felt that the British presence in India was a return to that origin.[25] To look eastward from Britain, Jones suggested, was to look deep into the cultural past, beyond Greece and Rome; space took on temporal dimensions.

The East contributed new models of poetic speakers and more intense appreciations of poetry. Jones argued that Arabians had a language adapted to poetry because they were "extremely addicted to the softer passions."[26] He was fascinated by Arabic poetry competitions, which he felt showed an appreciation for poetic forms and a "richness" of invention that he ascribed to the hot climate's creation of leisure time to engage in art. He described learned Hindus as "enthusiastick admirers of Poetry" and considered Sanskrit to be an original language, with texts that went "on to infinity."[27] Some of Jones's contemporaries did not share his fervor for these new reservoirs, believing them to be unsuitable to English literature.[28] However, by synthesizing climatological notions of poetic inspiration with the copiousness and antiquity of Sanskrit, Jones redefined the East, not as corrupt and despoiled, but as suffused with poetry, as a place where language was naturally rich and poets were appreciated. He thus produced another version of the persistent fantasy that the Eden of poetry was always elsewhere. What was remarkably different about his fantasy, when compared to Grays's medieval Wales or James Macpherson's Ossianic Scotland, was that Jones actually inhabited his poetic Eden.

The challenge of Jones's imagination of India is not just that it celebrates new voices but that it uses English literary forms to explain them and, as a consequence, to reconceive what East-West relationships can be. Jones found in India fresh images, allusions, and fables, a reserve from which "future scholars might explain, and future poets might imitate."[29] This alternate archive of poetic inspiration coincided with Jones's better-known scholarship as a linguist. His "Third Anniversary Discourse" (1786), which he delivered to the Asiatick Society in Calcutta, suggests that Sanskrit is "more perfect" than Greek and "more copious" than Latin. Yet there is such a "strong affinity" between these languages that they must have "sprung from a common source."[30] This idea of a single origin for all Indo-European languages would be Jones's lasting legacy, and it is still recognized by many modern linguists as an important contribution. Yet, few have noted that this thesis of a common origin also influenced his poetry. Jones legitimized his intellectual and artistic innovation by establishing a shared linguistic past; the Indo-European hypothesis is also a poetics.

Jones reoriented English poetry by connecting it with India, its fountainhead. His excitement about this connection inspired him to compose, during the 1780s, a series of nine "hymns," English poetic imitations of Hinduism's Sanskrit literature, particularly the Vedas, India's oldest sacred songs.[31] The Vedas were transmitted orally for thousands of years, combining regular meters with lyrics to produce a comprehensive vision of the universe.[32] Jones called these poems "hymns" in conscious allusion to their oral and religious origin. In them he devised English metrical and formal equivalents for Hindu sounds and myths by intermixing the more accessible address of the eighteenth-century English hymn with the ode, which had been an important source of innovation during the eighteenth century.[33] This syncretic hymning is particularly indebted to the verbal and speaking structures from Gray's Pindaric experiments, such as the "The Bard" and the "The Progress of Poesy," but Jones substituted Indian speakers for Welsh bards.

Jones's hymns offer a perspective on Anglo-Indian relations that seems also motivated by the kinds of collaborations at work in the Anglo-Welsh cultural revival. A lifelong advocate for Wales, Jones was a member of the Cymmrodorion Society, a society operating in London whose principles included the maintenance of traditional Welsh oral culture.[34] He had even fashioned himself a Welsh bard, creating an association named the Druids of Cardigan and installing himself as chief bard (*pencerdd*).[35] In his poetry, he tapped the Welsh cultural revival to establish his identity as a singer, interpreter, and translator, carefully combining elements of this cultural history with his interest in Sanskrit texts.[36]

But while in India, Jones clothed himself, literally and figuratively, in the knowledge, voices, and garb of Indianism, conjoining British and Indian cultural practices. At his retreat in Krishnagar, just north of Calcutta, he acted like a Brahman and at times addressed his English correspondents as though he were an "Indian Zemindar [*zamindar*]," a sovereign landowner who functioned almost like a prince.[37] It is easy to see his imitation of Brahman culture and style as equivalent to his imitations of Vedic songs. He dressed himself as an Indian prince and described his translations of Arabic poems as putting on them an "English dress," following a quite common eighteenth-century trope of translation as a change of clothes. He likely would have considered his imitations of Vedas as another opportunity for him to put on Indian garb. At the same time, he maintained clear characteristics of his Britishness, calling his vacation retreat a cottage, attempting to recreate a distinctly pastoral life. In Calcutta, he even kept a large pet turtle that he named Othello.[38]

The pretended Welsh bard was thus reclothed as an eighteenth-century orientalist scholar and administrator. By portraying himself as a bard with unique linguistic and cultural expertise and by "going native" in thought, dress, and text, Jones placed himself at the center of what Balanchandra Rajan has called the "multiple othernesses" that were at play in late-eighteenth-century Bengal.[39] But, rather than follow the usual relationship between colonizer and native in colonialism, in which the dominant person defines the subjected citizens as others and then further defines the self by excluding them, Jones attempted to establish a reciprocal rapport between Indian traditions and British poets. He created a kind of diversity that looks like multiculturalism, before that concept had been articulated, and yet he was already cognizant of its limitations. This reciprocity, Rajan says, resulted in Jones's "perplexed positionality."[40]

Jones's perplexities identify conceptual difficulties that theories of orientalism have been struggling with since their inception: how do we understand the appreciation that came with the eighteenth-century orientalism of scholars like Jones while also acknowledging the vital role it played in colonial expansion? Jones's representation of himself as a speaker—indeed, at times as an Indian speaker—gives us another way to consider this difficult question. His actions provide an example: He names his turtle Othello, suggesting that he understands the "perplexities" of his identity and his amalgamated social surroundings, calling to mind an alien Moorish figure made canonical in a play by English literature's most famous "bard." Similarly, in the cross-dressing of translation, he seeks out the affinities and connections between the spaces, social positions, and identities of his colonial life—his Welsh bardism, English education, multilingual training, and his status as a colonial jurist. He borrows from mid-eighteenth-century metaphors of poetic composition as an act of listening, and he describes himself as an exemplary auditor. He creates hymns that modernize and translate the performance traditions of Sanskrit songs. Such interest in working between cultures is made possible by his facility with languages, but it is not exclusively linguistic in its effects.[41] His insistence on "going native" is more than an imitation; it is also an act of colonial "re-signification" that takes native cultural materials and reinterprets them in contexts that for them are unusual.[42] Parama Roy suggests that assuming such a position of authenticity is a way of displacing the "native informant," but I think of it instead as a way of fabricating an informant where none formerly existed.[43] Drawing from Welsh traditions to personify Indian speakers and altering English literary forms to mediate Sanskrit songs allowed Jones to listen in on India without having to engage with the full complexity of actual Indian voices or to reproduce their sound with the same sense of accuracy that would dominate studies of oral traditions in ensuing centuries.[44] In fact, while Jones made himself knowledgeable about Hindu traditions, religion, and music, his poetry does not exhibit the fascination with recounting the scene of oral recitation or the significance of ethnographical authority and collection that would become so prominent in the nineteenth century.[45] Rather than seek to remove himself as an arbiter of these recast Hindu traditions, Jones fitted them into his English verse forms.

Jones's hymns thus are the conduit by which Vedic myths become verbal in English, with himself as the essential intermediary whose expertise is imagined as an ability to listen and sing. The Brahman speaker of the "Hymn to Surya" (1786) states that Jones "came . . . lisping our celestial tongue" (line 184); Jones does the "lisping" that Indian bards presumably cannot do for themselves. This lisping recalls Pope in his *An Epistle from Mr. Pope, to Dr. Arbuthnot* (1735), in which Pope explains why he writes by claiming that he "lisp'd in numbers, for the numbers came."[46] Pope's lisp is a moment of supreme self-confidence. Jones brought this image of confident inspiration with him to India, but in his version of authorial self-fashioning, Brahmans, rather than Jones himself, assert that the "numbers came." He routes his self-aggrandizement through the vitality of Indian voices. His knowledge becomes refigured as an aural acuity—an ability to hear Indian voices and turn them into printed poems with a specific accent, with the right lisp.

Likewise, in the "Hymn to Indra" (1785), a poem to the Hindu god of the skies, Jones refers to himself as an "isle-born bard" who "wakes" and "hears" the songs of Hindu speakers, which he records for English audiences (6). He includes himself among those "Sweet bards" who "shall hymn [Indra's] glory" in the future (92). Jones claimed that in "Hymn to Indra" he varied the stanzas with "a principle entirely new in modern lyrick poetry."[47] The newness of this lyric (presumably a result of his desire to capture Sanskrit's unique oral performances) created a particular accent that would bind English and India at the level of form long into the future.[48] And by using the term "hymn" as both a noun and a verb—a hymn that hymns Indra's glory—Jones identifies the genre and names the act of re-signification that together convert Sanskrit songs into English poetry. This hymning, moreover, is approved by those Indian speakers that Jones impersonates. The Brahmans he has created happily confirm the fidelity of his poetry and license its global circulation.

Many of Jones's contemporaries accepted this supreme confidence and orientalist expertise, asserting his authenticity and sometimes even arguing that he was a better representative of Eastern poetry than Eastern poets themselves. In an elegy written shortly after Jones's death, for example, an anonymous author claims that Jones's "magic voice" could unfold the "mysteries" of the East.[49] A memorialist writing in the early nineteenth century opined that "a sweeter lyre no eastern swain hath strung." And still another had this vision: seven "selected bards of Mecca stand / Mourning their western brother of the lyre."[50] These scenes construct an overdetermined orientalism in which the authenticity of Jones's poetry supersedes that of his own invented speakers. This anxious, contradictory position is possible only because British readers fantasized that Easterners themselves acknowledged Jones's superiority. While postcolonial criticism has recognized this as a familiar pose for the orientalist admirer, I would add that portraying Easterners as deferring to Jones's authority felt tenable to these celebrants because Jones's hymns were part of an ongoing series of poetic experiments (by Gray, Macpherson, and others) that grappled with how to mediate foreign voices into English texts.

Becoming the exemplary figure to extend these experiments to India required that Jones create new literary forms, and renovate old ones as well. For one crucial part of the "The Hymn to Durgá" (1788), for instance, Jones borrowed the final scene from Gray's "The Bard," in which the Welsh bard jumps from the cliffs of Mount Snowdon. The scene is resituated in the Himalayas to describe Shiva's courtship of Parvati, the exemplar of faith and devotion. Shiva, smitten by the beauty of Parvati, disguises himself as an old, lascivious Brahman with a "rude staff quiv'ring" in his "wither'd hand" (IV.3.7). He finds her dwelling on a cliff-face and tests her fidelity to him by exclaiming blasphemies. Unaware of his disguise, she rebukes the old Brahman, stating, "Who speaks, must agonize; who hears, must die" (V.3.5) and escapes by throwing herself from the mountainside.[51]

She spoke, and o'er the rifted rocks
Her lovely form with pious phrensy threw;
But beneath her floating locks
And waving robes a thousand breezes flew,
Knitting close their silky plumes,
And in mid-air a downy pillow spreading;
(VI.1.1–5)

At first glance, it might appear odd that a fatal plunge could express the romantic courtship of Indian deities, yet Jones echoes the concluding scene of "The Bard" to find a form with which to articulate Parvati's piety: she is willing to kill herself rather than be subjected to insults about her beloved. Unlike the last Welsh bard in Gray's poem, however, the fall in the "Hymn to Durgá" is interrupted; Parvati is saved by Shiva and transported "in clouds of rich perfumes" to a "mystick wood" where they consummate their love (VI.1.8–9). By being saved and transported, Parvati is able to dedicate herself to Shiva again and bear him children. Jones's adjustment of Gray's evocation of Welsh bardic traditions to celebrate and explain a central Hindu religious tale links this story with a crucial scene from eighteenth-century English poetry's experiment with translating foreign voices and speakers. The bard's suicidal loyalty to Wales becomes Parvati's selfless dedication to her husband. This point of contact between Britain and India, between European culture and Hindu religion, and the new poetical forms Jones created, are manifested in the cited yet altered final scene of Gray's poem.

In the "Hymn to Gangá" (1785), an encomium to the Ganges River (the Indian cultural equivalent to Mount Snowdon for Wales or Stonehenge for England), Jones likewise fitted principles from Gray's Pindaric odes to the particularities of Indian culture and geography. He embraced Gray's already unique Pindaric structure but enlarged it "by a line of *fourteen* syllables" to express the "solemn march of the great *Asiatick* rivers."[52] The languid, snaking motion of this central geographical feature necessitates a longer final line that properly captures the river's size and rhythm. The metrics of Gray's Pindarics thus are modified in Jones's hymn, taking on the stretching sublimity of Asian geography. Thinking of the Ganges as a heptameter line of poetry—a form most common in the sixteenth century and considered "sprawling" by the eighteenth century—demonstrates that conventional poetry was recharged by being pushed outward from Britain toward India.[53] Alloying Gray's Pindaric with a long line of "fourteener" verse creates an English form reshaped to India's geography. Even as Jones was objecting to the staleness of English literature, his modifications of it in the "Hymn to Gangá" led him back to an English common meter often found in the popular lyrics of religious hymns. This hymn provided him an opportunity to detail Indian geography, and detailing Indian geography supplied him with unusual content for his hymn.

As Gray's odes were an important formal inspiration for Jones's hymns, like the odes, the hymns were also a means of expressing politics. The "Hymn to Gangá" delivers a prophecy, as the last Welsh bard does in Gray's "The Bard." These two prophecies, however, convey notably different attitudes about the British. Whereas the last Welsh bard curses them in an expression of national resistance, the Brahman speaker of Jones's poem implores the goddess Ganges to acknowledge British efforts on behalf of Indians, efforts which indicate that the British are

> . . . a peerless race
> With lib'ral heart and martial grace,
> Wafted from the colder isles remote:
> As they preserve our laws, and bid our terror cease,
> So be their darling laws preserv'd in wealth, in joy, in peace
> (165–69)

The British are the "peerless race" with "lib'ral heart" that serendipitously is "wafted" in from across the globe. At first glance, this fawning address seems to praise the British and unashamedly legitimize their occupation of India. Appropriating Indian speakers to describe India's interactions with the British as providential and beneficent undoubtedly sanctions colonialism. The Indian speaker calling the British a "peerless race" implicitly maligns his own and credits the British with creating the "wealth . . . joy . . . [and] peace" that the speaker champions in the poem. And the speaker's claim that the British preserve Indian laws directly flatters Jones, a jurist who was central to that preservation. Jones advocated throughout his career that Muslim and Hindu legal complaints be decided according to those cultures' own customs, and to accomplish this he undertook, but was unable to complete, a multivolume digest of Muslim and Hindu laws. This passage suggests that Indians bless his efforts to codify their laws and to understand their cultural traditions.[54]

But more is at work in this impersonation of Indian voices and revision of Gray's bardic curse than first appears. Interceding with the "dread Goddess," the Hindu poet prays for the "peaceful duration" of British occupation "*under good laws well administered*."[55] This passage, often read as primary evidence of

Jones's colonialism, contains the potential for critique as well. Jones's Hindu speaker implicitly verbalizes his frustrations about justice by reminding the British that they are now responsible for the effective administration of "good laws," which have value in part because the natives bless them. The Brahman speaker's blessing, which makes up so much of the poem, is contingent upon this "just" administration, and Jones insinuates that the blessing of native Indians can be revoked as easily as it was given. While he appropriates the perspective of the native, he does so in such a way that at least some power still resides with that speaker.[56] Through this Brahman, Jones debates those members of the East India Company who, unlike him, would advocate for stronger British intervention in the legal affairs of Bengal's indigenous inhabitants.

The perplexities of Jones's identity as a colonizer and an appreciative orientalist are exemplified by instances like these, which orientalize English traditions as much as they anglicize Indian ones. Jones "goes native" in dress, learning, and writing, while maintaining his European heritage and consistently planning to return to England with a large fortune. Such ambivalence is now sometimes seen as characteristic of colonial discourse. In this case, however, his orientalist poetry is more than an act of simple appropriation or an aesthetic "conquest" in the service of British dominion. The complex identities Jones created in his poems and the recharged forms that he designed—the presentation of Vedic songs as Western hymns and odes; the refashioning of Welsh bardism as cultural intermediation—demonstrate the central place of Anglo-Indian poetry in the politics of orientalism.

This politics can be sensed in the circulation of printed texts and manuscripts that acted as relay points in a global system of communication through which the debate about colonialism took place. Jones read aloud the first hymn that he composed (the "Hymn to Camdeo") to great applause at the Asiatick Society of Bengal; it was eventually published in a Calcutta journal.[57] This success spurred him to send copies of three hymns to Hastings, who in the late 1780s was in London, after being recalled from his post as governor-general in India and impeached by Edmund Burke for corruption.[58] Jones was also corresponding with Burke, who applauded Jones's imitated hymns as an essential component of the "protection" of Indian "rights" and who described Jones as doing "justice" to Indian traditions, in much the same way that Burke felt he was exacting justice for Indians by impeaching Hastings.[59] Despite his physical distance from this debate, Jones seems to have been a part of it. He was sent a transcript of a dramatic speech in Parliament by the playwright, member of Parliament, and Burke ally Richard Brinsley Sheridan, in which Sheridan introduced part of the long list of criminal charges against Hastings.[60] Hastings, who read and approved of Jones's poetic imitations of Hindu voices, was counting on the written testimony of native Indian voices to exonerate him from charges of exploitation. Burke dismissed these testimonies as "forgeries," in part because the voices seemed to him too "European" in style.[61] The intricate material exchanges among Jones, Hastings, Burke, and Sheridan alert us to the role Indian voices played in the politics of late-eighteenth-century Britain. This network of texts, traveling back and forth between India and England in packet ships and mail carriages, shows that Indian voices were consistently put toward British political ends in concrete ways and with actual consequences. These exchanges give a material shape to Jones's theories that Eastern voices could revive English poetry and that voicing Indian speakers was a means of refurbishing English literature, which had become stale, while tying Britain and India ever more closely together. Literary forms still are often seen as primarily attached to a nation's own history, but Jones's poetry provides another example of how the study of English poetic form necessitates an understanding of its persistent internationalism.

MAKING THE SUBALTERN SPEAK

Impersonating Indians thus became one means of articulating colonial politics from new vantages and via revised literary forms. One of the most controversial instances of impersonation is Eyles Irwin's "Bedukah, or the Self-Devoted" (1776).[62] This poem, written in Madras, concerns a widow who commits self-immolation; it is part of a series of eclogues set in Asian locations, including places in China and India. "Bedukah" is the richest and most enigmatic effort in Irwin's collection. Like Jones, Irwin exemplified the multiple identities of Britain's colonial authors, whose professional and personal lives entwined poetry and colonial economy. Born in Calcutta but educated in England, Irwin eventually returned to India as an underwriter, surveyor, and revenue collector for the East India Company.[63] In each of these roles, he acted as one of those administrators whose purpose it was to transform Indian traditions into English forms of knowledge. At its core, "Bedukah" examines how British authors should represent Indian speakers and how well Indian subjects fit English forms of knowledge. Although "Bedukah" was not written as part of Irwin's professional portfolio, it nonetheless addresses many of the political issues facing him and his fellow officers, and it demonstrates how imaginative literature and colonial administration intersected in late-eighteenth-century India.

The poem begins with an invocation of a European muse. By using this conventional opening, Irwin situated his poem within contemporary British orientalism, in which Western forms of knowledge organized and acted upon Eastern subjects. Setting the events of the poem in comfortable, familiar forms of knowledge was necessary, because the poem presents the final moments of Bedukah, a devoted Hindu wife who is burned alive with her already deceased husband. *Sati,* the practice of widows burning themselves on their husbands' funeral pyres, was only somewhat familiar to British readers.[64] Often presented in the press as barbaric and tyrannical, it was used to justify intervention in India: public figures insisted that European gentlemen were needed to protect Indian women from various forms of oppression (none of which ever included European colonialism) and to educate Indian men about polite manners and chivalrous sentimentality.[65] In Irwin's poem, however, instead of British men saving Indian women, it is Bedukah who becomes exemplary, speaking with pleasure about the prospect of being burned alive and seeking to educate Westerners about the custom and to explain her decision. In the process, she teaches the poem's admiring male speaker and the female readers, to whom the poem is directed, the meaning of virtue and sacrifice. "Bedukah" allows Irwin to explore the contours of orientalism's representational scheme, in which Western authors speak on behalf of Eastern others. He offers a parable for the interaction of European poetry and colonial voices, a moral for European women to follow, and a fantasy about the advantages and limitations of using poetry to record the exotic elements of the Asian colonies.

Irwin described "Bedukah" as an "Indian pastoral." That he placed the horror of Indian self-immolation in the pastoral mode—typically reserved for leisure, enjoyment, and singing—shows some of the incongruity involved in English writers ventriloquizing Indian speakers. The "elasticity and responsiveness" of the pastoral made it an advantageous vehicle for the cultural imperatives of late-eighteenth-century colonialism.[66] Still, to write an "Indian pastoral" is to create a contradiction, and the poem quivers and cracks as it reconciles the customs of its content with the styles of its form. Irwin composed the poem in rhyming heroic couplets, a neoclassical configuration popular throughout the eighteenth century. Consequently, the dying declarations of its title character are spoken with the regularity of someone trained in the balanced harmonies of Pope. Bedukah ends up sounding like Belinda from *The Rape of the Lock,* if Belinda had been burned alive. In many ways, the precise attention to manifesting the acoustics of culturally situated vocal performances characteristic of Gray's imitations of Welsh prosody and the innovative printed forms of Macpherson's Ossian poems give way to placing alien speakers into more conventional English metrical structures. This does not mean that Irwin did not seek out his own types of invention with which to represent foreign voices. He refurbished the pastoral mode in this new climate by adapting it to the subject matter, scenes, and speakers of his poem, much as Jones adapted the Pindaric ode. In this "Indian pastoral," therefore, Irwin created a literary shape for what has been described as the hybridity of colonial discourse.[67] An Indian pastoral is a paradox—a Westernized tradition made Eastern—but it is also a double posture that permitted a British-Indian author like Irwin to speak in multiple voices to multiple audiences.

The poem gathers together a wide variety of voices, including Bedukah, her mother, a male European witness named Lycon, and the narrator. Each speaker offers a different perspective on this act of self-immolation. As a witness, Lycon is crucial to the logic of the poem. His voice assures readers that Bedukah's excellence shall be publicized by the "bewitching voice of fame" (III.113). The interplay of voices, within the poem and in its imagined afterlife of publication, indicates that speaking and hearing are significant tropes for the representation of the colonial encounter, turning reading the poem into an act of aural witnessing. The importance placed upon speaking and hearing in this poem coincides with a gradual erosion of seeing as a reliable form of witness in the course of the account. Throughout the poem, veils suddenly reveal or obstruct Lycon's view of Bedukah's death. These veils are metaphors for the difficulties of intercultural communication and the boundaries of what can and cannot be represented to Western readers. As Bedukah mounts the funeral pyre, she "casts her veil aside" (II.8). Once her veil is removed, Lycon notes: "One breast was slightly hid" and "one half-display'd, / Which, wild with youthful blood, luxuriant play'd"; the description of Bedukah's death thus allies the erotic and the exotic, sexualizing for British readers the Indian custom of sati (II.25–26). But Irwin's poem pulls aside this veil only momentarily before lowering it once again. As Bedukah begins to burn, "clouds of smoke" wreathe her body and obscure the scene:

> The priests with fragrant oil still feed the flame,
> Whose darkness round conceals the martyr'd dame.
> O! of this curtain let the Muse avail,
> Nor paint the sequel of the horrid tale.
> Enough of female faith is brought to light,
> Esteem, regard, and pity to excite.
>
> (III.81–85)

Since much of the poem anticipates the self-sacrificial display of Bedukah's "stubborn Virtue," the veiling of her death only magnifies its fascination and power (II.118). The speaker stops the poem—stops even the Muse—from penetrating the "curtain" that surrounds her burning body (III.83). The veil prevents us from seeing her immolation, and Irwin refuses to depict the final moments of her life. This is the limit beyond which the poem will not pass. The veil that had tantalized the reader with an exotic sexuality becomes a symbol of Western poetry's inability to represent the East.

The smoke might prevent us from seeing Bedukah's death, but it does not prevent us from hearing it. Bedukah sings until she dies, and Irwin gives a detailed aural description of her final moments.[68] When the signal to light the fire is given, it is as if

> At once a thousand trumpets rend the air,
> A thousand voices loud accordance bear:
> In Babel's tower not greater tumult rung,
> When strange confusion jarr'd from tongue to tongue.
> The signal giv'n!—-quick to the altar's side
> A thousand torches are at once applied.
>
> (III.73–78)

The thousand voices together with the thousand torches give the wife burning an acclamatory aspect. Lycon hears the signal to burn Bedukah "vibrate" on his ear (III.71–72), and her final words, he confesses, are "still trembling" there (III.99).[69] Chaos, Babel, and loudness were a central part of European accounts of sati, as Thomas Rowlandson's 1815 engraving *The Burning System Illustrated* demonstrates (Fig. 15). This engraving satirizes the debate about outlawing the practice of sati. British administrators, speaking to each other while Hindus prostrate themselves at their feet, claim to have "private reasons" for not suppressing the practice, reasons made clear by the small bags of money, labeled "rupees," that each of them holds. These bags are bribes paid by Hindus to allow the practice to continue. It is the left side of the illustration, however, that interests me. There, Rowlandson portrays a vivid carnival-like scene complete with drums, trumpets, singers, and acrobats, among other entertainments. Rowlandson's visual depiction is reminiscent of a public execution scene, which was used in comparisons that explained sati for European readers.[70]

Bedukah's voice pierces the tumult and gives a sermon on the moral improvement of English women. Her singing serves as an example of "Eastern Virtue and Religion's force," which Lycon hears, records, and transmits to his

Figure 15. Thomas Rowlandson, engraving, *The Burning System Illustrated* (1815). Courtesy of the British Library Board (C.59.f.11).

European readers in such fashion that her foreign voice resonates within this poem and for its readers (I.1). Her voice compels Lycon to speak out, to assure Bedukah and her family that he will value her memory and give her voice a form that Europeans can read. His account of sati, like Irwin's poem, translates her speech into a new cultural idiom that allows English readers to witness her example from afar. Bedukah herself encourages Lycon to see, hear, and remember. Not fearful at her death, she tells Lycon, as he is about to turn away, "make thee witness of BEDUKAH's end . . . [a]nd see a woman unsubdued by pain" (III.42, 44). Bedukah becomes a model for British women; her last words tell Lycon, "To Christian wives a Pagan's death relate, / And bid them envy, if not imitate" (III.51–52). Irwin suggests that English women, apparently more corrupt than India's devoted wives, have something to learn from Bedukah. He valorizes Indian women at the expense of British ones, and reverses the common sentiment that Britain should be horrified by this controversial Indian custom.

Yet Irwin also seems keenly interested in showing the potential of European art and aesthetics to record the voices of Asia. Bedukah's death is redeemed by the European witness and Irwin's poetic arts. This intercultural dialogue ultimately reaffirms poetry's ability to absorb the speakers and subjects of the East into traditional European literary forms. If, as Spivak contends, the colonial woman was always "doubly in shadow," then Irwin established an alternative in the idea that poetry, like Bedukah's self-immolation, brings her virtue "to light."[71] This light "melts" readers, the poem argues, reducing them to tears. These images of light and melting—oddly concordant with the topic of burning—appear repeatedly in the poem. Irwin describes Bedukah's voice as melting the crowd of onlookers.[72] Although Lycon initially describes widow burning as a "cruel custom" (I.88–89), by the end of the poem he thinks it an expression of the highest virtue, in which "female faith is brought to light" (III.85). Irwin himself dedicated the poem to "Eliza," saying that he had "melted o'er her funeral pyre" (I.16). Conceiving women as figures of inspiration, the poem's colonial poetics of gendered sentimentality revolves around the idea of men melting over female sacrifice. That Irwin voices an Indian woman who gladly displays her virtue by being burned alive makes his poem a fraught exercise of gender subordination. He created a type of spectacular femininity appreciated by listening men. This spectacle linked Indian women to their British counterparts by placing them in competition through sentimental expressions of virtuousness.[73] The spectacle of sati and of dying women's voices becomes a public good in this poem.

Spivak calls widow burning an ideological battleground and makes this battle a central example of the subaltern woman's inability to "speak."[74] Much of Spivak's "Can the Subaltern Speak?" and its expansion in *A Critique of Postcolonial Reason* concerns Western intellectuals who searched for colonial voices but invariably made them "mute" by repeating the primacy of the Western subject.[75] India, Spivak notes, is a "problem of representation" for British authors, who consistently construct it as a place that is "continuous and homogenous."[76] Unable to differentiate among Indians, the British, she claims, write them as if they were all the same. Irwin's "Bedukah" illustrates an eighteenth-century version of this problem. To make a colonial woman speak, Irwin transformed her into an uncomplicated subject—a selfless exemplar of womanly virtue coextensive with her husband. Any similarity between the subordinated position of Bedukah and her British counterparts is eradicated by his use of an Indian woman's voice to discipline those women. Irwin's poem reads like a confirmation of Spivak's argument about the primacy of the Western male subject. Despite the fact that in Irwin's poem European men use Indian women to criticize British women, it still offers something highly unusual in eighteenth-century poetry: a fictional version of what Spivak claims is absent from the debate about widow burning—"the testimony" of the "voice-consciousness" of the subaltern woman.[77] Spivak asks: "What is at stake when we insist that the subaltern woman speak?"[78] Irwin's poem offers one sort of answer by concocting the fiction that he has discovered and heard the voice-consciousness of Indian women. It co-opts what Spivak calls the "counter sentence" that the voices of Indian women would have provided in the debate among British and Indian men over the possession of women's bodies by composing that counter sentence for them. Composition of this counter sentence no doubt makes Irwin an example of Western male appropriation and subordination of both British and colonial women. In this sense, Spivak may be right that the subaltern woman's voice can never be heard. In this reading, the poem becomes an instance of this silencing, because it offers a fictive hope that her voice has been heard when it has not.

However, another interpretation might emphasize how notable it is that Bedukah dismisses the morality and virtue of British women. Her colonial voice is portrayed as being preserved by the (male) Western subject, but Bedukah is also invested with a power that supersedes that of her Western audience. Assuming the speaking position of an Indian woman allowed Irwin to critique what he perceived as corrupted English culture. Figuring her voice as a final, suicidal vocal performance makes her voice akin to the dying enunciations of the last Welsh bard. Moreover, her performance is set in India but directed within the poem to an English-language audience, making the poem a vessel by which dead Indian voices travel overseas. India thus becomes a place from which an author can authoritatively examine and satirize British women by using another's voice as a proxy. Bedukah seeks to educate and to conform British women, a radical position for the 1770s. Sanctified by her performance of virtuous sacrifice, associated with the authenticity of colonial speakers, her voice provides opportunities for Irwin to criticize European women. In this formulation, subaltern speech and the exotic colonial woman are powerful weapons, and ones as effective in the European world as in the Asian one.

As this analysis of "Bedukah" shows, reading for the subaltern voice presents an ethical quandary for literary critics. The impersonation of Indian speakers by British writers during the colonial period raises questions about collaboration between ostensibly antagonistic political constituencies, much as it does in the cases of Welsh and Scottish cultural nationalists. Is it still foolish to think of impersonation as categorically similar to "authentic" voice? Is there anything redemptive about Western men representing the voices of Indian women or is it always a moment of suppression, no matter what her voice says? These difficult questions are magnified in John Leyden's "Song of the Telinga Dancing Girl. Addressed to an European Gentleman, in the Company of Some European Ladies" (1803).[79] The "Song of the Telinga Dancing Girl" explores the subjectivity of a colonial Indian woman, as "Bedukah" does, except that Leyden embraces the language of sati to access her internal thoughts. What readers find in her mind is a moment of cross-racial desire. Before the rigid separation exemplified by Thomas Macaulay's 1835 "Minute on Indian Education"—which calls for the creation of a "class" of Indians with English manners who would act as "interpreters" between the British and those "millions whom [they] govern"[80]—these kinds of relationships were known, and they indicated another link between British colonists and Indians.[81] Describing this cross-racial desire with the discourse of sati makes the gender competition of "Bedukah" explicit and produces a potentially massive disruption of the sexual politics of Eastern colonialism.

Leyden, like Irwin, was an administrator with the East India Company. As a translator and linguist in India, Java, and Malaysia, with knowledge of numerous languages, Leyden had a career that necessitated interacting with others' voices. He arrived in Madras in 1803 and in 1807 became the Chair of Hindostani at Fort William College, an educational institution established for the purpose of training East India Company employees. He composed poetry, much of it from the perspective of ethnic others, including Africans, Malaysians, and his Afghan servant, Pushto. Nearly all of his poems are in conventional English verse forms; much like Irwin, Leyden revised these different ethnic voices to fit into standard poetic English. This is true for Rad'ha, the dancing woman referred to in this three-stanza poem, who admires and longs for her white Englishman in a form of iambic tetrameter:

Dear youth, whose features bland declare
A milder clime than India's air,
These ardent glances hither turn!
For thee, for thee alone, I burn.

Ah! If these kindling eyes could see
No dearer beauty here than me,
I vow by this impassion'd sigh,
For thee, for thee, would Rad'ha die!

Ah me! Where'er I turn my view,
Bright rivals rise of fairer hue,
Whose charms a milder sun declare.—
Ah! Rad'ha yields to sad despair.

The language of this poem reads as a familiar repetition of romantic conceits found in Petrarch, Sidney, and Shakespeare. Yet, when set in an interracial context and interpreted through the sort of spectacular femininity of sati, the language of burning and desire takes on a heightened significance. Following Leask, we might read this poem as an expression of a familiar colonial logic, whereby the exotic woman is an object of orientalist desire. In this reading, Rad'ha is a foil by which the male colonizer can vocalize his own sexual appetites by displacing them onto a sexually excited woman. Such exotic desires are directed toward an imagined male reader who is meant to "enjoy" the admiration of a native girl.[82] Put in the position of the "European Gentleman," readers participate virtually in the exotic pleasures of the East, including native women dancing for him. Rad'ha's internal thoughts are equivalent to her alluring dance. Her voice, like her body and her desire for white men, must be interpreted as fetishized and highly racialized.

Rad'ha, like Bedukah, is undoubtedly a British fantasy of Indian women as available and submissive, but it may be possible to see in Leyden's use of the language of sati a representation of cross-racial desire as unsettling. Rad'ha's desire is strong, even violent. She "burns" for her admirer; she vows with an "impassion'd sigh" that she would "die" without him, placing herself in the position of the virtuous wife. By setting the language of sati alongside that of more traditional discourse of romantic love, Leyden produces a sense of cross-racial desire as gender competition; Indian women want what white women have: white men. In this interpretation, the poem interrupts the unilateral focus on the reproduction of whiteness among the British colonizers of India. The poem's singular voice and its narrow attention on her internal thoughts align the sympathies of readers with a sentimentalized, desiring woman. Rather than a fantasy of an available exotic woman, she becomes a figure of pity, a lover who is unrequited because of the gendered and racial politics of colonialism.

Lycon's assertion that Bedukah should be a model for British women and Rad'ha's competition with white women for white men suggest how Indian colonialism raised anxious questions about what it meant to be British. If sati was an ideological battleground in eighteenth- and early-nineteenth-century India, then Irwin and Leyden extended that battleground to the sexual politics of Britain as it played out in its colonies. The consequences of this struggle had their fullest manifestation when Anglo-Indian authors absorbed Indian customs and voices into their poems, making the subaltern speak rather than keeping them silent. These poems show that, before the nineteenth-century shift in Indian colonial politics that rigidly separated white culture from Indian culture, British authors were intrigued by poetry's ability to create Indian voices that they could then use to evaluate their own colonial policies and sexual desires. The poetic techniques of speaker and voice were used to extend colonialism's ideological dominion and to examine critically its effect on Western subjects. Conferring voices on Indian women made them into speaking subjects, but only temporarily and for the explicit purpose of allowing the British to speak to themselves about themselves. Quite often, the innovations of these poetic forms revolved around the identity of the speaker as much as the structure of the verse. Nonetheless, these poems turn what appear to be conventional genres and forms toward disruptive ends, transforming their speakers' performances for their audiences of English readers. Thus, their speakers cannot help but speak in an English accent, even if this accent is a strategic first step—clumsy as it may be—to exploring Eastern consciousness. At a moment when colonial domination was less rigid and encompassing than it would be a century later, it may be that the subaltern voice had more possibilities to be recognized and to upset what we now assume to have been the orthodox dynamics of colonialism.

REWRITING GRAY'S "THE BARD" IN INDIA

Irwin's Bedukah and Leyden's Rad'ha are examples of Eastern speakers' being fit into Western cultural patterns. Bedukah's peculiar "accent" is created by putting her speech in a pastoral form and in neoclassical heroic couplets, creating someone who sounds familiar while describing notably alien things. This combination of familiarity and exoticism was a motivating paradox of Anglo-Indian poetry, and it explains why authors replaced actual Indian women's voices with fictional ones. Another significant but often overlooked way that India was made familiar to English readers is by orientalizing English literary texts and traditions. To investigate this dynamic and its effects, I return to Thomas Gray's "The Bard" and assess how it was imaginatively transported to India in the late eighteenth century. Jones rewrote this poem as part of his attempt to fashion an intermediary position between Indian traditions and English poetry, harnessing Sanskrit to recast some of the eighteenth-century's most popular literary forms. In this process, Jones orientalized English verse forms by circuiting them through India, before returning them to England again as print. The poems examined next also orientalize Gray's "The Bard," but in remaking Gray's images and literary forms they created an extremely precise analytic for the contemporary debate about British governance of eastern India. In these recitations, Gray's poem becomes something like a fossilized relic in which we can see the accumulating sedimentary lines of the debate about colonialism.

"The Bard" was a good candidate to be relocated to India because it narrates indigenous resistance to English occupation. As I note in Chapter 1, with this difficult poem dense with historical references, Gray interprets the legend that the English king Edward I murdered all of the Welsh bards after he invaded and subdued Wales during the thirteenth century. Welsh bards were seen by many mid-eighteenth-century authors as artists and historians who had significant political power in traditional Celtic and Nordic cultures. Indeed, the majority of "The Bard" is spoken by the last living Welsh bard, who tries to resist the invading English army with his voice. At a crucial point in the poem, he is joined by the ghosts of his fellow bards, who form an apparitional choir and amplify his song. At the end of the poem, the Welsh bard leaps to his death in front of the advancing English army as a final act of defiance. Anglo-Indian authors globalized the political concerns that Gray had localized in this English-Welsh antagonism; they rewrote the scenes, images, and voices of "The Bard" from an Indian perspective. They carried Gray's impersonations of Welsh bards into the Indian sphere, using them as a part of their program to imitate Indian voices while assessing the consequences of doing so. These authors adapted Gray's poem because it provided a model within which to consider whether speech acts, like curses and prophecies, could resist military and economic might. "The Bard" supplied a template upon which the notion of speaking out could be overlaid so as to comment on the twined issues of cultural preservation and political collision. The resistance of Welsh bards to English invasion became a metaphor for the British occupation of India, leading Anglo-Indian authors to focus on the conclusion of Gray's poem and the identity of his speakers.

That does not mean these rewritings were always critical of European colonialism. Irwin composed one version of "The Bard" that celebrates British dominion. His poem, "Ramah: Or The Brahman" (1780) borrows many of its features from Gray's poem but substitutes a Brahman speaker for the Welsh bard.[83] In front of a crowd, Ramah delivers a lengthy lesson on the history of India and prophesizes about its future as part of the British imperium, before leaping to his death. His "dying words" recapitulate the Indian subcontinent's subjection (line 34). He describes the struggle between Hinduism and Islam, lamenting that Hindu holy temples were defiled by the Muslim Mughal Empire. These Mughals are overthrown by what Ramah calls Hinduism's "all-righteous Gods," who get their revenge through the British, who are in turn characterized as "Christians sent to give our tyrants laws" (66). At this moment, Ramah establishes an alliance between Hinduism and Christianity against Islam.

Yet Ramah's poem ends with an ominous prophecy that the "crescent" (Islam) will overtake the "cross" (Christianity). Immediately after this pronouncement, Ramah throws himself from the top of the Hindu temple on which he has been speaking. This conclusion is nearly identical in language, attitude, and style to the description of the last Welsh bard plummeting from Mount Snowdon.

> He spake—and headlong darted from the height,
> Swift as the falling meteor cleaves the night.
> The hollow pavement to the fall resounds;
> The body streams with undistinguish'd wounds:
> The martyr's end the temple's records own,
> And leaves a lesson to the British throne!
>
> (115–20)[84]

One notable difference between this poem and Gray's "The Bard" is that Irwin does not produce the equivalent of an Indian accent. There is no attempt to imitate Indian oral poetry, as Gray imitates medieval Welsh prosody in his poem, and little effort to create English-language equivalents, as Jones does. Gray's idiosyncratic, irregular Pindaric ode is replaced with the more conventional heroic couplet. But Irwin nevertheless elaborates on the sense that the Welsh bard's suicide is a political act by writing his poem beyond the point when his Brahman speaker has hit the ground, offering in the sound of his body a "lesson to the British throne."

But what lessons are the British meant to learn from a falling Hindu body? Is Ramah's voice a thinly disguised confession of British anxieties about being overthrown by Muslims in India? Or is this a suggestion that the British should listen more closely to native speakers as a way to refine their dominion and thus avoid failing in the way their predecessors did? Answers to these questions do not exist within the poem. Instead, some clues are found in the poem's footnotes, which introduce a British voice to frame Ramah's poetic enunciations. Paratexts, such as prefaces and footnotes, were an important means by which Anglo-Indian poets made their poems intelligible to a diverse range of audiences.[85] Here, Irwin's footnotes seek to justify British colonialism. One footnote, for example, reassures readers that if the East India Company is "attentive" to native Indians it will "obviate the prophecy of our Bramin" (Irwin, p. 25). The use of "our" reveals much about the perspective of the poem. "Our" Brahman, the British speaker says, shows what can be avoided only with well-crafted colonial policies. These policies are explained in another footnote, which insists that "the balance of power should be the principal object of every state," arguing that the British only created an Indian empire out of "self-defence against the attacks of native and foreign enemies" (p. 25). The East India Company is described as supporting their colony "as much by the exercise of moderation and justice as by the terror of their arms" (p. 23). Appealing to patriotic British readers, another footnote states that "every lover of his country must consider with pleasure the conduct and success of the English" in ejecting other powers from the Asian subcontinent (p. 23). The British, in fact, are put in direct contrast to other nationalities, like "the Hollander" who "spreads his toils / Fawns like a friend, and seizes all the spoils. / His ill-got scepter blossoms but to fade, / By fraud secur'd, and with injustice sway'd" (lines 73–76). Oppression is always identified with local Muslim rulers or other European powers rather than with the Christian British.

These examples illustrate the stark differences between Gray's poem of Welsh resistance and Irwin's poem of British colonialism. Ramah, rather than inciting the crowd to resist, as the Welsh bard does, instead lectures the mass of listeners who surround him about the virtues of the "generous Briton" (line 78). The Indians are lucky to have escaped from the Mughals' grip to the protection of such a law-abiding and benevolent people, Irwin wheedles. Thus, Irwin rewrites "The Bard" to speak enthusiastically colonial propaganda in poetry. While structured as an address to his fellow countrymen, Ramah's pronouncements double as a set of instructions to East India Company administrators. Irwin creates a memorandum on British governance, using the poem to argue that the British should control India, but they should do so by listening to Indians, especially those Indians British authors have impersonated in their literature.

The textual apparatus of the poem thus repeats, in rather startling ways, the colonial dynamic between Britain and India. Irwin qualifies Ramah's enthusiastic poetic propaganda with the prose of colonial administration. The British perspective—in the form of Irwin's editorial voice in the footnotes—is removed to the margins of the text, but this marginal voice possesses inordinate power. From these margins, Irwin offers an imaginative reconciliation of British ambitions and Indian goals. His need for these footnotes might reveal the limits of his ability to contort Hindu speakers into a celebration of occupation. Alternately, the footnotes could be considered a technique of printed voice, a way of reconciling multiple speech acts, much like Gray's use of quotation marks and Macpherson's creation of a participatory poetics. Regardless, the poem presents itself as a technology for arbitrating between these two constituencies. Ramah legitimizes British dominion, even offers his own death as a "lesson," without actually threatening his position as a colonized subject. British political principles are put into a colonial poetic form: they are offered by an Indian speaker who is continually corrected and explained by a European one, even as the English language and its verse forms are appointed to smooth out those differences. In addition to mediating for readers what are allegedly Indian voices, Irwin's poem is a way to understand the relationship between colonizers and those colonized. It enlists native voices to justify British colonialism while simultaneously chastising the British for specific colonial practices. It listens into the past of Muslim despotism and into the future of British dominion, contrasting the two in poetry and prose, in Indian poetic enthusiasm and prosaic British rationality.

Irwin was not the only poet who turned to Gray's poem and its representation of Welsh oral traditions to anticipate the future relationship between Britain and India. The anticolonial Quaker poet John Scott rewrote "The Bard" out of sympathy with the colonized inhabitants of India and out of Christian concern for the ethics of the British nation. Scott longed for the time when Britain was unencumbered by overseas possessions and thus independent of attachment to the world—isolated, yet happily self-sufficient.[86] Scott worried also that colonialism endangered British liberties.

His poem "Serim; Or, the Artificial Famine" (1782) describes a famine that occurred during the 1760s in Bengal and may have starved up to thirty million people.[87] When this knowledge began to circulate in British newspapers and political pamphlets, many readers were shocked. Some accused the East India Company of exacerbating the famine to assert their control, a charge that is central to the poem. Ultimately, Scott summoned the famine victims' specters, depicting them as a supernatural choir, like the Welsh bardic ghosts who sing in "The Bard" to resist the oncoming English army. Like those Welsh singers, the voices of apparitional Indians haunt the British as punishment for their crimes.

The speaker of Scott's poem is Serim, a Hindu who relentlessly insults the British. The British are called "insatiate plunderers" who in the poem command the Hindus to "bring gold, bring gems . . . who hoards his wealth by Hunger's rage shall / die" (p. 140). The depiction of insatiable Englishmen who starve those who won't pay them tribute confirmed some popular sentiments. It also creates a bizarre disembodied virtuality within the poem: Serim ventriloquizes English voices, in a complex variation of what Homi Bhabha has described as colonial mimicry.[88] In this case, however, a Quaker author (who anxiously admits at the beginning of his poem that he has never visited India but that he is an admirer of William Jones) creates a Hindu speaker who in turn mimics his British oppressors. Scott's cited voices cite yet other voices in a string of quotations that is as disorienting as it is politically rich. An anticolonial English author speaks on behalf of Indians who in turn parody the brutality of their colonizers by having them sound rapacious, unfeeling, unforgiving, interested only in wealth.

Serim's response is to curse the British, just as the Welsh bard curses the English invaders in "The Bard." Serim calls out to the British, warning, "'Yet you, ye oppressors! Uninvok'd on you, / 'Your steps, the steps of Justice will pursue'" (p. 150). And this curse of justice is delivered in the form of ghostly haunting that will be felt in Britain's most hallowed private space, the domestic sphere. In Serim's prophecy, the gaudy rooms, smooth couches, and rich tapestries of British life—supplied by "Luxury's hand" (p. 150)—will be steeped in the vocal sounds of empire:

'. . . Night's kind calm in vain shall sleep invite,
'While fancied omens warn, and specters fright:
'Sad sounds shall issue from your guilty walls,
'The widow's wife's, the sonless mother's calls;
'An infant Rajah's bleeding form shall rise,
'And lift to you their supplicating eyes.
(p. 150)

Britain, Serim claims, will be haunted by the ghosts of those it has subjected. Seeping from the elegant walls and cushions of drawing rooms and bedrooms, the voices of colonials will follow their oppressors back to their homes. He offers a nightmare of a Britain overrun by foreign voices that are the aural and visual hallucinations of imperial excess. The Indomania that captured the attention of the 1770s and 1780s English-language reading public primarily took the form of printed texts—travel narratives, epistolary collections, and, to a lesser extent, Anglo-Indian poetry—that British readers purchased and put in their polite drawing rooms and on their tea tables. Scott sketches out a fantasy in which these silent literary voices, safely closed up in books, locked away in ink, come back to life, animated again to publicize the tragedy going on across the globe in India. There is no apparent escape, and no boundary is too great; this is invasion in reverse.

The fantasy of India's voices disturbing British tranquility shows one colonial effect of eighteenth-century printed voice's ability to transcend the boundaries of space and time. We might think of Serim, then, not as a colonial mimic, but as a predecessor to the postcolonial critic. So, when Serim is killed at the end of Scott's poem, it is clear that the British have exacted their revenge.

Enrapt he spoke—then ceas'd the lofty strain,
And Orel's rocks return'd the sound again.—
A British ruffian, near in ambush laid,
Rush'd sudden from the cane-isle's secret shade;
'Go to thy Gods!' with rage infernal cried,
And headlong plung'd the hapless Sage into the
foaming tide. (pp. 151–52)

Serim's death is described as a direct result of colonial violence. Whereas Ramah's suicide is a self-sacrificial lesson, Serim's is a product of terror. And with the assassin screaming "Go to thy Gods" the British get the last word. Scott makes the politics of speaking explicit and unglamorous: the English not only speak, they silence their adversaries. But Serim does in fact "go to his gods," adding his voice to the spectral choir. His voice is preserved and retrieved by a sympathetic author to haunt the drawing rooms of Britain. Serim is resurrected by the poem and the dead speak again, engaging one of the classic metaphors for what literature can accomplish. Gray's form, with its explicit attention to the ability of spectral voices to transcend death, supplies an opening through which to imagine Serim's ultimate victory. The rewritten "Bard" becomes a machine, a reproducible technology, by which the voices of the dead are not just recorded but reanimated, transmitted across boundaries, and converted into forms that are emotionally intelligible to readers of English. The voices of the dead possessed an enormous imaginative power for an anticolonial author like Scott. As with the Welsh antiquarians described in Chapter 2, Scott used these revived voices to create a sense of passionate political speech and to connect the concerns of an alien culture with the wider celebration of liberty. This strategy sentimentalizes the dead, making their voices into an uncannily perpetual memorial.

DISLOCATED ORIENTALISM

What are we to make of the literary transpositions and cultural translations involved in rewriting "The Bard" in India? What happens when medieval Welsh bardic history is dislocated and set within the orientalism of eighteenth-century India? According to some scholars, these types of poems manifest an effort to fashion a ventriloquized poetic voice, which suggests an attempt to legitimize or obscure the violence of colonialism with literature.[89] Anglo-Indian poetry makes evident that literary voice and speaking position, authenticity and appropriation must be understood to evaluate the interventionist modes of eighteenth-century British imperialism. I would add, however, that all revisions of "The Bard" in India raise fundamental questions about literature's roles in extending and understanding imperial interventions. By appropriating Gray's popularization of Welsh oral traditions, Jones, Irwin, and Scott associated Indian speakers with Welsh bards. All three authors used the image of the performing Brahman, thus reconfiguring the symbolism of the Welsh bardic past and reinterpreting native speakers as commentators on and participants in, rather than as silent victims of, British colonialism. These Brahman speakers were undoubtedly intended to authenticate English imitations as genuinely oriental and thus can be interpreted as an effort to borrow Indian culture for British political goals. Still, these poems emerge from the intersection of Welsh traditions and European notions of Asian poetics. At a point when the status of British dominion in India was still undecided and Britons were anxious about their success on the subcontinent, Gray's "The Bard" provided these authors a rich set of metaphors with which to consider questions of cultural interaction and political liberty. English poets' wild experiments with voice and the innovative poetic forms were used to reconsider questions of colonial agency, literary appreciation, and cultural interaction.

When we note that Welsh oral culture was orientalized, we are called to reimagine the role of voice and appropriation in orientalism itself. "The Bard" in India is another spectral version of its supposedly Welsh origin. The apparitional chorus, which delivers so much of the critique in Gray's poem, is an analogue for these later acts of revision, in which Britain's empire is haunted by speakers who are outside of traditional temporalities and yet refer to contemporaneous events. These rewritten versions of "The Bard" verbalized British uncertainties about its colonial future by appealing to the Welsh past. The images, literary forms, and voices (both printed and oral) found in these rewritings circulated globally, forcing us to reflect on the role of foreign speakers and oral culture in our assessments of Britain's colonial project. If spectrality is an analogue for the act of revising, then the politics of citation is lodged in the traceable reference that is carried across borders by the intertextuality of these poems. We might think of "The Bard," therefore, as the deep structure of these Anglo-Indian revisions, whose differing politics are each revealed precisely at the moment of citation, at the moment when they allude to, but alter, Gray's poem, their original model. Stuart Hall describes the deep structure of artistic works as consisting of "connotational chains" that refer to the ideological foundations with which each artwork is made.[90] These connotations are reproduced by users of artworks, whether they intend it or not, and often without their knowing they are doing it. The politics of these artworks are overwritten or even galvanized by new contexts. (Hall's example is James Thomson's "Rule Britannia," whose nationalistic chorus includes the line "Britons never will be slaves" yet was written while Britain was an important factor in the transatlantic slave trade.) Recontextualizations of Gray's poem proliferated because of the deep structure that it offered to other authors. The generic features and literary representations of oral voices in "The Bard" provide numerous paths for evaluating and responding to British colonialism. For an author like Irwin, this led to a positive assessment of British superiority. For Scott, it resulted in disgust for the colonial economics of resource extraction that he warned would register as a vocal haunting that could not be escaped. For Jones, it appeared as a tempered vision of Anglo-Indian cooperation, with himself as the ultimate arbiter.

All of these poets, however, shared an interest in citing earlier poetic forms as a way of legitimizing their impersonated speakers and establishing them in multiple disparate cultural contexts and political discourses. Since citationality sanctions the possibility of literary adaption as an intervention in colonial politics, their revisions are never simply reiterations of earlier templates and scenes—they are never "simply replicas of the same."[91] Rather, these citations function as a series of formal and cultural conjunctions meant to cross temporal and spatial boundaries, like the ghosts of Gray's bardic chorus and the haunting phantoms in Scott's "Serim." These conjunctions and crossings open up possibilities for the kind of "re-adaptation" and "interactive dynamism" that Gauri Viswanathan asserts was crucial for the British-Indian relationship during this colonial period.[92] My notion of a dislocated orientalism expands on this dynamism, revealing points of contact in the intersecting pattern of Anglo-Indian poetry's readapted literary forms and cultural appropriations. In the ways Anglo-Indian poetry modified these earlier experiments with mediating oral voices and foreign speakers we can also see its role within the mechanisms of colonial power.

Anglo-Indian poets therefore are significant for eighteenth-century experiments with poetic voice because they listened to India, seeking new traditions to borrow and imitate. Raymond Schwab has named this historical process the "oriental Renaissance" and believes that the textual and cultural exchanges from India utterly transformed Europe, ushering in its modern artistic age.[93] This version of orientalism coincides with Jones's perception that native Indian voices might rejuvenate flagging Western traditions. But if there was an "oriental Renaissance" in which Eastern texts reinvigorated Western culture, then we must note that it was powered by British authors who orientalized European traditions as much as they imitated Asian poetries. English authors like Jones, Irwin, and Leyden transported English literary forms and traditions to India, renovating them by mixing them with Indian idioms. These forms were "Indianized" as a way of energizing English literary traditions that some authors felt had become politically corrupt and artistically repetitive. Anglo-Indian poets then borrowed back these Indianized traditions, and thus the "reawakening" of the "oriental Renaissance" is at least in part self-made and fantastical.[94]

In my readings of Anglo-Indian poetry, therefore, I follow a labile and plastic model of orientalism that perceives it as more than a unidirectional system imposing Western forms of knowledge. Orientalism, Michael Dodson reminds us, was not "directed solely at the construction of ruling authority upon European terms, but rather, was also a series of strategies to co-opt, control, and adjust elements of established Indian social, cultural, and political authority."[95] Anglo-Indian poetry was part of that strategy to co-opt and control Indian society, and in this process it relied on traditions outside of India, like those of Wales, to construct and understand India. These appeals connected Britain and India not just thematically or metaphorically but in concrete ways that can be read. Additionally, these traditions were often used to criticize the very orientalism that made Anglo-Indian poetry possible in the first place. At this stage, Anglo-Indian poets subjected India to the most modern and fashionable of British aesthetic techniques, using exotic Indian voices to create innovative literary forms as an extension of their will to control their subjects.

These rewritings, therefore, were more than an "annexation" of Indian materials to be put in European forms, as Kate Teltscher has called this process.[96] The aesthetic innovations involved in making Indians speak were inextricably linked to political affinities and cross-identifications with Britain that are inadequately express by our current notions of cultural appropriation or translation. As discussed in Chapter 2, the language of appropriation mischaracterizes the collaboration between Welsh cultural nationalists and the English poets that represented Welsh traditions. Rather than reject the English authors as appropriators of their culture and English poetry as inauthentic, as Katie Trumpener suggests occurred, the Welsh themselves borrow liberally from English traditions as a way to revive their own. In late-eighteenth-century India, the language of cultural appropriation once again misses crucial details of colonialism's cross-cultural exchange. Anglo-Indian poetry cannot escape the label of orientalism, of course; I do not argue that British authors avoided the pitfalls of appropriation simply because they were sincerely interested in Asian culture. But some ways in which they bore the marks of their wide cultural borrowing are difficult to identify in readings dependent on theories of a rigid nationalism and an appropriative colonialism. The complex reframing of texts and speakers evident in rewriting "The Bard" in India or in impersonating women's subjectivities demonstrates that British colonialism disinterred voices from other localities as a way to consider the myriad consequences of interventions in India. The literary forms that resulted are oriented in multiple directions. They are highly mobile texts rooted in many places at once.

In the 1770s and 1780s, when both the perception and the inevitability of British dominion in India were still unsure, it might have been possible to see in the impersonation of subaltern voices a struggle for the future of India as a colony, motivated by the British but with indigenous participation, even if that participation was virtual. Of course, the recognition of the subaltern's voice as having a part to play in this debate about the structure of British colonialism or about transnational gender subordination did not happen on terms that subalterns would choose. I do not suggest that the reconstructions of subaltern voices in Anglo-Indian poetry are "pure" or authentic. In fact, a quite convincing argument can be made that these impersonations were among the most insidious strategies of co-optation available to colonialism because they could convince readers they had encountered Indian voices when they had not. Yet, one of the troubles of identifying subaltern speech, as Spivak notes, is "the assumption that there *is* a pure form of consciousness" that can be identified and recovered at some sedimentary level—a "form of consciousness," I would add, that is attended by and reinforced with the notion of voice as unmediated authentic self-expression.[97] By representing William Jones as an Eastern bard, or by utilizing the language of sati to reveal impediments to interracial desire, or by adapting the "The Bard" to India, Anglo-Indian poetry demonstrates that the ventriloquism of native voices can be put to many different political ends, whose instrumentality in advancing colonialism cannot always be assumed. Since the authenticity of these indigenous speakers is constructed, it is also elusive and extremely contingent for those who would seek to possess it. At some admittedly high level of abstraction, Ramah, Serim, Bedukah, Rad'ha, even the last Welsh bard are fungible. What remains is the speaking figure, and the literary structures that these authors employed—the techniques of poetic voice mediated as print; the impersonations and cross-identifications these techniques permit and extend—to create the myth of authentic performance and the permanence of cultural translatability that connected the different nodes of colonialism.

Ultimately, then, we may need to reconsider the relationship between the global and the local, between Britain's overseas colonialism and the formation of the British national literature. Robert Crawford introduced the idea of devolution to conceptualize the emergence of English literature in the eighteenth century as an interaction among the (at times contentious) parts of the British Isles. But what if we pushed further, devolving English literature to the Indian colonies and back again? What view of English poetry then appears? Recombining the postcolonial vocabulary of marginality, transoceanic peripheries, and flows of culture and power developed by earlier scholars and attending to influence, generic transformation, and intertextuality allows us to appreciate better the connections and exchanges between Britain and India at an early moment of colonial dominion. We should continue to develop our sense of the interpenetration between these places, and of the processes of literary adaptation which construct this sense, by devolving the generic and printed elements that were involved in the impersonation of native Indian voices. At the same time, we must keep in mind the parallel historical transformations at work during the eighteenth century, especially as they relate to colonialism and to the global circulation of capital that mirrored, and in some important ways diverged from, the global circulation of voices and texts described in this book. While the meanings of Englishness and Britishness were being contested in the national cultural movements of Wales, Scotland, and Ireland, all of these cultural and national identifications were also being transported to the colonies, where they were transformed, debated, and reassessed. At the same time, they were used to evaluate the effects of colonialism and, in some instances, to critique it. From this vantage, the collaboration between ostensibly antagonistic nationalist traditions, like those found in Wales, Scotland, and England, seems also to have been at work in India, pursued by, of all people, Anglo-Indian authors writing in English. We should think about the connections among these cultural traditions as outlining a vast transoceanic periphery linking locations along the circumference rather than always orienting our attention toward the center or through the metropole. We might think of this circulation along the circumference as how cultural exchange was imagined by eighteenth-century poets—as instances of speaking and hearing, as moments of dialogue, as listening in on native peoples—but also how cultural exchange is given material shape through the revision and adaptation of familiar genres and texts. Noting precisely how English writers structured Indian voices by recalling Welsh ones, or how male authors constructed Indian female speakers, is ultimately to note the quite real politics invested in the establishment of new literary forms through the renovation of old ones. These transformations reveal that the voice of eighteenth-century Anglo-Indian poetry concerns the political relationship of different cultures flung across the vast expanse of the globe.

Coda: Reading the Archive of the Inauthentic

Oral traditions and foreign voices from the edges of the British Empire revitalized eighteenth-century English literature as poets experimented with various ways to represent these traditions and voices on the printed page. The techniques they developed were a response to the period's shifting relationship to cultural media: the positive revaluation of folk traditions as heroic, not vulgar; the reconsideration of what mass readership meant for authors; the growing importance of colonial locales for poetic inspiration. By evoking the sense of immediacy associated with oral performance, the collective belonging of folk traditions, and the excitement of exotic places, these experiments attempted to mitigate the social isolation that authors worried had derived from the growing prevalence of silent, solitary reading. Thomas Gray's later poetry set an example, cultivating a relationship to reading texts that resembles listening to song and imagining that the intimacy of oral performance can be achieved by readers attuned to texts' aural possibilities. His poetry served as a vital origin for a number of experimental offshoots: the elocutionists, who sought to use the printed text to revive what Thomas Sheridan called the "living voice," and those poets in Wales, Scotland, and India who turned to Gray's model when rewriting foreign voices to register the politics at work in the debate about British colonialism. By offering an alternate genealogy of eighteenth-century experimentalism, I seek to establish a heuristic for understanding the formation of poetic voice in relationship to colonialism, one that can be extended to other topics and locales, such as the highly sexualized imitations of Tahitian islanders that circulated during the 1770s and 1780s or the impersonation of African slaves found in abolitionist poetry. I see this heuristic as both adding to and troubling our understanding of Britain's national canon as being organized around the desire for a unifying culture that shifted from classical to vernacular literacies during this period of rapid expansion of colonial governance overseas.

This alternate literary genealogy necessarily returns us to questions about the relationship between our conceptions of voice and colonial subjectivity. Previously, scholars have emphasized the importance of discriminating between the authentic traditions of Wales, Scotland, and Ireland and their appropriation by English authors. While these readings have generated crucial new theories about the emergence of Britishness, they have also caused us to overlook the rise of transnational literary forms whose voices result from vital collaborations between these ostensibly antithetical authors and traditions. The impulse to seek cultural resources outside and away from literary England led to the formation of a global aesthetics of poetic voice. The competing national and international allegiances of the poetry explored here contain pioneering attitudes toward literary form and generic adaptation. Gray, Collins, Hemans, and others utilized the ode and blank verse, genres and techniques that we currently understand as innovative in the late eighteenth century; but others, such as Anglo-Indian authors from the 1770s and 1780s, also renovated neoclassical conventions rather than abandoning them. Therefore, the "invention" of voice referred to in Chapter 3 should also be understood as a *reinvention* of recognizable forms and genres. This renovation of well-known genres and this adaptation of conventional techniques were not simple exercises in emptying and refilling literary forms. These verbal structures carried with them the vestigial politics of their initial making and their subsequent transformations. These politics were conveyed through the genres, scenes, and techniques of earlier poems that were incorporated in and tailored to the circumstances of new localities and speakers. Multiple and at times discordant voices structured the contemporary disputes about the evolution of the British state and the consequences of its rapidly shifting empire. Poetic form is a quite specific record of these debates about nationalism on the British Isles and imperial expansion overseas.

If poetry was a valuable medium within which to debate nationalism and empire, then the ventriloquism of non-British speakers was an important (if flawed) way to imagine their part in this debate. Reflecting on what we might learn from reading these voices and figures, Lynn Festa warns that, "in composing accounts of eighteenth-century colonialism that seek to avoid making objects of others," we should "be cautious about making the semblance of subjects as well."[1] Even as we recognize that colonial figures were not always oppressed objects at the mercy of imperial power, we must avoid anachronistically projecting our fantasies of meeting idealized colonial figures from the past. Festa advocates for a "sentimental model of recognition" which "might be incorporated into a form of subject making that does not just involve puppetry or wish fulfillment."[2]

Ventriloquism and impersonation, however, unsettle our current descriptions of eighteenth-century forms of subject making. How should we read colonial texts and understand the connection between the voices evoked within them and those historical subjects they claim to represent? In reappraising our methods of reading the colonial archive, we might turn to William Lisle Bowles's first-person poetic monologue "Abba Thule's Lament for his Son Prince Lee Boo" (1794), which engages many of the technologies of impersonation and metaphorics of voice discussed in previous chapters.[3] As with the Anglo-Welsh collaborations and the works of the Brahman bards, Bowles's poem presents a subject who is neither an oppressed figure of empire ("puppetry") nor a dependably resisting agent ("wish fulfillment"). The poem, based on real events, recounts a mournful soliloquy by Abba Thule for his son Lee Boo, a prince who traveled from Palau, a Pacific island group near the Philippines, to England on an East India Company ship in 1784.[4] After six months in England, Lee Boo died of smallpox and was buried in a London cemetery. The tragic story of Lee Boo was well known in Britain because of a popular travel narrative published in 1788.[5] This narrative refers to his father as "Abba Thulle" (neither name was correct) and is illustrated with an engraving that depicts him shirtless and muscular, with tattoos across his chest and shoulders. An earring dangles from his elongated earlobe and a hatchet is propped on his shoulder (Fig. 16). This is a depiction of an alluringly exotic Micronesian placed within the well understood conventions of eighteenth-century portraiture, such as its three-quarters profile. This collision of exotic and familiar appears in the narration as well: Captain Wilson, a British explorer who traveled back to England with Lee Boo, reports that when he first met Abba Thulle he was "perfectly naked," had no "ornament of distinction," and disliked English tea.[6] But Wilson also professes his respect for Abba Thulle's humanity. Another narrative repeated this description, claiming that Abba Thulle was a "man of great humanity as well as extraordinary natural understanding," who felt deeply for the sailors and saw them as friends.[7] It is impossible to know definitively Abba Thulle's perspective, but he did feed the shipwrecked sailors, ask them to aid his military campaigns, help them to build a new ship, and entrust his son to their care, showing some level of attachment to them.

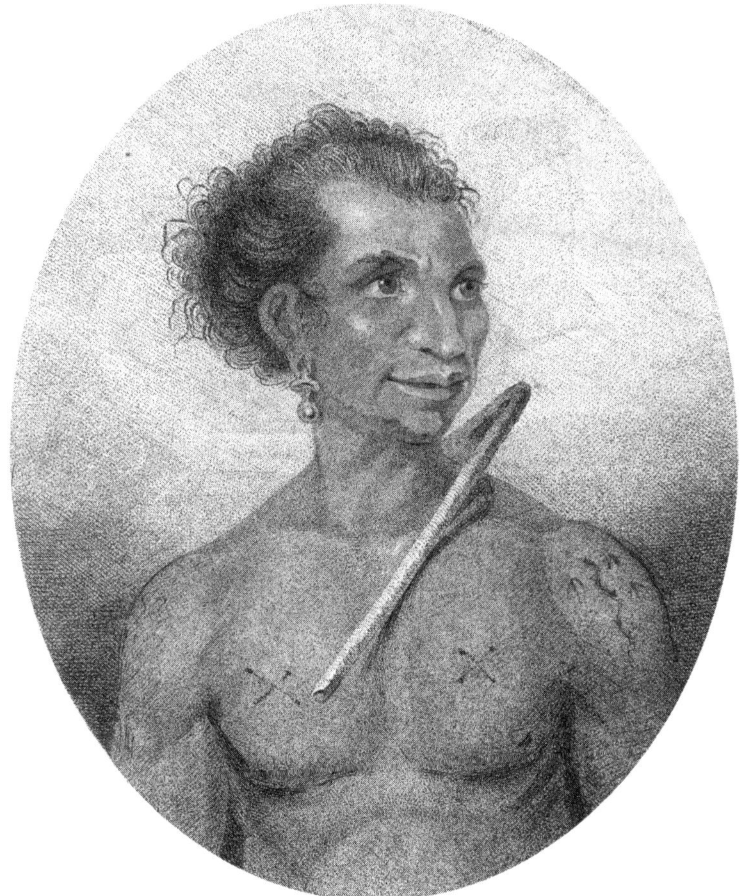

Figure 16. An engraved drawing of "Abba Thulle," by Henry Kingsbury (after one by Arthur William Devis), which appeared in George Keate's *An Account of the Pelew Islands . . .* (1788). Courtesy of the National Library of Australia (an9024483).

Bowles's poem, likely inspired by these narratives, uses the immediacy of the monologue to dramatize Abba Thule's sorrow at his son's departure and the unsuccessful wait for his return. The sense of exoticism mixed with admiration that Captain Wilson felt comes through in the Bowles's portrayal of Abba Thule's pathos. Abba Thule stands at the water's edge and casts his voice out over the ocean to his son, then waits for a reply that he never will receive. He weeps in disappointment as ships pass by without returning his son. Bowles's poem presents Abba Thule's voice in an attempt to connect Britain with distant locales by conducting its speaker into the global circulation of voices. He hears the "sound of the encircling seas" (line 18). Its "falling surge" is "mournful" because it carried Lee Boo away, yet in its sound Abba Thule still thinks he can "listen to [Boo's] echoing shell" (32). He hears warnings in the articulate ocean: "Methought the wild waves said, amidst their roar / At midnight, Thou shalt see thy son no more!" (48–49). He loses faith, exclaiming, "Oh! I shall never, never hear his voice" (61) and lingers "on the desert rock alone, / Heartless, and cry for thee, my son, my son" (71–72). He implores the sun "beneath whose eye / The worlds unknown, and out-stretched waters lie" (9–10) if it can see Lee Boo in some far-off land, standing on the

> . . . rude shore
> Around whose crags the cheerless billows roar,
> Watching the unwearied surges doth he stand,
> And think upon his father's distant land!
>
> (11–14)

The parallel positions of Abba Thule and his son on distant shores yet facing the same ever-circling ocean endow voice with the ability to traverse vast distances, much as Gray hoped his imitation of Welsh and Scandinavian bards would do. As Gray's voices traveled widely, due to the efforts of his poetic adapters and imitators, the voice of Abba Thule traversed the globe in Bowles's imaginative rewriting of it.

Lee Boo's silence in comparison to Abba Thule's extensive speech expresses some of the complexities of their extended aural intimacy that Bowles's poem tries to capture. Abba Thule hopes to transcend the boundaries of space and time and hear his son's voice again. However, while he believes he can almost discern his son's voice in the ocean, Lee Boo's reply never reaches him. Bowles did not create specific accents or metrical forms in which to present the cultural uniqueness of his speaker's voice. Instead, like many of the authors discussed here, he utilized the idea of speech, the metaphorics of voice, and renovated generic forms to create an impersonation with which to understand the effects of colonial encounters on an increasingly interconnected planet. In this instance, Bowles adopted the dramatic monologue to devise a frustrated call-and-response, an incomplete, one-sided conversation that satisfied the persistent desire among eighteenth-century readers to be addressed by an exotic speaker. There is an explicitly political dimension to this choice of the dramatic monologue. A contemporary of Bowles, Joseph Cottle, a Bristol poet and the printer of Samuel Taylor Coleridge's and William Wordsworth's 1798 edition of *Lyrical Ballads*, placed Abba Thule in dialogue with his son in his poetic version of this encounter.[8] Bowles chose the monologue to capture the deleterious impact on Pacific culture of European contact, which takes away Abba Thule's son and removes his sound from him. Uncompleted calls thus become a trope for the sinuous currents and counterflows of global travel and colonialism that often are themselves intercepted or arrested midstream, to the detriment of indigenous populations.

Bowles's poem reaches English-language readers, intending to excite their pity and sympathy with the father's cries of "my son, my son" and with his exclamatory weeping. The circuit of speaking and hearing between Abba Thule and his son, interrupted by the vast distances, is completed instead by readers, who are recruited by the poem's dramatic address to be the recipients—the audience—of what was intended for Lee Boo. What does it mean to "hear" the voice of Abba Thule that was intended for Lee Boo but is diverted to us? That eighteenth-century authors employed subaltern voices raises questions about how we are supposed to understand ventriloquism and impersonation in relation to forms of subject making. Postcolonial criticism has extensively theorized the dangers of scholars' desire to recover subaltern voices and reconnect them with those texts that claim to represent them. Gayatri Chakravorty Spivak even wonders what is at stake when we ask subalterns to speak in the first place.[9] The attempt to discover subaltern speakers in the colonial archive, she asserts, demonstrates the desire for the "useful fiction" of a "self-consolidating other" who appears from the archives, like a ghost, just at the moment when it is needed.[10]

I agree with Spivak's cautions; in fact, as I have pointed out in preceding chapters, we will not find any actual voices within any of these texts. Yet, because the concept of voice underwrites our understandings of individuality, interiority, and personhood (especially political personhood), even in forms ostensibly resistant to European subjectivity, an analysis of how authors experiment with poetic voice, and how it evolves as a result, offers us fertile terrain for exploring the role of ventriloquism in colonial discourse. Additionally, it allows us to reassess how we read eighteenth-century British impersonations of foreign speakers for evidence of colonial agency. To what degree does it matter if these texts are not authentic (or authenticated) enunciations of subaltern figures or resistant nationalists? Can we recover subaltern subjects from European impersonations of their voices? Is it possible to advance an anticolonial agency through European imitations of colonial subjectivities? How compromised is the anticolonial representation if its speaker is not an actual colonized subject but a ventriloquized one? Is this fictive subject so compromised that we must declare it an extension of British imperialism?

One valid set of answers to these questions would insist that these evocations of oral voices and impersonations of foreign speakers are instances of outright appropriation that have been pointed to for years as the motor of colonial discourse and imperial policy making. In this reading, these evocations and impersonations are not translations of oral performances or the voices of actual subalterns like Abba Thule—whose name cannot even be agreed on by his English authors—and therefore should be separated from all the different kinds of enunciations we could study in the presence of better archival evidence. Appropriation is a misrepresentation of others, limiting the opportunities for them to represent themselves. This view of impersonation as solely disruptive asserts that imitation is always an asset to British colonialism at some fundamental substratum, even if authors critique or resist it. From this perspective, our time would be better spent attempting to rediscover the texts of native speakers and explaining those voices rather than comprehending texts that impersonate them.[11]

Conversely, the printed voices and literary impersonations analyzed here complicate our still rigid dichotomy of voice as either imperial projection or recognition of unalloyed oppositional figures. We need to acknowledge more readily that there is continuity between these two positions while considering some of the ways that colonial impersonations both construct and constrain the experiences of indigenous or subaltern subjects. I suggest that we see these impersonations of foreign speakers and imitations of oral voicing as elements of a reconceived colonial archive. To do so would further expand discursive boundaries and retool our interpretive techniques, permitting us to reexamine projection, virtualization, and voice as modes of colonial reading. This view does not regard the colonial impersonations described here as a reliable historical archive, if that term implies authenticity or verifiability. Instead, such an archive is designed from the inauthentic: it is a set of associated stories and characters, virtual projections and appropriations that circulated through British society, near and far, during the eighteenth century. To read this archive of the inauthentic not only expands our sense of the colonial archive but also relates historical beings with their numerous virtual and literary companions who are constructed and given voice in English-language poetry and travel narratives. From this vantage, these impersonations of non-English voices constitute colonized speakers and contribute to this archive in significant ways, especially when they usurp sovereign native subjects and replace them with their own representations.

Untangling the literary forms of impersonation provides an opportunity for further understanding the multiple exchanges enacted by the adoption of foreign voices. Striving to describe a middle range between colonial complicity and anticolonial native resistance can be found in a host of British textual practices akin to resistant colonized subjects but clearly not produced by them. The conferral of voice and the personification of speakers introduce powerful if slippery hints at subjectivity. Fashioning the illusion of being addressed by alien subjects in their own voices was clearly an act of appropriation and of virtualization by European authors. Nevertheless, it established an unstable yet reciprocal intimacy among readers and fantasized colonial voices. This is why the literary text is aptly poised to register types of anticolonial thought that are complexly intermixed with imperial power. Reading such texts closely and situating them in global cultures unite intimate moments and relationships—especially evocations of bodily effects like the voice that occur through generic adaptation and formal innovation—with more virtual and imaginative considerations, such as ethnic and national belonging, shared reading, persona, and other techniques involved in the formation (and constraint) of subjectivity.

Representation, Srinivas Aravamudan counsels, "should not be read as politics tout court, but as *vicariously* so," especially with colonized subjects who are both European projections and "beings leaving stubborn material traces even as they are discursively deconstructed."[12] Reading for certain tropes of representation opens "the discussion of a wide range of representational and rhetorical techniques used by metropolitan cultures (sometimes erratically, at other times systematically) to comprehend the colonized."[13] The archive of the inauthentic refocuses our attention on the vicariousness and virtuality of these impersonated colonial voices and the politics that comes with them. From these residues, which stand beside and in place of indigenous voices, we may be able to reconstruct the obfuscated picture of colonial agency as it is mutually constituted. Confining ourselves to repeating the impossibility of recovering "authentic" voices involves losing a level of richness that could expand our study of subalterns. Bowles's depiction of "Abba Thule," for example, is composed from elements that resemble those of Gray's last Welsh bard, Macpherson's Ossianic speakers, and the Brahman bards of late-eighteenth-century Anglo-Indian poetry. If we are unable to read these affiliations, we neglect the deep affinities among groups—Welsh nationalists, Brahman impersonators, Pacific islanders—that worked against disciplinary regimes of British imperialism, even though each of them functioned within it and was affected by it quite differently. We might note how these poems and their elaborate literary impersonations insinuate that their authors understood the invented nature of these voices. These writers' innovative poetic practices correspond with an equally innovative cultural politics of borrowing, exchange, and collaboration.

Recuperating the archive of the inauthentic therefore requires that we continue to press upon the contours and function of the colonial archive. Recent debates about the colonial archive have theorized its positivistic history and have tried to comprehend its limitations. I suggest that we will find refreshed possibilities if we combine techniques like virtualization and retroactive reading with these new theories of the colonial archive, in the process discovering alternate routes backwards to subjectivity and agency. As Jenny Sharpe notes, resistance too often is equated solely with possessing an "oppositional consciousness," which is difficult for scholars to determine because we cannot know the intentions of individual subjects and because agency is always a negotiation and is often compromised.[14] Anjali Arondekar likewise calls for a theory of archival reading that moves away from the idea that discovering an object leads to formulation of a subject, that if we read a body or a text we can somehow recover the person who authored it.[15] We must "work with the empirical status of materials even as that status is rendered fictive," Arondekar explains.[16] Reading the archive as providing us not with empirical truth but with narratives will necessitate that we engage with all the difficulties and advantages wrapped up in textual interpretation. Betty Joseph pursues such a strategy in her call for a "globalized reading of the transnational archive of British rule," not to "excavate the past" but rather to reveal the "arenas, agendas, and subjects that are hidden when history is told one way or another."[17] She rejects the argument that we need in our research to portray the native speaker as a "sovereign subject or nothing" at all.[18] Joseph's method of reading proposes that literature can function as a supplement to the "official" archive. By focusing on the use of intertextuality, citation, and quotation in the official archive, she argues, scholars can imagine what is absent and who remains uncertainly reported in its pages.

Throughout this book, I have remained acutely aware of impersonation as a mode of virtualization along the lines that Aravamudan, Arondekar, and Joseph describe. I have sought these material traces and signs of resistance in literary form, in the allusive collaboration between Wales and English literature, the intimate publics of Scottish nationalism, and the impersonation of Indian voices in English poetry as an exponent of colonial politics. Preserved in poetic form and activated by it, we can hear the virtualized voices of native speakers shaped by metropolitan cultures and we can listen to the distortions of those voices. In reading these voices, I have sought to describe the transformations in genre and style that make the mediations culturally intelligible and politically vibrant to English audiences. In short, I read these impersonated voices as powerful instances of virtualization that can be submitted to the procedures of retroactive reading. By thinking through how voices are made in a text and how alien speakers are impersonated, we might broaden an already existent avenue through which to comprehend the mechanisms of British colonialism and the effects it has on colonized subjects. I suggest that the production of virtual and colonial speakers in English-language texts is thus a form of resistance housed within the dynamics of affirmative colonial discourse and in the practices that created colonial space and systems of regimentation. These texts have been neglected for too long, either because we assume that they do not have anything to say to us or because what they say is perceived simply to reinforce notions of European cultural superiority. What appears to be a substantive problem is in fact a methodological one, causing us to discount evidence by classifying it as not actually evidence at all.

It is time to reexamine the sinewy and uncomfortable connections between appropriation and collaboration, authenticity and inauthenticity, as a way to describe the link between colonized subjects and the inhabitants and descendants of colonizing countries who appropriated their voices. In this type of reading, we might see that a material trace of subaltern resistance to colonialism exists within the ventriloquism of British authors. If we can tactically suspend our attempts to differentiate between the rightful possession of cultures and vernaculars and their theft by ostensibly inappropriate authors, we can investigate more closely the networks of formal and aesthetic experimentation that both supported colonialism and gave voice to the debate about its consequences. Ventriloquism, therefore, was not always an instrument of colonial co-optation, of anglicizing, of domination. Voice instead was transpersonal, in much the same way Adela Pinch has argued that sentimentality and feeling were seen as transpersonal in the eighteenth century, roving contagiously among individuals, with an agency that traverses texts.[19] Transpersonal voices were associated with specific bodies and persons but were also detached from them, impersonated, and then satirized, celebrated, mourned; they were continually revised and distributed throughout the print marketplace and across oceans as virtual representations of themselves. Voices leapt from one person to another and connected disparate persons and locales while communicating between them. Of course, this was not a new technological or cultural condition in the late eighteenth century. To some extent, all textual voices are transpersonal because they are citable, able to be set in new contexts. But the portability of voice as a printed product increased during this period, due to the confluence of literary, economic, and social factors, all of which impelled the self-conscious experimentation with printed poetic voice discussed here.

This is not to suggest that we should suspend our attention to appropriation as a venue from which to theorize European colonization, or that the study of English-language literature is always best able to advance postcolonial thinking. The shift that this kind of reading requires is fragile, because the possible interpretations are highly fluid and open to misunderstanding. Nonetheless, one of the many consequences of reading the archive of the inauthentic is an awareness of the global aesthetics of printed voice developed throughout this book. While English literature was being constituted through the collaboration of traditions and speakers in Wales, Scotland, and Britain's overseas colonies, it was also being harnessed as a means of theorizing practical resistance to colonialism. These movements were happening simultaneously and were dependent on one another. Uncovering eighteenth-century experiments with poetic voice provides not only an additional tool for illuminating the contradictions in British colonial texts from our present position in history, but it also further reveals the benefits of performing retroactive reading on new colonial archives. These archives, and the way we read them, can be tied to actual speakers who imagined resistant political possibilities and practices, "including those not yet realized or realizable in their own historical moment."[20] While these historical moments will always remain tantalizingly out of reach, I hope that by embracing the possibilities latent in the virtual, the vicarious, and the performative—indeed what we think of as inauthentic and forged—we might be able to conjure new critical practices for the future.

Notes

INTRODUCTION. THE GLOBAL AESTHETICS OF POETIC VOICE

1. Diderot, *Selected Writings*, 106.

2. Pinkerton, *Scottish Tragic Ballads*, xvii.

3. For a much longer exposition on the fantasy of unmediated voices, see Friedrich Kittler, *Gramophone, Film, Typewriter.*

4. Elizabeth D. Hervey makes a similar point in *Ventriloquized Voices*, 6.

5. Bronson, "Strange Relations," 299.

6. See Zionkowski, *Men's Work*. For other descriptions of the professionalization of authorship, see Woodmansee, *The Author, Art, and the Market*; and Hammond, *Professional Imaginative Writing in England, 1670–1740*.

7. Trumpener, *Bardic Nationalism*, 33.

8. For a recent consideration of what has been called the lyricization of poetry and its relationship to the Romantic lyric, see Jackson, "Who Reads Poetry?" esp. 183.

9. See Doody, *The Daring Muse: Augustan Poetry Reconsidered*, 10–11. According to Doody, Augustan poets saw themselves as "dashing and experimental," not "musty," "correct," or "stiff" (10).

10. For a brief yet detailed description of Gray's importance in the eighteenth century, see Patey, " 'Aesthetics' and the Rise of the Lyric in the Eighteenth Century," 589.

11. See Tadié, *Sterne's Whimsical Theatres of Language*, 8.

12. Tadié, 5. See also pages 1–47 for more on the conversational models of Sterne's fiction.

13. Aravamudan, *Tropicopolitans*, 269.

14. Aravamudan, *Tropicopolitans*, 274–75. His use of the factish derives from the scholarship of Bruno Latour.

15. Crawford, *Devolving English Literature.*

16. This is the commonly known title of the poem, as it circulated in the late eighteenth century after its manuscript was discovered and published posthumously. It should probably more accurately be known as "Ode to a Friend, &c.," the title William Collins scrawled atop his manuscript. See *Poems of Thomas Gray, William Collins, and Oliver Goldsmith*, ed. Lonsdale, 492–501.

17. *The Works of William Collins*, ed. Wendorf and Ryskamp, lines 45, 39, 53. Subsequent citations of this poem refer to this edition and are cited in the text by line number.

18. The Highlands Ode, Howard Weinbrot notes, is a poem about "the variously reconciling effects of the British imagination that does not need classical inspiration";

see *Britannia's Issue*, 381. Collins adapted the ode by linking it to the local mythology of Scotland and, in the process, articulated how such adaptation energized Britain's flagging imaginative power (Weinbrot, 381–85). Collins expressed fears about the decline of poetry, in a dream that he reported to school friends about climbing the "Tree of Poetry." In the dream, after he climbed out on a limb, the limb could not support him and he fell to the ground. See Wendorf, *William Collins and Eighteenth-Century English Poetry*, 9. Wendorf reads this as an allegory of Collins's own fears of poetic failure; I see it as also representative of Collins's sense of dissatisfaction with the current state of poetry.

19. Susan Stewart, *Crimes of Writing*, 91. Stewart continues that "it makes little difference whether the artifact is real or a forgery: distressed genres are characterized by counterfeit materiality and an authentic nostalgia" (91). But, as I show later in this chapter, the way Collins "counterfeits materiality"—by juxtaposing representations of Scottish relics with oral traditions—makes a great deal of difference for the poem.

20. Ibid., 103.

21. Ibid., 105.

22. Ibid., 68. Stewart warns, however, that "there is no 'natural' " in these genres, meaning there is no pure expression, no original authentic past that we can trace (38). Instead there are persistent attempts to recreate the natural as something absent but made available again through the power of writing.

23. Ibid., 122. Stewart makes this remark about English ballads, and I pair her idea with poetry, even though she does not explicitly link them.

24. John Home came to London in 1749 hoping to have David Garrick stage his play *Agis*, a Grecian allegory for the contemporary relationship between Scotland and England, after the Act of Union in 1707. For more on Home's trip to London in 1749, see Henry Mackenzie's *An Account of the Life and Writings of John Home, Esq.*, 35.

25. Wendorf and Ryskamp, *Works of William Collins*, lines 3–4.

26. McLane, *Balladeering, Minstrelsy, and the Making of British Romantic Poetry*, 30–32. See also Bolter and Grusin, *Remediation*.

27. McLane, 24, 32. Friedrich Kittler, *Discourse Networks 1800/1900*, esp. 265–73.

28. Kittler, *Discourse Networks*, 265.

29. In 1600 Edward Fairfax translated Tasso's *Gerusalemme Liberata* as *Godfrey of Bulloigne, or the Recoverie of Jerusalem*. His was the first English translation of this text, and it remained popular into the eighteenth century. For more, see *Godfrey of Bulloigne*, ed. Lea and Gang, 3–65.

30. Other scholars have made versions of this argument. Weinbrot warns, however, that this relationship begins as an asymmetrically authoritative one; throughout the ode, Collins informs Home what he "must do," and the irony of this imperative is that Collins embodies the type of English authority that Home had just encountered while in London (382). Still, by the end of the poem both the speaker and Home have undergone a "Scottish-induced metamorphosis": Home has been transformed from an observer of Highlands culture to a participant in it, which he then shares with the English speaker, who likewise has become "educated and imaginatively rejuvenated while telling Home about Scottish imaginative power" (383–84).

31. Evan Gottlieb argues that these layers of mediation defuse and neutralize oral voices that appear in print. See *Feeling British*, 137–41. Collins's mediation, he suggests, means that the "original folk material will be disciplined and domesticated into a nonthreatening literary form for the consumption of leisured readers" (141).

32. For an overview of these metaphors of voice, see Lesley Wheeler's *Voicing American Poetry*, 1–3, 17–38.

33. See Connor, *Dumbstruck*; Bloom, *Voice in Motion*; Kreilkamp, *Voice and the Victorian Storyteller*; Picker, *Victorian Soundscapes*; Prins, "Voice Inverse"; Smith, *The Acoustic World of Early Modern England*; Garrett Stewart, *Reading Voices*; as well as the entire issue of *New Literary History* 32, 3 (Summer 2001), titled "Voice and the Human Experience."

34. This renewed attention to aurality, speech, voice, and sound reproduction is especially felt in the study of poetry, which, as Susan Stewart notes, "is a form of verbal representation" that "even in its written form evokes aspects of aurality in production and reception"; Susan Stewart, *Poetry and the Fate of the Senses*, 60. "Poetry," Stewart says, "presents an image of the speaker in relation to a listener," which then "begins the social work of making that relation intelligible through its own projected conditions of reception" (67).

35. Connor, 30, 3, 4.

36. Susan Stewart, *Poetry and the Fate of the Senses*, ix.

37. Berry, *Poetry and the Physical Voice*, 196. Berry calls this the "physical voice" of poetry, which is intimately linked to the personal, even physiological, characteristics of the author. A related conception of voice comes from T. S. Eliot's *The Three Voices of Poetry*, which allows that the poet can speak to himself, an audience, or as a character.

38. Wimsatt, *The Verbal Icon*, 5. Emphasis in original.

39. Brower, *The Fields of Light*, 19, 29. See Brower's entire chapter "The Speaking Voice" for an excellent description of mid-twentieth-century notions of poetic voice.

40. Wimsatt, xv–xvi.

41. There is still a debate about the degree to which New Criticism separated authors and readers from the text. Perhaps the most famous formulation is Terry Eagleton's assertion in *Literary Theory* that, "if the poem was really to become an object in itself, New Criticism had to sever it from both author and reader" (47). See also Jancovich, "The Southern New Critics," and Mao, "The New Critics and the Text-Object."

42. Ong, *The Presence of the Word*, 168.

43. Ong, *Writing and Orality*, 82, 131, 44. Ong argues that print "reinforces and transforms the effects of writing" (117).

44. See Derrida, *"Speech and Phenomena" and other Essays on the Husserl's Theory of Signs*, as well as his *Of Grammatology*.

45. See in particular Bakhtin, *Problems of Dostoyevsky's Poetics* and *The Dialogic Imagination: Four Essays*.

46. Cixous, "The Laugh of the Medusa," 347, 351, 350.

47. See Brathwaite, "The History of the Voice." "Nation language," Brathwaite says, "is a strategy [of the slave] . . . to retain his culture" (270). Brathwaite points out that the oral plays a large role in nation language because "oral literature is our oldest form of auriture" (267). "Auriture," as I see it, is a term meant to combine the oral with literature and to recall Derrida's idea of *écriture*. See also Glissant, *Caribbean Discourses*, 163–65, 182–88.

48. See, as one example, *Landmark Essays in Voice and Writing*, ed. Peter Elbow, especially his introduction, "About Voice and Writing."

49. In *Problems in General Linguistics*, Émile Benveniste sees the self and the speaking subject as a product of the pronouns used in a language. Charles Hartmann (*Jazz Text: Voice and Improvisation in Poetry, Jazz, and Song*) proposes that voice is "the physical medium of identification," an "abstract idea of selfhood," and the "vibration of air in a

particular throat," all of which are not "metaphorically juxtaposed" but interwoven (3). Voice is a "sentience or intentionality unfolding in time" (113), a consciousness constructed through relations to other voices, since "no fully recognized voice is ever single" (146) but is "born . . . in a matrix of other voices" (47).

50. Barthes asks, "Is it not the truth of the voice to be hallucinated?" ("Music, Voice, Language," 272).

51. Griffiths, *The Printed Voice of Victorian Poetry*, 67, 13, 38, 61. "Printed voice," as Griffiths defines it, is still limited in many ways, and my project seeks to improve upon this term. For example, he claims that "the reader must inform with a sense of the writer it [the voice] calls up—an ideal body, a plausible voice"; in other words, while Griffiths concedes that one can never recover (or even truly discover) an author's voice, he still maintains that the physical voice of the author should inform the reader's interpretation of a poem (60). The text, in this sense, is a series of "hints at voicing, whose centre in utterance lies outside itself, and also an achieved pattern on the page, salvaged from the evanescence of the air" (60). The printed poem too closely resembles a script for a performance that the reader must call into an existence, a performance without which the text seems to be incomplete. My position about printed voice differs from Griffiths's at those moments when he underemphasizes print's independence from actual speaking or singing voices. He argues, for instance, that "literature aspires to recreate in a sublimed atmosphere the conditions of speech" (36). I do not think it necessarily follows from his analysis that print aspires to actual speech or singing, so that one could characterize print as incomplete. Readers do not "deduce" a voice encoded or imprinted within the text. Instead, authors use particular textual techniques to construct the evocation of voice that readers imagine during the act of reading.

In 'Difficulties of the Bardic Voice," Donald Wesling offers a theory of voice similar to that of Griffiths when he argues that "silent reading must *supply the voice* on the basis of what is known about speaking and about style in writing" (71). Yet, Wesling's comments show that for him voice is fundamentally commensurate with style in the way that style "preserves," as he says, a writer's voice (70).

52. See Zumthor, "The Text and the Voice" and *Oral Poetry*, esp. 97.

53. Zumthor, "The Text and the Voice," 67, 71.

54. Sterne, *The Audible Past*, 2.

55. Bacon, *Sylva Sylvarum*, 56, no. 199; 42, no. 125. Even as he suggested them, Bacon's theories were being questioned in dramatic texts and in anatomical explorations. For more on this early modern debate, see Bloom, 73–79.

56. Bloom, 6, 9–10.

57. Ibid., 3, 16.

58. Della Porta qtd. in Connor, 5–6.

59. Morland, *Tuba Stentoro-Phonica, An Instrument of Excellent Use*. This instrument was in essence an early version of the megaphone, made first of glass, then brass, and eventually copper.

60. See Connor, 5, 199–200.

61. See, von Kempelen, *Mechanismus der menschlichen Sprache nebst Beschreibung einer sprechenden Maschine*. For more, see Lastra, *Sound Technology and the American Cinema*, 31–35.

62. The advantages of his ear trumpet, Hooke noted, after presenting samples at the Royal Society, were that a "stronger sound was conveyed by it"; see *Early Science at Oxford*, vol. 11: 330–31.

63. See Gouk, "English Theories of Hearing in the Seventeenth Century," esp. 145–47.

64. See Tyerman, *The Life and Times of the Rev. John Wesley, Founder of the Methodists*, vol. 1: 108.

65. Sterne writes in *The Audible Past* that "attempts to represent sound visually were themselves artifacts of a larger process through which sound was isolated as a phenomenon and by means of which it would become an object of theoretical and practical knowledge in its own right" (42). Sterne dates this process to the mid-eighteenth century, though its origins may be even earlier.

66. Ascham qtd. in Woolf, "Hearing Renaissance England," 120.

67. Ascham qtd. in Smith, *The Acoustic World of Early Modern England*, 117.

68. Smith, 119. The lack of space between words in many medieval and early Renaissance texts makes evident this philosophy: the texts were meant to be read aloud without interruption, not perused silently in one's room. See Elsky, *Authorizing Words*, 4.

69. As Smith describes it, "paper and ink as material entities stand in for muscles and air as material entities" (121); in essence, he says, these are interchangeable entities that would be brought into question in the eighteenth century.

70. Smith, 96–129. As Smith argues, however, in the seventeenth century print stood "at the farthest remove from the speaking body" (125). See also Gaskell, *A New Introduction to Bibliography*, 10–12.

71. Hudson, "Constructing Oral Tradition," 241.

72. See Fliegelman, *Declaring Independence*.

73. Fox, *Oral and Literate Culture in England, 1500–1700*, 39, 5.

74. Rath, *How Early America Sounded*, x.

75. Fox, 6, 258.

76. Hudson, "Constructing Oral Tradition," 252.

77. McDowell, "Mediating Media Past and Present," 246.

78. For more on these broad shifts, see Steve Newman, *Ballad Collection, Lyric, and the Canon*, chaps. 2 and 4, and esp. pp. 10–11, 57–58, 183–84.

79. McDowell, 246; emphasis in original.

80. Morganwg, *Poems, Lyrical and Pastoral*, vol. 2: 220.

81. McLane, *Balladeering*, 72. McLane calls this the "ascendancy of ethnographic authority." This ascendancy entails that "what had been considered a deficit in the cultural politics of the 1760s and 1770s," the "perceived reliance on merely oral tradition, merely living reciters," had become by the nineteenth century "a criterion of ethno-poetic authority" (13).

82. Blackwell, *An Enquiry in the Life and Writings of Homer*, 103, 107–9; and Wood, *An Essay on the Original Genius of Homer*, liv, lvii, lxi.

83. For representative works on historicism, medieval revivalism, and eighteenth-century antiquarianism, see Johnston, *Enchanted Ground*; Snyder, *The Celtic Revival in English Literature, 1760–1800*; Joseph Levine, *Humanism and History*, 190–213.

84. Sheridan, *A Course of Lectures on Elocution*, 39, 71, 8.

85. Fenning, *A New Grammar of the English Language* (1771), and Blair, *Lectures on Rhetoric and Belles Lettres* (1783) are quoted in Hudson, *Writing and European Thought, 1600–1830*, 106, 108.

86. Harold Love writes that "oral delivery becomes . . . an act of scribal publication by dictation" ("Oral and Scribal Texts in Early Modern England," 99).

87. George, "Public Reading and Lyric Pleasure," 388.

88. Johnson, *A Journey to the Western Islands of Scotland*, 117.

89. *Johnson's Dictionary*, 4–5.

90. For more on Johnson's concerns about an impure English language, see Baucom, *Out of Place*, 26–29.

91. For more on stadial and climatological theories of cultural difference, see Wheeler, *The Complexion of Race*, 176–233; and Nussbaum, *Torrid Zones*, esp. 1–22.

92. Novak, "Primitivism," 465. See also Hudson, "Theories of Language" and *Writing and European Thought*, 119–42.

93. See Ballaster, *Fabulous Orients*, 17. Ballaster asserts that the decisive period in orientalism was the early eighteenth century, when understandings of the East as similar or analogous to Europe gave way to the idea that the East was ineluctably different (24).

94. Joseph Trapp qtd. in Rothstein, *Restoration and Eighteenth-Century Poetry, 1660–1780*, 112.

95. Percy, *The Song of Solomon, Newly Translated from the Original Hebrew*, xxxii–xxxiii.

96. Blair, *Lectures on Rhetoric and Belles Lettres* (ed. Harding), 112.

97. *The Letters of William Jones*, vol. 2: 716.

98. Hayley, *An Essay on Epic Poetry*, canto III, lines 14–15, 16, 17, 21.

99. Ibid., III.23, 28.

100. Kurasawa, *The Ethnological Imagination*, ix.

101. See Pagden, *The Fall of Natural Man*.

102. *The Correspondence of Edmund Burke*, vol. 3: 351.

103. Horace Walpole (to Horace Mann), in *The Yale Edition of Horace Walpole's Correspondence*, vol. 24: 21 (July 10, 1774).

104. Marshall and Williams, *The Great Map of Mankind: Perceptions of New Worlds in the Age of Enlightenment*, 258; and Michael J. Franklin, "Sir William Jones, the Celtic Revival and the Oriental Renaissance," 37.

105. William Shenstone qtd. in Ross, *The Old Norse Poetic Translations of Thomas Percy*, 7.

106. Trumpener, xi, xii.

107. Sorensen, *The Grammar of Empire in Eighteenth-Century British Writing*, 3.

108. Kaul, *Poems of Nation, Anthems of Empire*. For many different views on the coalescence of Britain as a nation, see Colley, *Britons*; Lucas, *England and Englishness*; and Hugh Kearney, *The British Isles*.

109. Karen O'Brien, "Poetry and Political Thought," 168–70.

110. Kaul, *Poems of Nation, Anthems of Empire*, 18, 1.

111. Ibid., 85, 89.

CHAPTER 1. THOMAS GRAY, VIRTUAL AUTHORSHIP, AND THE PERFORMED VOICE

1. McDowell, "Mediating Media Past and Present," 233–34.

2. Zaret, *Origins of Democratic Culture*, 69–72.

3. See St. Clair, *The Reading Nation in the Romantic Period*, 11.

4. Zionkowski, *Men's Work*, 170. For more on patronage, see Griffin, *Literary Patronage in England, 1650–1800*. For more on how shifts in the literary marketplace changed authorship, see Kernan, *Printing Technology, Letters, and Samuel Johnson*; Hammond, *Professional Imaginative Writing in England, 1670–1740*; and Woodmansee, *The Author,*

Art, and the Market. There are numerous books about this shift from an early modern to an Enlightenment sense of authorship. For a listing of more see, Wall, *The Imprint of Gender: Authorship and Publication in the English Renaissance*, 13–17.

5. This separation of the text from the author has often been equated to childbirth, in which the text becomes an independent entity, alive in its own right. John Milton warned in *Areopagitica* (1644), his treatise on the printing press, that "books are not absolutely dead things, but doe contain a potencie of life in them to be as active as that soule was whose progeny they are; nay they do preserve as in a violl [vial] the purest efficacie and extraction of that living intellect that bred them" (4) (page citation from 1644 edition). James Kearney offers a slightly different sense of the relationship when he suggests that the Reformation English book was an "incarnate text" tethered, in an umbilical fashion, to its producer. See *The Incarnate Text*, 1–41.

6. McKeon, *The Secret History of Domesticity*, 54 and passim.

7. Rose, "The Author as Proprietor," 75.

8. Cooper, *Characteristics of Men, Manners, Opinions, Times*, 78.

9. Boswell, *Life of Johnson*, ed. Chapman, 731. On Gray's retiring ambivalence to the literary marketplace, Linda Zionkowski writes in *Men's Work* that Gray tried "to reclaim a cultural position for poets that would render them not marginal but central, not mercantile but heroic. And in so doing, he defined resistance to commerce, not participation in it, as the truly masculine stance for writers" (147). Suvir Kaul argues that Gray's relation to arts and class is marked by "radical ambivalence" but that he can be seen as part of the shift from "gentleman-poet" to "man of letters" (*Thomas Gray and Literary Authority*, 9); for these moments of ambivalence, see 4–12, 157, 224. In addition to these sources, see William Levine, "'Beyond the Limits of a Vulgar Fate'"; and especially Scott Hess, *Authoring the Self*, 109–13, in which Hess argues that the "Elegy" reflects "Gray's ambivalent authorial identity and relationship to commercial print culture" (109).

10. I have borrowed the term "printed voice" from Eric Griffiths's *The Printed Voice of Victorian Poetry*. Griffiths argues that the "provision of voices for lines of print has to be done with every text" and that this is fundamentally an "exercise of imagination" (7). As he points out, the "poet's voice is not the voice of the person who is the poet" and the "voice is that which is decided in reading a text" (67). It is this act of "imaginative voicing" that turns readers into an audience (38).

11. Montagu, "Verses Address'd to the Imitator of the First Satire of the Second Book of Horace," www.nlx.com/collections/86 (accessed January 17, 2010).

12. Montagu always denied authoring the *Verses*. Regardless, the public consistently assumed that the poem was composed by her, no doubt because of the evident animosity between her and Pope. See Grundy, "*Verses Address'd to the Imitator of Horace*," 108. James McLaverty has suggested that Pope orchestrated the publication of poetry against himself to legitimize his desire to compose a public response against his many detractors("'Of Which being publick the Publick Judge.'"

13. Deutsch, *Resemblance and Disgrace*, 23.

14. Maynard Mack, *Alexander Pope*.

15. Pope, "An Epistle from Mr. Pope, to Dr. Arbuthnot," lines 125–28.

16. Deutsch, 11.

17. See Deutsch, 11–39. For more on the ways Pope controlled his public representation, see Stephanson, *The Yard of Wit*, chap. 4; and Donaldson, "Concealing and Revealing."

18. Swift, *The Complete Poems*.

19. *The Correspondence of Thomas Gray*, vol. 2: 372 (February 13, 1753). Hereafter cited in the text as *Corr.*

20. Swift, "Thoughts on Various Subjects," vol. 4: 489.

21. Gray's attempt to disassociate himself from the voices of the poem was not always successful, as one reaction from Leigh Hunt demonstrates. Hunt's reading of the poem's epitaph is as for Gray himself: "The epitaph is on the author . . . We suspect, that the 'cross'd in love' of the previous lines might very well apply to Gray. He had secret griefs of some kind, perhaps of disease, perhaps of sympathy with a good mother, and distress at having a bad father (for such, alas! was the case)" (Hunt, *A Book for a Corner*, 222).

22. Frank Ellis was the first to suggest that Gray's revisions were an attempt to "depersonalize" the poem. These attempts have been ignored by critics, Ellis argues, who insist on using the "Elegy" to reconstruct his biography, a misinterpretation that Ellis calls the "biographical fallacy." See Ellis, "Gray's *Elegy*."

23. See Guillory, *Cultural Capital*, 85–133. Guillory argues that the peasant poet of Gray's poem ("mute, inglorious Milton") is not silenced by death but by illiteracy, constraining literary production and poetic success (116). He claims that Gray's "Elegy" represents the increasing importance of vernacular over classical literacy, which permits a complexly intertextual poem like the "Elegy" to become an indicator of "cultural capital" (101).

24. In *Thomas Gray and Literary Authority*, Kaul claims that Gray's references to the "simple poor" and "unlettr'd muse" indicate that "what the *Elegy* really mourns . . . is that poetic practice uninflected by the logic of commodity is not possible" (127, 141–42). Scott Hess argues that authorship is constructed in the contest between the orality of the swain and the literacy of the author, understanding the epitaph as Gray's attempt to control his audience's reaction; *Authoring the Self*, 110–13.

25. Lonsdale, ed., *The Poems of Thomas Gray, William Collins, and Oliver Goldsmith*, 113.

26. For more on the "birth," see Robert Mack, *Thomas Gray*, 424. For more on the queerness of collaboration in the creation of printed texts, see Masten, *Textual Intercourse*, 4–7, 12–62. For queer readings of Gray's poetry, see Hagstrum, "Gray's Sensibility"; and Rousseau, "The Pursuit of Homosexuality in the Eighteenth Century." George E. Haggerty offers Gray's potential same-sex desire as a reason why he avoided public exposure, claiming "the physical expression and the public exposure are written into Gray's poetry of feeling, where they tremble with the frustration that they must already imply" ("*O lachrymarum fons*," 85). See also Haggerty, " 'The Voice of Nature' in Gray's *Elegy*."

27. Austin, *Chironomia; or, A Treatise on Rhetorical Delivery*, iv. Thanks to Danielle Bobker for bringing this work to my attention.

28. The prevalence of oratorical manuals showed that this movement toward speech was at least in part dependent on print. Print extended and enlivened rhetoric and public speech. Austin is in this movement since, as Ben McCorkle argues, print came to stand in as the "exemplary standard for oral delivery," which included the "mechanical standardization of delivery" and differed from the audience-centered oratory of antiquity (35); see McCorkle, "Harbingers of the Printed Page."

29. Austin, 528–29.

30. Ibid., 522.

31. Austin writes in *Chironomia* that he seeks "to produce a language of symbols so simple and so perfect as to render it possible with facility to represent every action of an orator throughout his speech, or of an actor throughout the whole drama, and to record them for posterity, and for repetition and practice" (274–75). His diagrams constitute a system for performing what begins as written text.

32. Burgh, *The Art of Speaking*, 29.

33. Sheridan, *A Course of Lectures on Elocution*, xii.

34. For more, see Fliegelman, *Declaring Independence*, 26.

35. Jefferson, despite his aversion to public speaking—he never delivered the State of the Union Address in person while president, preferring to send a handwritten letter—seems to have been an avid student of elocution, concluding, for example, that oral recitation was unique to each human being and that "no two persons will accent the same passage alike." He thought characteristics of voice, such as tone, were integral to a human's personality and that a text sounded "an author's sentiments or revealed his character" (qtd. in Fliegelman, 20).

36. Benjamin Franklin wrote this in a letter to Noah Webster. See "all these improvements backwards" (December 26, 1789), in *Autobiography, Poor Richard, and Later Writings*, 437–38.

37. Steele, *An Essay Towards Establishing the Melody and Measure of Speech*.

38. Tedlock, *The Spoken Word and the Work of Interpretation*, 6.

39. Ibid., 7. Emphasis in original.

40. Tedlock, "Toward an Oral Poetics," 517.

41. Ibid., 515.

42. Fabian, "Keep Listening."

43. Ibid., 90.

44. Ibid., 91, 89.

45. Julien, *African Novels and the Question of Orality*, 46.

46. Ibid., 10. For a longer discussion of reading at the intersection of the formal and the ideological, see Kaul, *Thomas Gray and Literary Authority*, 1–15.

47. Zionkowski, 170. The shift toward a more professional model of authorship based on paying readers rather than patronage was expressed as a loss of status for authors in the wider culture. Zionkowski suggests that some authors, most notably Samuel Johnson, combated this loss by instituting a gender ideology that saw involvement in the commercial marketplace of print as a reassertion of masculinity and cultural authority (9–10).

48. Kaul, *Thomas Gray and Literary Authority*, 239.

49. See Genette, *Paratexts*, 1.

50. Gray composed "The Bard" in fits and starts. He wrote that after abandoning the poem for some time he found the impetus to complete it after seeing John Parry perform Welsh songs in 1757. For a detailed history of the poem and its composition, see Lonsdale, ed., *Poems of Thomas Gray, William Collins, and Oliver Goldsmith*, 177–83.

51. Gray, "Argument" in *Poetic Commonplace Books and Manuscripts of Thomas Gray, 1716–1771*, 932. The "Argument" was not published with the poem.

52. Gray felt that bards occupied a public office that was conferred and fully sanctioned by the reigning political authority. See Martin, *Chronologie de la Vie et de L'Oeuvre de Thomas Gray*, 186. Gray's evidence derives from his research with medieval manuscripts that claim to describe accurately the role and function of medieval bards, for instance, that bards' importance in the political structure is indicated by their being allowed to sit with kings and queens.

53. These details are included in Norton Nicholls's "reminiscences" of Gray from 1805. See Gray, *The Correspondence of Thomas Gray*, vol. 3: 1290.

54. Eugene McCarthy writes that Gray's "poetic voice was liberated" after he assumed the "voice of the poet/bard" (*Thomas Gray*, 229). Arthur Johnston claims in *Thomas Gray*

and the Bard that "The Bard" shows Gray "swinging" toward a concept of the poet that was "as far removed as possible from the figure he had represented in his earlier poems," and that through the Bard Gray was "speaking in character" (8–10). In *The Poetry of Thomas Gray: Versions of the Self,* Roger Lonsdale argues that Gray escaped from himself by imagining himself as a bard, which is an instance of "total self-projection" (16). In *Britannia's Issue,* Howard Weinbrot considers "The Bard" to be Gray's affirmative departure from the private inspiriting muse of earlier poems (like the "Sonnet on West") in favor of the "public voice of nation" and of a poet who, like the bard, evokes a unified community (385, 397).

55. In *Gray Agonistes,* Robert F. Gleckner identifies the Bard as Gray, though he sees this identification as the terminus of Gray's "Miltonic agon"—the culmination of Gray's struggle with Milton's continuous influence, which, for Gleckner, also marks the tragic end of Gray's poetic career (90). His reading of the poem's conclusion, where the Bard hurls himself off Mount Snowdon to his death, says it all: "The Bard enacts in his plunge the willful sinking of Gray himself into the depths of eternal night and silence from which [he] will never be repaired nor his voice speak, much less sing" (92). Likewise, Wallace Jackson argues that Gray petitions "[reflect] the poet's uncertain claim to voice" and that "his own poetry is vocal to a few . . . or to none" ("Thomas Gray: Drowning in Human Voices?" 369).

56. Trumpener, *Bardic Nationalism,* 6. English poets, Trumpener argues, tried to "impersonate" bardic voice and to "imitate bardic materials" without an understanding of their cultural situatedness or their historical significance (6). She claims that this "refunctioning" of the bard by English authors like Gray simply displays "the nominalism of imperialism in a new, aesthetic register" (33).

57. John Parry is best remembered now from Gray's comments about him in his letters. Blind at birth, Parry was a practicing harpist throughout his life. His patrons were the family of Sir Watkin William Wynn. Parry edited and published some of the earliest collections of Welsh music, including *British Harmony, Being a Collection of Antient Welsh Airs, The Traditional Remains of those Originally Sung By the Bards of Wales, carefully compiled and now first published with some additional Variations, by John Parry* (London, 1781). For more information on his life, see Griffith, "Introduction" to *Four Lessons for Harp or Harpsichord by John Parry,* iv–vii; and Williams, *John Parry (1710?–1782).*

58. The reference to "this learned body" is ambiguous. While it seems likely from the context that "this body" refers to Gray's body, it is also possible that "this body" could refer to the body of scholars at Cambridge, the audience of Parry's performance, of which Gray was a member.

59. Gray wrote: "the thought, w[ch] you applaud, in those lines, <u>Loose his beard &c</u>: is borrow'd from painting. Rafael in his Vision of Ezekiel (in the Duke of Orleans' Collection) has given the air of head, w[ch] I tried to express, To God the Father; or (if you have been at Parma) you may remember Moses breaking the Tables by the Parmeggiano, w[ch] comes still nearer to my meaning" (*Corr.,* 2: 476–77 [August 27, 1756]). He probably saw both of these art objects while touring Italy with Horace Walpole between 1739 and 1741. For more on this tour, see Robert Mack, *Thomas Gray,* 220–70.

60. Cowley, *The English Writings of Abraham Cowley,* vol. 2: 214.

61. Gray's complete comment about Dodsley's *Collection* is: "You know I was of the publishing side, and thought your reasons against it none . . . the *still small voice* of Poetry was not made to be heard in a crowd; yet Satire will be heard, for all her audience are by nature her friends" (*Corr.,* 1: 296). Gray's statement about poetry's "still small voice" alludes to a passage from 1 Kings 19:12: "and after the earthquake a fire, but the

Lord was not in the fire; and after the fire a still small voice." See *Holy Bible* (King James Version), 321.

62. "The Bard," in *Thomas Gray and William Collins: Poetical Works*, ed. Lonsdale, line 1. Hereafter cited parenthetically by line number. Most citations of Gray's poetry are from this Lonsdale edition and are cited below as *Poetical Works*.

63. Gray's verse evokes elements of Welsh prosody rather than replicating them exactly. See McCarthy, 194–201.

64. The term "double cadence" is Gray's and is meant to suggest an affinity with a type of Welsh verse called *Gorchest y Beirdh*, which Gray translated as the "Excellent of the Bards" in his *Poetic Commonplace Books* (799). He observed in his commonplace book that Welsh compositions were "generally in stanzas regularly answering one another; & there is a conceal'd harmony, arising from the regular return of similar letters or syllables in the beginning or middle of a Verse, doubtless very pleasing to ears accustom'd to the Cadence of their Poetry & Language" (799). But Gray was partly mistaken in his use of *Gorchest y Beirdh*. As Arthur Johnston points out, this Welsh verse pattern was not formed until the fifteenth century, after the historical period in which "The Bard" is set ("Gray's Use of the Gorchest y Beirdd in 'The Bard,'" 335–38.

65. Gray felt that Welsh oral poetry was naturally melodic and thus enticing; at one point he wrote in his commonplace book that Welsh poems had "excellent Prosodia, & wch is perhaps the finest, that any Language affords, [and] were admirably contrived for assisting the memory. [T]hey were all adapted to Musick, every word being harmonious, the strongest and most expressive repeated in a beautiful manner" (*Poetic Commonplace Books*, 799).

66. Ibid.

67. Pennant, *Tour in Wales*.

68. Charnell-White, *Bardic Circles*, 46.

69. Richards, *Wallography*, 122. Richards does concede that the Welsh language is pure, because it was not "deflowr'd by the Mixture of any other Dialect" (121), so I suppose he considers it "pure" gibberish.

70. An anonymous travel writer qtd. in Michael Franklin, "The Colony Writes Back," 13.

71. Johnson, *The Lives of the Most Eminent English Poets*, vol. 4: 183.

72. In the 1768 edition of this poem, Gray added a footnote to the line "A Voice, as of the Cherub-Choir" that simply declared "Milton" (*Poetical Works*, 199). This understated, seemingly self-explanatory footnote says a great deal about the importance and familiarity of Milton's "voice." Next to "distant warblings" Gray included another footnote: "The succession of Poets after Milton's time" (199).

73. See Garber, *Quotation Marks*, 13–15, 19. These quotation marks also appear in the fair copy of the poem which Gray penned into his commonplace book. He was careful that they appeared as well in the printed text.

74. For more, see de Grazia, "Sanctioning Voice," 288. See also de Grazia's article "Shakespeare in Quotation Marks." According to Robert Bringhurst, movable type representing quotation marks was not even produced until the mid-sixteenth century, which was about a century after the introduction of printing to Europe; see *The Elements of Typographic Style, version 2.5*, 86. For a related study of quotation marks in poetry, see Gregory, *Quotation and American Poetry*.

75. De Grazia, "Sanctioning Voice," 289. The discussion over using quotation marks to indicate who speaks parallels the contentious debate about copyright and intellectual property that went on in eighteenth-century print culture. For more on this, see Rose,

Authors and Owners; and Saunders and Hunter, "Authorship and Copyright, and Lessons from the 'Literatory.'"

76. This resistance to Gray's use of unusual typographical techniques and meters reflects the general response to his *Odes* (the collection in which "The Bard" first appeared), which was at once enthusiastic and confused. "The Bard" was one of two poems collected in *Odes*, published in 1757. William Powell Jones gives a suitably complex assessment of the reading public's reception of *Odes* when he says that, though the poems might not have been universally appreciated, they were widely read and bought; see Jones, "The Contemporary Reception of Gray's *Odes*."

77. Bickley, ed., *The Diaries of Sylvester Douglas, Lord Glenbervie*, vol. 1: 135. This anecdote might also suggest the particularly textual nature of Gray's orality and its difference from actual oral performance.

78. See the anonymous review "Odes of Mr. Gray." The importance of Spitalfields grew after French Huguenots settled there during the 1700s. With this influx of foreign labor, it was converted from open or cultivated fields into tenement housing for silk-weavers, a population that came to dominate the area. Scholars estimate that there were between forty and fifty thousand workers involved in the British silk trade in the early eighteenth century, mostly in London. For more, see Sheppard, *London: A History*, 129, 172, 230; Hibbert, *London: The Biography of a City*, 122; Inwood, *A History of London*, 332–33; and Richardson, *London and Its People*, 152.

79. Waller, *1700: Scenes from London Life*, 271. Waller's evidence consists of the records of the French Huguenots who made up most of the population of Spitalfields. She notes that they still spoke and wrote in French, or a combination of French and English that Frenchified English words: one silk-weaver, for example, wrote his address as "dans la rue Lyon Rouge, paroisse Stepney, Spitlefeilds hameau" (271). These populations were not fully assimilated until three or four generations had passed; see Waller, 274.

80. Gray claims, in a handwritten note in his personal copy of the *Odes*, that Welsh metrics convey a "wild spirit." See Lonsdale, *Poems*, 188.

81. Gray selected this motto from Pindar's *Olympian Odes*. For more information about Pindar's odes and their role in Gray's poetry, see Lonsdale, *Poems*, 157; and McCarthy, 167.

82. Gray provided detailed instructions about how the volume was to be constructed, how his poems were to be presented, and in what order they were to appear, further evidence that he remained interested in and involved with his printed works until the end of his life. He instructed his printers to place the three imitations near the end of the book, and he remarked to Walpole that *Poems* provided him with a sense of an ending, noting sardonically, "What has one to do, when *turned of fifty*, but really to think of finishing" (*Corr.*, 3: 1018 [February 25, 1768]).

83. See William Powell Jones, *Thomas Gray, Scholar*, 102.

84. Although the evidence is not conclusive, it seems that Gray could not read Old Welsh or Old Norse, the languages of the original poems he was evoking; hence, he relied almost exclusively on the Latin translations. Most scholars agree, however, that Gray had some small knowledge of the two languages, particularly their rhythms, on which he capitalized when devising the metrical forms of his imitations and "The Bard." For more, see Snyder, *The Celtic Revival in English Literature, 1760–1800*, 34; Starr and Hendrickson, eds., *The Complete Poems of Thomas Gray; English, Latin and Greek*, x; Kittredge, "Gray's Knowledge of Old Norse," xli–l; and William Powell Jones, *Thomas Gray, Scholar*, 98–99, 101.

85. For ideas about translation in the late seventeenth and early eighteenth century, see Judith Sloman, *Dryden: The Poetics of Translation.*

86. Gray made this comment about adding notes to "The Bard" in particular. He claimed to be spiteful toward his readers because the material of the bards' prophecy could be found in any "six-penny History of England" (*Corr.* 3: 1002 [February 1, 1768]).

87. In the overall "Advertisement" for the imitations, Gray explains that they were meant to be "some specimens of the Style that reigned in ancient times among the neighbouring nations . . . and . . . our Progenitors" (*The Complete Poems,* 33).

88. *Poetical Works,* 63. For complete information about "The Fatal Sisters," see Lonsdale, ed., *Poems,* 210–13. The origin of "The Fatal Sisters," first titled by Gray "The Song of the Valkyries," was an Icelandic legend *Davraðer Lioð* from the eleventh century. Gray translated from Bartolin's *Antiquitatum Danicum de Causis Contemptae Mortis,* a volume of Norse poems with Latin translations which was published in Copenhagen in 1689.

89. "The Fatal Sisters," in *Poetical Works,* line 63.

90. Ibid., lines 57–60.

91. Kaul, *Thomas Gray and Literary Authority,* 241.

92. Millner, *Thomas Gray's Welsh and Norse Poetry,* 80. In his discussion Millner refers particularly to contemporary reviews of Gray's later poetry in *Critical Review* 25 (1768), 367; and in *Monthly Review* (May 1768), 408.

93. "The Triumphs of Owen," in *Poetical Works,* line 1.

CHAPTER 2. WALES, PUBLIC POETRY, AND THE POLITICS OF COLLECTIVE VOICE

1. "Eisteddfod" translates roughly as "sitting together"; in *The Eisteddfod,* Hywel Teifi Edwards further defines it as a meeting, a singing session of national songs (4). Thought to date from the twelfth century, these meetings were competitive from the beginning; later they tested and licensed performers in the metrical traditions of Wales (Edwards, 6–7). The last significant eisteddfod before the eighteenth century occurred in 1567, but its importance endured: similar yet much smaller gatherings were held sporadically, most often in pubs, until the early eighteenth century; see Edwards, "The Eisteddfod Poet," 9. The first modern eisteddfod was organized in 1789, after which it evolved into the National Eisteddfod that continues annually.

2. *The Cambro-Briton,* vol. 3: 442.

3. Ibid., 3: 504.

4. Ibid., 1: 58.

5. See Hughes, "St. David's Day," 139.

6. As Shawna Lichtenwalner notes, oral festivals like the eisteddfod helped the Welsh "re-envision and codify a positive cultural identity that was historically based but modernized" (*Claiming Cambria,* 142 and throughout).

7. Schwyzer, *Literature, Nationalism, and Memory in Early Modern England and Wales,* 81.

8. I have adopted the term "resistant nationalisms" from Janet Sorensen's *The Grammar of Empire in Eighteenth-Century British Writing* (24). She in turn developed her term from the work of David Lloyd and Paratha Chatterjee. For more on resistant nationalisms in the British Isles, see Pittock, *Inventing and Resisting Britain*; and Kidd, *British Identities before Nationalism.*

9. See Benedict Anderson's discussion of the role between print and the formation of the nation as an "imagined community" in *Imagined Communities*, 1–37.

10. Morgan, "From a Death to a View," 99. E. D. Evans notes that by the eighteenth century, "bardic learning, handed down by oral tradition, was waning but far from extinct" (*A History of Wales*, 235). For more on Wales in the eighteenth century, see Davies, *A History of Wales*.

11. Trumpener, *Bardic Nationalism*.

12. Ibid., xi.

13. Ibid., xv.

14. Ibid., 6, 33.

15. Ibid., 6.

16. Ibid., 34.

17. The exact composition date of Evans's "Paraphrase" is unknown. Sarah Prescott dates it from sometime between Gray's initial publication in 1757 and 1765. For her rationale, see "'Gray's Pale Spectre,'" 89, fn. 45.

18. For more on the Cymmrodorion Society and other antiquarian societies, see Sarah Prescott's *Eighteenth-Century Writing from Wales*, chap. 1; and "'What Foes more dang'rous than too strong Allies?'"; as well as the society's website: www.cymmrodorion1751.org.uk/ (accessed February 3, 2010).

19. Psalm 137:2–6 tells that upon reaching Babylon the Jews "hanged our harps upon the willows." When the Babylonians asked the Jews to entertain them with a song, they refused, reaffirming their faith and invoking dire outcomes should they sing to their captors or forget their homes in Jerusalem: "let my right hand forget her cunning . . . let my tongue cleave to the roof of my mouth." The question the Jews ask themselves—"How shall we sing the LORD's song in a strange land?"—is the same question Evans attempts to answer in his poem, on behalf of Welsh national authors.

20. Trumpener, 4.

21. Ibid., 4.

22. Lichtenwalner, 20.

23. Prescott, "'Gray's Pale Spectre,'" 80, 93.

24. "Proclamation for a Meeting of the Bards, *At Midsummer*, 1798."

25. This translation appeared in W. Owen Pughe's *Palestine, a Poem by Heber, and The Bard, by Gray, Translated into Welsh*, published in London in 1822. The review appeared in the *Cambro-Briton* 3: 307, 312.

26. *OED*, s.v. "transfusion."

27. The first successful blood transfusion occurred in 1818, just a few years before this reviewer lauded Pughe's poem. For a discussion of the transfusion supposed to have been provided for Pope Innocent VIII, see W. J. Bishop, *The Early History of Surgery*, 112–14.

28. Morganwg experimented with a number of bardic identities throughout his life before settling on "Iolo Morganwg," a name by which he is still commonly known. See Charnell-White, *Bardic Circles*, 10. For more on Morganwg, see Jenkins, ed., *A Rattleskull Genius*; Constantine, *The Truth Against the World*; and Hutton, *Blood and Mistletoe*, 146–82. See also the website of "Iolo Morganwg and the Romantic Tradition in Wales," University of Wales, Aberystwyth, http://iolomorganwg.wales.ac.uk/ (accessed December 19, 2009).

29. Iolo Morganwg [Edward Williams], *Poems, Lyrical and Pastoral*, vol. 2: 7. Both names—Edward Williams and Iolo Morganwg—appear on the title page of this collection, Morganwg's own publication, perhaps demonstrating his dual readership.

30. Morganwg, 1: 7.

31. For more on the Enlightenment suggestion that oral traditional cultures were the state of nature, see Neil Rennie, *Far-Fetched Facts*, 113.

32. Morganwg qtd. in Charnell-White, *The Truth against the World*, 36, 68, 153.

33. Merians, *Envisioning the Worst*, 13–14.

34. *The Gentleman's Magazine* LIX, part 2, 1789, 976–77. Morganwg, 2: 195. Although Morganwg claimed to detest Gray's poem, he may have been the printer and publisher of Pughe's Welsh translation of it. He was a printer, and the publisher of Pughe's translation is listed on the title page as "E. Williams."

35. Charnell-White, 38.

36. Ibid., 20.

37. Charnell-White notes that the gorsedd mixed a number of traditions, particularly from the eisteddfod, so that there was little practical difference between these occasions (121). These two models show that the societies and constituencies of Welsh bardism, while often overlapping, could also be in conflict as they struggled to determine regional identity.

38. Hutton, 159.

39. In a note appended to the title and to the conclusion of his poem "The Swain of the Mountains," Morganwg describes the "specimen of the old national Manner of the Welsh in their poems" (*Poems, Lyrical and Pastoral*, 1: 92, 95).

40. Morganwg qtd. in Charnell-White, 38. As of 2009, there was a memorial to Morganwg and the gorsedd on Primrose Hill.

41. There is a description of this early gathering in *The Morning Chronicle* (September 26, 1792) and in Morganwg, *Poems, Lyrical and Pastoral* 2: 39. For more on the role of Celtic antiquarianism in Morganwg's bardic revival, see Branwen Jarvis, "Iolo Morganwg and the Welsh Cultural Background."

42. Edward Jones, Miscellany. Charnell-White claims that there is no corroborating evidence that this event happened (138). Nonetheless, the note gives a picture of how Morganwg's performances may have been organized.

43. *The Monthly Review of Literature; or magazine de savans* (London: 1792–1793), 16.

44. Ibid., 17.

45. Edward Jones, Miscellany. This mixture of sources leads Charnell-White to conclude that, while literary primitivism may have provided Morganwg with a "ready-made framework," he borrowed from non-Welsh traditions as well to fill in that frame (79).

46. Of course, it is possible as well that the idea of holding them "dear" is merely metaphorical.

47. A description of this meeting can be found in *Cambro-Briton*, 3: 504.

48. Reproduced in Wu, ed., *Romantic Women Poets*, 508–10 (lines 8, 24, 33–34). It was originally titled "Lines on the Eisteddfod of the Cymmrodorion." The reaction to Hemans's poem on its publication was strongly dismissive. One reviewer claimed it was "better left deposited in the archives of that foolish people" and that the eisteddfod was one of the "two greatest humbugs" in London at the time (Wu, 508, fn. 3).

49. Roach, *Cities of the Dead*, xiii.

50. Several critics have noted Hemans's enormous sensitivity to how texts mediate specific sounds, voices, locales, and contexts. Nanora Sweet and Julie Melnyk characterize all of Hemans's poetry as an "echoing intertextuality" (*Felicia Hemans*, 3). In "'A Deeper and Richer Music,'" Diego Saglia extends this notion of sound and text, arguing that Hemans's verse is a "complex interweaving of human and natural location . . . mediated

by other texts and voices" (351). Rather than access "a world of absolute transcendental values," Hemans's textual voices are "situated within cultural and ideological contexts drawn from history or historically grounded literary and non-literary sources or connected with men and women in identifiable settings and situations" (352).

51. George Gordon, Lord Byron, *Byron's Letters and Journals*, ed. Marchand, vol. 7: 182 (September 28, 1820).

52. Lootens, "Hemans at Home."

53. For an excellent discussion of Hemans's life, reputation, and critical heritage, see Susan Wolfson, *Felicia Hemans*, xii–xix. For more on Hemans and the eisteddfod, see Lichtenwalner, 148–60.

54. *Cambro-Briton*, 3: 61.

55. Aaron, "'Saxon, Think not All is Won.'"

56. Hemans, *Poems, England and Spain, Modern Greece*, 73–74. See also Brewer, "Felicia Hemans, Byronic Cosmopolitanism and the Ancient Welsh Bards," 173–74.

57. Hemans, *Poems*, 73–74, 76.

58. See the preamble to "The Rock of Cader Idris" in Wu, ed., *Romanticism*, 1247.

59. Trinder, *Mrs. Hemans*, 30.

60. Hemans, *Tales and Historic Scenes*, "Advertisement." References to Hemans's poems in *A Selection of Welsh Melodies* are from this edition and are cited by line number.

61. Lichtenwalner, 152.

62. See, for example, Sweet and Melnyk, *Felicia Hemans*, 3; Saglia, "'A Deeper and Richer Music'"; and Rudy, "Hemans's Passion." The work of Paula Feldman, Tricia Lootens, and Susan Wolfson has also been significant in bringing Hemans back to our attention.

63. See Bogel, *Literature and Insubstantiality in Later Eighteenth-Century England*.

64. For more on this connection between nationalism and the memorializing of the dead, see Schwyzer, 97–98.

65. Taussig, *The Magic of the State*, 4. Taussig qtd. in Schwyzer, 98.

66. Rhys Jones, *Gorchestion Beirdd Cymru*. The English translation of Jones's preface is provided by Prys Morgan in "From Death to a View" (70).

CHAPTER 3. SCOTLAND AND THE INVENTION OF VOICE

1. Macpherson. *Fragments of Ancient Poetry*, a2. All references to the *Fragments* are to this edition; quotations are cited parenthetically in the text.

2. *The Correspondence of Thomas Gray*, ed. Toynbee and Whibley, vol. 2: 680.

3. See Gaskill, ed., *The Reception of Macpherson's Ossian in Europe*. For a consideration of the effect of the Ossian myth on interest in "native" British traditions, see Weinbrot, *Britannia's Issue*.

4. For a description of assessments of *Fragments*, see Stafford, *The Sublime Savage*, 40–60, 79–80.

5. Johnson, *The Major Works*, ed. Greene, 637–38.

6. Performance, Janet Sorensen notes, was an essential part of this connective relationship, since "performing bodies were seen as facilitating the affective bond of spectators" among the wide variety of Scottish publics ("Varieties of Public Performance," 134).

7. Adam Fox argues that, in the reciprocal relationship of orality and writing, the written word augments and reinvents the spoken word, "making it anew, propagating its

contents, heightening its exposure, and ensuring its continued vitality" although in different forms. See Fox, *Oral and Literate Culture in England, 1500–1700*, 5 and passim. See also Hudson, "Constructing Oral Tradition," 240–55.

8. Here, I am borrowing from Eric Havelock, who suggests that ancient Greek oral poetry functioned as a "total technology of the preserved word" which maintained and transmitted culture across time (*Preface to Plato*, 43).

9. Fielding, *Writing and Orality*, 9.

10. Davis and McLane, "Oral and Public Poetry," 125, 128. Davis and McLane even go so far as to suggest that Scotland was the first place to theorize orality, though, as I point out, Scottish authors were in conversation with and were developing techniques alongside English and Anglo-Welsh writers.

11. For more on the importance of songs and song culture in Scotland, see Pittock, *Poetry and Jacobite Politics in Eighteenth-Century Britain and Ireland*, esp. 1–9; and Davis, "At 'san about': Scottish Song and the Challenge to British Culture." The publication of Scots songs, Davis notes, dates back to at least the 1680s. Many of these were "fake" or invented, creating a refreshing air of exoticism for primarily urban English consumers. Unlike English scholars and antiquarians, Scottish song-makers and collectors thought of songs as a "renewable resource" that involved "community activity" and the "interaction between oral and print sources" (Davis, 194).

12. There are numerous scholarly works that discuss the debate about the authenticity of the Ossian poems. For an excellent overview, see Howard Gaskill's introduction to *The Poems of Ossian and Related Works*.

13. Ballad traditions, Donald Meek argues, were an important source of cultural creativity in Scotland and thus "enjoy[ed] a conspicuous place" of "respect." Despite significant revisions between the medieval period and the eighteenth century, these ballads maintained their "intrinsic vitality." Macpherson drew on this vitality as he devised a system by which to present the oral voices as printed text. See Meek, "The Gaelic Ballads of Scotland," 20, 43.

14. Ephemerality, Johnson asserted, was to be expected from nonwritten learning; for him, "speech becomes embodied and permanent" through writing. To Johnson, human memory seemed so fallible that the recollection of ancient traditions would be impossible. After questing through Scotland for bards, he announced that it was hopeless "to find any traces of Highland learning. Nor are their primitive customs and ancient manner of life otherwise than very faintly and uncertainly remembered by the present race." See Johnson, *A Journey to the Western Islands of Scotland* (117, 114). For more on Johnson's rejection of the existence of oral poetry, see Hudson, "Oral Tradition," 161–76.

15. Johnson, *Journey*, 117.

16. Stone makes these claims in "Albin and the Daughter of Mey," 15.

17. Also, Crawford, *The Modern Poet*," 40; and Stone, 15.

18. Blair, *Lectures on Rhetoric and Belles Lettres*, ed. Harding, 124–25.

19. Ibid., 113.

20. Macpherson, *The Works of Ossian*, vol. 1: 24.

21. Sinclair, *The Poems of Ossian*, xv.

22. The poems in Smith's collection closely resemble Macpherson's Ossian publications, and a collection of the ostensibly "original" Ossian poems was published by Smith, which included Gaelic poems with English explanatory notes. More interesting, perhaps, is Smith's assertion that one of the state functions of the bard was to sing the clan

chief to sleep at night (Smith, *Sean Dana; le Oisian, Orran, Ulann &c. / Ancient Poems of Ossian, Orran, Ullin, &c. Collected in the Western Highlands and Isles; Being the Originals of the Translations Some Time Ago Published in the Gaelic Antiquities.* Edinburgh, 1787), 162.

23. John Smith, 157, 12, 93.

24. Moore, ed., *Ossian and Ossianism*, vol. 2: 84.

25. Ibid., 2: 84.

26. Haywood, *The Making of History*, 79.

27. Moore, 2: 8.

28. According to Robert Lass, the history of the second person case is "intricate . . . not well understood" and "possibly incoherent," but the prevailing thought is that in Middle English the second person included both "ye/you" and "thou"; the former suggested formality and the latter familiarity. By the end of the sixteenth century, "thou" and its possessives, "thee" and "thy," were increasingly rare; and by the eighteenth century, "*you* was the only normal spoken form; *thou* . . . [was] restricted to high-register discourse," even though it had once signified a "heightened emotional tone" or "intimacy." See, Lass, *The Cambridge History of the English Language*, vol. 3: 148–53. See also Burnley, *The History of the English Language*, 200; Stevick, *English and Its History*, 140; and Pyles, *The Origins and Development of the English Language*, 201.

29. Moore, 2: 6.

30. Elfenbein, *Romanticism and the Rise of English*, 66–71.

31. It was common for authors and scholars to translate ancient poetry, especially oral poetry or folkloric genres, into unlineated prose.

32. Manning, "Ghost-Writing Tradition," 92, 96.

33. Ibid., 99.

34. Connor, *Dumbstruck*, 3.

35. Ghosts come to represent this because Ossian's world is meant to be a "preliterate, and therefore prehistorical, attempt to think about history" (Underwood, "Romantic Historicism and the Afterlife," 238).

36. Meek, 28.

37. Roach, *Cities of the Dead*, 13. Roach's argument about performance as re-performance is based in part on Richard Schechner's description of performance as "twice-behaved behavior" or "restored behavior" (qtd. in Roach, 3). For a fuller discussion of the features of oral traditions in Macpherson, see Fitzgerald, "The Style of Ossian"; Stafford, 103–11; and Groom, *The Making of Percy's Reliques*, 77.

38. Roach writes that "the process of surrogation does not begin or end but continues as actual or perceived vacancies occur in the network of relations that constitutes the social fabric" (2). This process, Roach notes, is inexact, and happens through trial and error.

39. Moore, 2: 14.

40. Macpherson, *Works of Ossian*, 2: 340, 349, 389.

41. Frances Sheridan's reaction was recorded by James Boswell in his journal during his early years in London. See *Boswell's London Journal: 1762–1763*, 182. See also an argument by Fiona Stafford in which she claims that reactions like these "belong to the 'age of sensibility' " and demonstrate that the Ossian poems expertly elicited sentimentality from their readers (172).

42. Lamport, "Goethe, Ossian, and *Werther*," 98.

43. For more on the notion of the heart in literature, see Erickson, *The Language of the Heart, 1600–1750;* and Jager, *Book of the Heart*.

44. Vendler, *Invisible Listeners*, 3.

45. Recent studies of intimacy have addressed this split between public and more private forms of relationships. Niklas Luhmann argues in *Love as Passion* that modern companionate love modeled on passionate intensity between two people is a recent invention. Lauren Berlant, however, defines intimacy as "something [to be] shared"; in explaining the link between an individual and a collectivity, she emphasizes the bonds of common experiences (*Intimacy*, 281–83).

46. Warner, *Publics and Counterpublics*, 75.

47. Berlant, *The Female Complaint*, viii. While Berlant distinguishes intimate publics from counterpublics, she admits that they share features (7–8).

48. Pinch, *Strange Fits of Passion*, 3, 187.

49. For an excellent overview of Pinch's argument, see Cottom, review of *Strange Fits of Passion* in *Nineteenth-Century Literature.*

50. John Sitter, *Literary Loneliness in Mid-Eighteenth-Century England;* and Irlam, *Elations*, 17 and passim.

51. The sensation of intimacy felt at a distance was familiar to those writing letters to loved ones, but the concept derived from Leopold Rosenmayr's study of family life (*Sociology in Austria*), in which he explores how family members who do not reside together still feel effects that they describe as proximate intimacy.

52. Runciman, *The Blind Ossian Singing and Accompanying Himself on the Harp*. See Macdonald, *Scottish Art*, 70. This sketch was for a mural painted in 1772 which was destroyed by fire in 1899.

53. Potter, ed., *The Poetry of Nature; Comprising a Selection of the Most Beautiful Apostrophes, Histories, Songs, Elegies, &c., from the Works of the Caledonian Bards. The Typographical Execution in a Style Entirely New, and Decorated with the Superb Ornaments of the Celebrated Caslon* (London 1789). *The English Review* scathingly remarked that, despite the claims of newness in the title, its italic presentation was common to "elections" and to "canvasses of different kinds, and in the circular letter of tradesmen" (vol. 16 [1795], 263), that is, it was vulgar and common.

54. McGill, "The Duplicity of the Pen," 42.

55. Zuk, ed., *Bluestocking Feminism*, vol. 3: 13.

56. DeLucia, "Far Other Times Are These," 40, 43.

57. Ibid., 40. See also Potkay, "Virtue and Manners in Macpherson's *Poems of Ossian*," 121, 125.

58. Pinch, 55.

59. For more on how the shift from oral delivery and manuscript to print-based culture changed notions of past and present, see Elizabeth Eisenstein's *The Printing Press as an Agent of Change.*

CHAPTER 4. IMPERSONATING NATIVE VOICES IN ANGLO-INDIAN POETRY

1. Alexander Dalrymple, an employee of the East India Company, enthusiastically called his company a "great Machine!" in "Fragment on the India Trade" (5).

2. For an extensive discussion of the process of recording and preserving ostensibly disappearing Indian traditions, see Ronald Inden, *Imagining India.*

3. Said, *Orientalism*. For an excellent overview of the many responses to Said's *Orientalism*, see Cass, "Interrogating Orientalism," 25–45. See also Macfie, *Orientalism*, esp. 181–326, 345–74.

4. Cohn, *Colonialism and Its Forms of Knowledge*, 21.

5. For a compelling synthesis of how orientalism advanced British economics, see Siraj Ahmed, "Orientalism and the Permanent Fix of War."

6. Michael Franklin, "Sir William Jones, the Celtic Revival and the Oriental Renaissance," 37.

7. For the best account of the need to read eighteenth-century poetry internationally, see Suvir Kaul, *Poems of Nation, Anthems of Empire*, esp. 1–43. For an instance in regard to Augustan formal "expansiveness," see Margaret Anne Doody, *The Daring Muse*, 13–18.

8. See, for instance, Leask, "Towards an Anglo-Indian Poetry?"

9. Gibson, *Indian Angles*, 6–10.

10. Tara Ghoshal Wallace, challenging Edward Said's sense that resistance to imperialism was small, argues that "popular and authoritative British writers from Alexander Pope to Walter Scott warn that imperial power poses grave social and moral dangers for the metropole" (*Imperial Characters*, 18). As Wallace notes in particular, India becomes an opportunity for contradictory political claims about Britain (141–42).

11. Here, of course, I am consciously adapting the language of "speaking back" typically associated with native colonized peoples to describe the position of Anglo-Indian authors. See, for example, *The Empire Writes Back: Theory and Practice in Post-Colonial Literatures*, ed. Bill Ashcroft, Gareth Griffiths, and Helen Tiffin.

12. See Linda Colley's *Captives: Britain, Empire, and the World, 1600–1850*, esp. 251. Other estimates place the number higher. The number of British civil servants in India is difficult to know, since it fluctuated. This number does not include other Europeans who resided there as independent merchants, traders, and mercenaries.

The relationship between the Mughal Empire, the East India Company, and the British government was complex, especially after the company took on a more governmental role beginning in the 1760s. Although the British East India Company technically acted as an administrative agent on behalf of the Mughal Empire, the company exerted outsized influence because of its bribery and militarism. The British Parliament, anxious about the increasing power of the East India Company, added direct oversight beginning in the 1770s. Ultimately, the East India Company was removed entirely in favor of crown control of India, in 1857. For a short and lucid account of this complex relationship, see Rajat Kanta Ray, "Indian Society and the Establishment of British Supremacy, 1765–1818," 513.

13. Rocher, "British Orientalism in the Eighteenth Century," 217. For an excellent comprehensive history of these years of colonialism in India, see Marshall, *The Oxford History of the British Empire*, vol. 2: *The Eighteenth Century*.

14. For more, see Steadman, "The Asiatick Society of Bengal." The Asiatick Society, Steadman argues, could "hardly have existed without official recognition of the importance of native languages and literature for the effective government of the growing British empire in India and a conscious attempt to embody this recognition in permanent or semipermanent institutions" (469–70).

15. See *The Letters of William Jones*, vol. 2: 880 (January 23, 1791). Hereafter abbreviated *LWJ* and cited by volume and page number.

16. The Asiatick Society and the personal and literary relationships of scholars, more generally, were part of the "new institutions of sociality" that Mary Ellis Gibson argues were crucial to the literary culture and political economy of India (*Indian Angles*, 22).

17. Rocher, 228.

18. William Jones's role in orientalism and British colonialism has been fiercely debated. Said suggests that Jones is an origin for European orientalists (*Orientalism*, 78). Garland Cannon argues that Jones does not fit into Said's notion of orientalism because he appreciated Eastern culture; see Cannon and Brine, eds., *Objects of Inquiry*, 25–50. Michael Franklin, for his part, has pointed out that Jones appreciated Indian culture at a moment when many discounted its significance. Without denying Jones's role in colonialism, Franklin considers Jones's hymns an example of his "benign imperialism" ("Accessing India," 64). In *India Inscribed: European and British Writing on India, 1600–1800*, Kate Teltscher disagrees, instead describing the numerous ways in which Jones was complicit with and even extended British systems of colonialism in India by acquiring oriental knowledge (192–228). For more on William Jones generally, see also Franklin, *Sir William Jones* and *Orientalist Jones;* Cannon, *The Life and Mind of Oriental Jones;* Drew, *India and the Romantic Imagination;* and Mukerjee, *Sir William Jones*.

19. *LWJ*, 2: 747 (August 12, 1787).

20. Franklin, *Sir William Jones*, 74.

21. *LWJ*, 2: 747 (August 9, 1787).

22. Franklin, *Sir William Jones: Selected Poetical and Prose Works*, 336. Thomas Percy suggested similar sentiments when he complained that "cold European imaginations" might find "somewhat extravagant" the images and metaphors of his *Song of Solomon* (xxxii–iii).

23. *LWJ*, 2: 714 (October 5, 1786.) There is a longer genealogy to this notion that goes back to early British orientalism in India. See Ahmed, 179–80.

24. *LWJ*, 2: 898 (October 19, 1791).

25. Jones felt the literature of Arabia and India to be a literature of "originals"; Ibid.: 716 (October 12, 1786).

26. Franklin, *Sir William Jones: Selected Poetical and Prose Works*, 326.

27. Ibid., 164; *LWJ* 2: 747.

28. Thomas Warton complained that Arabic poetry was "extravagant and romantic" and Edward Gibbon thought that Eastern authors lacked "the temperate dignity of style, the graceful proportions of art, the forms of visible and intellectual beauty"; see Marshall and Williams, *The Great Map of Mankind*, 73.

29. Jones, *The Works of William Jones*, ed. Shipley vol. 3: 547. In his written poetry, Jones tried to model this imitation of Sanskrit texts and popularize the study of the language. He was also involved in printing Sanskrit, publishing in 1792 the first Sanskrit text to appear in the *Calcutta Gazette*. For a discussion of Jones's dual investment in imitating Eastern voices to create original innovations, see Zak Sitter, "William Jones, 'Eastern' Poetry, and the Problem of Imitation."

30. Franklin, *Sir William Jones: Selected Poetical and Prose Works*, 361.

31. Often mistakenly received as translations, Jones's "hymns" were published piecemeal in Britain after having circulated among the orientalist community in Calcutta. A draft of "Hymn to Camdeo" and the first stanza of "Hymn to Indra" were sent to Charles Wilkins (*LWJ*, 2: 624–25 [December 15, 1783]). As Jones began to compose his hymns, he appealed to his fellow orientalists, like Wilkins, to supply him with "some *more of his names &c.*" of entities in Hindu mythology (*LWJ*, 2: 669 [April 14, 1785]). These instances show that orientalism, while certainly a "textual attitude," as Said argues in *Orientalism* (93–94), was also embedded in material circumstances that operated through conversation and the circulation of texts among specific individuals.

32. For an introduction to the history and structure of the Vedic tradition, see William K. Mahony, *The Artful Universe*, esp. 1–16. The particular attraction of Sanskrit for English poetry's experiments with poetic voice might be best summed up in Mahony's sense that the poet in the Vedic tradition hears "the primordial, divine Word sounding in the background of all existence" and then gives "voice to that Word in poetic songs . . . ." (12).

33. For a description of the Pindaric as arguably the most innovative genre of the eighteenth century, see Douglas Lane Patey, " 'Aesthetics' and the Rise of the Lyric in the Eighteenth Century," 588–89. For more on changes to the hymn in the eighteenth century, see Margaret Anne Doody, *The Daring Muse*, 75.

34. Franklin, *Sir William Jones*, 63.

35. Franklin, "Celtic Revival," 30. Franklin suggests that Jones may have been more interested in socializing than reviving bardism, though his interest still shows Jones's sensitivity to Welsh culture; see, Franklin, *Orientalist Jones*, 105–6.

36. Franklin argues that Jones, throughout his hymns, poses as a "Hindu poet." These poems legitimize British rule, and thus, as Franklin says, the "objectives of the poet, Orientalist, lawyer, and patriot can be seen to coalesce" (*Sir William Jones: Selected Poetical and Prose Works*, 123). While my own readings have benefited enormously from Franklin's research, I differ with him on how Jones presents himself in these hymns.

37. Franklin, *Sir William Jones*, 88; and *LWJ*, 2: 811 (September 19, 1788). For a discussion of the zamindar, see Betty Joseph, *Reading the East India Company, 1720–1840*, 127.

38. *LWJ*, 2: 783 (October 8, 1787).

39. Rajan, *Under Western Eyes*, 3.

40. Rajan, review of *Tropicopolitans*, 73. It is Jones's attempt to serve as an intermediary among conflicting voices and traditions that leads Rajan to conclude that Jones was "perplexed."

41. For more on the relationship between linguistic and cultural translation, see Talal Asad, "The Concept of Cultural Translation in British Social Anthropology."

42. Roy, *Indian Traffic*, 8.

43. Ibid., 18.

44. Performance culture, C. A. Bayly points out, was a significant avenue of commentary on British colonialism. Festivals, for example, served as an essential part of intra-Indian political communication, which linked widespread elements of the populace in the enjoyment of traditional culture. Such performances included recitations of songs, chants, prayers, and homilies, all of which promoted the exchange of knowledge. The media presented at these performances were complex; part written and part oral, they included heroic ballads of warrior culture, epics told by traveling storytellers, and social comedies. These "written media and their 'shadow' verbal forms," at times performed by traditional Indian bards (*bhats* and *charans*), added up to multitudinous ways in which Indians used oral forms to share information, conduct debates, and offer critical comment. See Bayly, *Empire and Information: Intelligence Gathering and Social Communication in India, 1780–1870*, esp. 207–8.

45. For more on this historical shift toward what Maureen McLane calls the "ascendancy of ethnographic authority" in ballad collecting and other examinations of oral traditions, see *Balladeering, Minstrelsy, and the Making of British Romantic Poetry*, 72–75.

46. Alexander Pope, "An Epistle from Mr. Pope, to Dr. Arbuthnot," 602, line 128.

47. Jones makes this claim but does not explain exactly how his "variations," as he calls them, are entirely new. See Franklin, *Sir William Jones: Selected Poetical and Prose Works*, 135.

48. For more on the performative history of the classical ode and its influence on English poetry, see Fry, *The Poet's Calling in the English Ode.*

49. "Encomiums on Sir W. Jones," 2.

50. Ibid., 3, 6.

51. Franklin, *Sir William Jones: Selected Poetical and Prose Works,* 168. Franklin retains Jones's original stanza numbering, which includes the three part unit of the Pindaric: strophe, antistrophe, and epode. My numbering corresponds to stanza and line.

52. Ibid., 126. While it is not clear, I believe that the stanza structure of "Hymn to Gangá" is revised from Gray's "The Progress of Poesy: A Pindaric Ode" as much as it is from "The Bard."

53. Capell, *Notes and Various Readings of Shakespeare,* 72. For another instance of heptameter as an extensive elongated line, see Aaron Hill, *Gideon; or, The Patriot,* 60.

54. These efforts were not necessarily unselfish or unpolitical. Jones's judgeship required him to operate within and therefore to understand Hindu and Muslim legal tenets. His willingness to do so played a role in the debate about how best to administer Britain's Indian possessions, a debate which included members of the East India Company, the British Parliament, and native Indians. For more on the place of Jones's legal studies in this debate, see Loomba, *Colonialism/Postcolonialism,* 168–69.

55. Franklin, *Sir William Jones: Selected Poetical and Prose Works,* 124.

56. My position contrasts notably with those of other scholars of Jones and Indian orientalism. Franklin, for example, argues that in Jones's writings he denies Indians the power to represent themselves but also blurs the difference between self and other (*Sir William Jones: Selected Poetical and Prose Works,* 8). Nandini Das suggests, in "'[A] Place Among the Hindu Poets': Orientalism and the Poetry of Sir William Jones (1746–1794)," that Jones brought the "alien space" of India within the familiar frame of European culture, which was an assertion of the "comprehensive and superior knowledge" of the European scholar (1245). Teltscher in *India Inscribed* discusses the "literary annexation" in which Indian materials are recast in light of European traditions (211).

57. Cannon, *Life and Mind,* 233.

58. *LWJ,* 2: 719.

59. Edmund Burke qtd. in Michael Franklin, "Accessing India," 49.

60. *LWJ,* 2: 778.

61. For more on the use of Indian voices in the Hastings impeachment, see Teltscher, 177–79.

62. Irwin, "Bedukah, or the Self-Devoted. An Indian Pastoral." This poem was published in London by J. Dodsley, the son of the well-known literary publisher. While it was written in India, it is unclear to me if it was also published there. Quotations from "Bedukah" are cited in the text by canto and line number.

63. See *Oxford Dictionary of National Biography,* s.v. "Irwin, Eyles." Irwin spent most of his life in India, although many significant events, such as his marriage, occurred in Britain; and after leaving the company's service, he retired to Bristol. He was stationed at Fort St. George in Madras (currently Chennai) and was an emissary to China in the 1790s.

64. The English called the custom *suttee,* an incorrect transcription of the Hindu word *sati,* meaning "good wife." For examinations of sati see, Major, *Pious Flames*; Weinberger-Thomas, *Ashes of Immortality*; Mani, *Contentious Traditions*; and Hawley, ed., *Sati, The Blessing and the Curse.*

65. East India Company recruits being educated at Calcutta's Fort William College, for instance, were asked to debate in Hindi whether sati was "repugnant to natural feelings"

or "inconsistent with moral duty" as a way to improve their language skills and familiarity with the country. See Rocher, 219.

66. McKeon, "The Pastoral Revolution," 289. With his emphasis on place and space, McKeon talks about the pastoral as perhaps the most expert form of "discursive imperialism." For additional information about the pastoral in foreign settings, see Stuart Curran, *Poetic Form and British Romanticism*, 95–99.

67. See Bhabha, *The Location of Culture*, esp. 145–74.

68. The idea of the wife celebrating her choice to burn by singing until dead was a common feature of European accounts of sati. See Ballaster, *Fabulous Orients*, 291. It was also a common feature of some Scandinavian poetry. See, for example, Thomas Percy's "The Dying Ode of Regner Lodbrog."

69. In Lycon's account, sound is impressive; his description of hearing as a vibration and "trembling" is aligned with what were then the most advanced accounts of human hearing, which emphasized the ear as an organ of resonance upon which sounds impressed themselves. For more, see Gouk, "English Theories of Hearing in the Seventeenth Century."

70. See Banerjee, *Burning Women*, esp. 173–210, where Banerjee discusses the idea of sati as "dying" to speak.

71. Spivak, "Can the Subaltern Speak?" 84.

72. Melting is an important metaphor for the emotional relationship among Bedukah, her listeners, and the English readers of the poem. For example, Irwin writes that, in response to her tales, her audience "melted of distress" (III.15). In another instance, the poem's witness and narrator, Lycon, states, "[T]hro' the crowd her melting accents steal" (III.1).

73. See Schürer, "The Impartial Spectator of Sati, 1757–1784," in which he argues that one stance toward sati taken during this period was what he calls the "sentimental impartial spectator"—the Western onlooker who judged the meaning of sati in "moral and aesthetic" rather than "political" terms (22). Schürer is right to point us toward the importance of moral and aesthetic categories in the representation of sati. These categories, however, should not be considered apolitical. In fact, as this chapter shows, the aesthetic was mobilized in the service of evaluating colonialism's politics.

74. Spivak, "Can the Subaltern Speak?" 98.

75. Ibid., 90.

76. Ibid., 101.

77. Ibid., 93. See also Spivak's ambivalent elaboration of this concept in *A Critique of Postcolonial Reason*, 269–311.

78. Spivak, *A Critique of Postcolonial Reason*, 309.

79. Leyden, *The Poetical Remains of the Late Dr. John Leyden*.

80. *Macaulay: Prose and Poetry*, 729.

81. For one account of these interracial relationships, see William Dalrymple's *White Mughals*.

82. For Leask, Leyden's "screen" of "fair" European women who shield the European man indicates that Rad'ha's desire should be seen as "transgressive" (Leask, "Towards an Anglo-Indian Poetry?" 60).

83. Irwin, "Ramah: Or The Brahman."

84. The final couplet of "The Bard" is: "He spoke, and headlong from the mountains height, / Deep in the roaring tide he plunged to endless night." See Lonsdale, ed., *Thomas Gray and William Collins: Poetical Works*, lines 143–44.

85. Gibson, *Indian Angles*, 21–22.

86. Imperial expansion made many Britons feel that the nation was over extending its boundaries. The writer and critic Horace Walpole grimly joked, in a letter written in 1762, that Britons "were full as happy, when we were a peaceable quiet set of tradesfolks, as now [when] we . . . are overrunning East and West Indies" (*The Yale Edition of Horace Walpole's Correspondence*, vol. 22: 16). Playwright and member of Parliament Edmund Burke, who for much of his career worked against the East India Company, worried that "young men, (almost boys) govern there [India], without society and without sympathy with the natives," their only goal, he grieved, being the "rapid accumulation of wealth" (qtd. in Suleri, *The Rhetoric of English India*, 32).

87. *The Poetical Works of John Scott, Esq.*, 137–52.

88. See Bhabha, 121–25. Bhabha famously notes that the anglicizing of India created individuals who were "almost the same, but not quite" (122).

89. For two versions that expand on this argument about poetry ventriloquizing Indian voices and using those voices to obscure the violence of colonialism, see Das, " '[A] Place Among the Hindu Poets' " and Teltscher, *India Inscribed*.

90. See Hall, "Signification, Representation, Ideology," 106. Said, too, discusses deep structure, claiming that orientalism has "a kind of deep structure . . . able to multiply and proliferate in all kinds of ways." He compares this deep structure to syntax, which can produce enormous variety "out of a very small number of elements." See Goldberg and Quayson, eds., *Relocating Postcolonialism*, 4.

91. Butler, *Bodies that Matter: On the Discursive Limits of "Sex,"* 226.

92. See Viswanathan, *Masks of Conquest*, 8–9. The "re-adaptation" that Viswanathan describes operates according to a "principle of complementarity," with its "capacity for transference, in criss-cross fashion." This complementing creates an "interactive dynamism" between the British and Indian traditions.

93. See Schwab, *The Oriental Renaissance*. The "arrival of Sanskrit texts in Europe," Schwab argues, revived an "atmosphere" that connected parts of the globe that had been separate, effecting an enormous cultural shift in Europe, the likes of which had not been experienced since the Italian Renaissance (11).

94. Ibid., 15.

95. Dodson, *Orientalism, Empire, and National Culture*, 5.

96. Teltscher, 211.

97. Spivak, *A Critique of Postcolonial Reason*, 274.

CODA: READING THE ARCHIVE OF THE INAUTHENTIC

1. Festa, *Sentimental Figures of Empire in Eighteenth-Century Britain and France*, 240.

2. Ibid., 241.

3. Bowles, *Sonnets, with other Poems*.

4. The island is also known as Belau.

5. Keate, *An Account of the Pelew Islands*. This account described the shipwreck of the British ship *Antelope*, interactions with the natives of Palau, and the ship's return, carrying Lee Boo, to England.

6. Ibid., 26, 55.

7. *The Interesting and Affecting History of Prince Lee Boo . . .*, 8. This claims to be a compilation of Keate's narrative.

8. Cottle, "Lee Boo. A Poem."

9. Spivak, *A Critique of Postcolonial Reason*, 308–9.

10. Spivak, "The Rani of Sirmur," 250–51.

11. That appropriation reduces opportunities for accurate self-expression by colonized peoples certainly seems to be demonstrated in the case of Bowles's "Abba Thule," a literary historical construction whose name we cannot even be sure of. For example, his name in Bowles's poem is likely the English misinterpretation of the Palauan word "ibedúl," meaning chieftain. (Josephs, *New Palauan-English Dictionary*, s.v. "ibedúl.")

12. Aravamudan, *Tropicopolitans*, 9, 6; emphasis added. Rather than "reifying *a* voice of resistance or dissent," Aravamudan suggests, "the act of reading makes available the differing mechanisms of agency that traverse texts, contexts, and agents themselves" (14; emphasis in original).

13. Ibid., 9.

14. Sharpe, *Ghosts of Slavery*, xv.

15. Arondekar, "Without a Trace," 21.

16. Ibid., 22.

17. Joseph, *Reading the East India Company*, 2, 3.

18. Ibid., 21.

19. Adela Pinch varies this theme by arguing that, in the eighteenth century, emotions were "transpersonal," at times perceived as "autonomous entities . . . that wander extravagantly from one person to another" (*Strange Fits of Passion*, 3).

20. Kaul, "Provincials and Tropicopolitans," 431.

Bibliography

Aaron, Jane. "'Saxon, Think not All is Won': Felicia Hemans and the Making of Britons." *Cardiff Corvey: Reading the Romantic Text* 4, 1: 1–3.

Ahmed, Siraj. "Orientalism and the Permanent Fix of War." In *The Postcolonial Enlightenment: Eighteenth-Century Colonialism and Postcolonial Theory*. Ed. Daniel Carey and Lynn Festa, 167–203. Oxford: Oxford University Press, 2009.

Anderson, Benedict. *Imagined Communities: Reflections on the Origin and Spread of Nationalism*. London: Verso, 1991.

Aravamudan, Srinivas. *Tropicopolitans: Colonialism and Agency, 1688–1804*. Durham: Duke University Press, 1999.

———. *Enlightenment Orientalism: Resisting the Rise of the Novel*. Chicago: University of Chicago Press, 2012.

Arondekar, Anjali. "Without a Trace: Sexuality and the Colonial Archive." *Journal of the History of Sexuality* 14, 1/2 (January–April 2005): 10–27.

Asad, Talal. "The Concept of Cultural Translation in British Social Anthropology." In *Writing Culture: The Poetics and Politics of Ethnography*. Ed. James Clifford and George E. Marcus, 141–64. Berkeley: University of California Press, 1991.

Ashcroft, Bill, Gareth Griffiths, and Helen Tiffin, eds. *The Empire Writes Back: Theory and Practice in Post-Colonial Literatures*. London: Routledge, 1989.

Austin, Gilbert. *Chironomia; or, A Treatise on Rhetorical Delivery*. Ed. Mary Margaret Robb and Lester Thonssen. Carbondale: Southern Illinois University Press, 1966.

Backscheider, Paula. *Eighteenth-Century Women Poets and Their Poetry: Inventing Agency, Inventing Genre*. Baltimore: Johns Hopkins University Press, 2005.

Bacon, Francis. *Sylva Sylvarum*. London, 1627.

Bakhtin, Mikhail. *Problems of Dostoyevsky's Poetics*. Ed. and trans. Caryl Emerson. Minneapolis: University of Minnesota Press, 1973.

———. *The Dialogic Imagination: Four Essays*. Trans. Michael Holquist. Austin: University of Texas Press, 1981.

Ballaster, Ros. *Fabulous Orients: Fictions of the East in England, 1662–1785*. Oxford: Oxford University Press, 2005.

Banerjee, Pompa. *Burning Women: Widows, Witches, and Early Modern European Travelers in India*. New York: Palgrave Macmillan, 2003.

Barthes, Roland. "Music, Voice, Language." In *The Responsibility of Forms: Critical Essays on Music, Art, and Representation*. Trans. Richard Howard, 278–85. Berkeley: University of California Press, 1991.

Baucom, Ian. *Out of Place: Englishness, Empire, and the Locations of Identity*. Princeton: Princeton University Press, 1999.

Bayly, C. A. *Empire and Information: Intelligence Gathering and Social Communication in India, 1780–1870*. Cambridge: Cambridge University Press, 1996.

Benveniste, Émile. *Problems in General Linguistics*. Trans. Mary Elizabeth Meek. Coral Gables: University of Miami Press, 1971.

Berlant, Lauren. *Intimacy*. Chicago: University of Chicago Press, 2000.

———. *The Female Complaint: The Unfinished Business of Sentimentality in America*. Durham: Duke University Press, 2008.

Berry, Francis. *Poetry and the Physical Voice*. London: Routledge and Kegan Paul, 1962.

Bhabha, Homi K. *The Location of Culture*. London: Routledge, 1994.

Bickley, Francis, ed. *The Diaries of Sylvester Douglas, Lord Glenbervie*. 2 vols. London: Constable, 1928.

Bishop, W. J. *The Early History of Surgery*. London: R. Hale, 1960.

Blackwell, Thomas. *An Enquiry in the Life and Writings of Homer*. London, 1735.

Blair, Hugh. *Lectures on Rhetoric and Belles Lettres*. London, 1783.

———. *Lectures on Rhetoric and Belles Lettres*. Ed. Harold F. Harding, foreword by David Potter. Carbondale: Southern Illinois University Press, 1965.

Bloom, Gina. *Voice in Motion: Staging Gender, Shaping Sound in Early Modern England*. Philadelphia: University of Pennsylvania Press, 2007.

Bogel, Frederic. *Literature and Insubstantiality in Later Eighteenth-Century England*. Princeton: Princeton University Press, 1984.

Bolter, Jay David, and Richard Grusin, eds. *Remediation: Understanding the New Media*. Cambridge, MA: MIT Press, 1999.

Boswell, James. *Boswell's London Journal: 1762-1763*. Ed. Frederick A. Pottle. New Haven: Yale University Press, 1992.

———. *Life of Johnson*. Ed. R. W. Chapman. Oxford: Oxford University Press, 1998.

Bowles, William Lisle. *Sonnets, with other Poems*, 3rd ed. Bath, 1794.

Brathwaite, Kamau. "The History of the Voice." In *Roots*, 259–304. Ann Arbor: University of Michigan, 1993.

Brewer, William. "Felicia Hemans, Byronic Cosmopolitanism and the Ancient Welsh Bards." In *English Romanticism and the Celtic World*. Ed. Gerard Carruthers and Alan Rawes, 167–81. Cambridge: Cambridge University Press, 2003.

Bringhurst, Robert. *The Elements of Typographic Style, version 2.5*. Vancouver: Hartley and Marks, 2002.

Bronson, Bertrand. "Strange Relations: The Author and His Audience." In *Facets of Enlightenment: Studies in English Literature and Its Contexts*, 298–325. Berkeley: University of California Press, 1968.

Brower, Ruben. *The Fields of Light: An Experiment in Critical Reading*. London: Oxford University Press, 1951.

Burgh, James. *The Art of Speaking*. London, 1761.

Burke, Edmund. *The Correspondence of Edmund Burke*. Vol. 3. Ed. George H. Guttridge. Cambridge: Cambridge University Press, 1961.

Burnley, David. *The History of the English Language: A Source Book*. London: Longman, 1992.

Butler, Judith. *Bodies that Matter: On the Discursive Limits of "Sex."* New York: Routledge, 1993.

Calder, Alexander, Jonathan Lamb, and Bridget Orr, eds. *Voyages and Beaches: Pacific Encounters, 1769–1840*. Honolulu: University of Hawai'i Press, 1999.

The Cambro-Briton. 3 vols. London: 1822.

Cannon, Garland. *The Life and Mind of Oriental Jones: Sir William Jones, the Father of Modern Linguistics*. Cambridge: Cambridge University Press, 1990.

Cannon, Garland, and Kevin R. Brine, eds. *Objects of Inquiry: The Life, Contributions, and Influences of Sir William Jones, 1746–1794*. New York: New York University Press, 1995.

Capell, Edward. *Notes and Various Readings of Shakespeare, part the first; . . . With a General Glossary*. London, 1774.

Cass, Jeffrey. "Interrogating Orientalism: Theories and Practices." In *Interrogating Orientalism: Contextual Approaches and Pedagogical Practices*. Ed. Diane Long Hoeveler and Jeffrey Cass, 25–45. Columbus: Ohio State University Press, 2006.

Charnell-White, Cathyrn. *Bardic Circles: National, Regional, and Personal Identity in the Bardic Vision of Iolo Morganwg*. Aberystwyth: University of Wales Press, 2007.

Cheek, Pamela. *Sexual Antipodes: Enlightenment Globalization and the Placing of Sex*. Stanford: Stanford University Press, 2003.

Cixous, Hélène. "The Laugh of the Medusa." In *Feminisms: An Anthology of Literary Criticism and Theory*. Ed. Robyn R. Warhol and Diane Price Herndl, 347–62. New Brunswick: Rutgers University Press, 1997.

Cohn, Bernard. *Colonialism and Its Forms of Knowledge: The British in India*. Princeton: Princeton University Press, 1996.

Colley, Linda. *Britons: Forging the Nation, 1707–1837*. New Haven: Yale University Press, 1992.

———. *Captives: Britain, Empire, and the World, 1600–1850*. New York: Anchor Books, 2002.

Connor, Steven. *Dumbstruck: A Cultural History of Ventriloquism*. Oxford: Oxford University Press, 2000.

Constantine, Mary-Ann. *The Truth against the World: Iolo Morganwg and Romantic Forgery*. Cardiff: University of Wales Press, 2007.

Cooper, Anthony Ashleigh, Earl of Shaftesbury. *Characteristics of Men, Manners, Opinions, Times*. Ed. Lawrence E. Klein. Cambridge: Cambridge University Press, 1999.

Cottle, Joseph. "Lee Boo. A Poem." In *Poems*. 148–92. Bristol, 1796.

Cottom, Daniel. Review of *Strange Fits of Passion*. In *Nineteenth-Century Literature* 52, 3 (December 1997), 372–74.

Cowley, Abraham. *The English Writings of Abraham Cowley*. Vol. 2, *Poems: Miscellanies, The Mistress, Pindarique Odes, Davideis, Verses Written on Several Occasions*. Ed. A. R. Waller. Cambridge: Cambridge University Press, 1905.

Crawford, Robert, *Devolving English Literature*. 2nd ed. Edinburgh: Edinburgh University Press, 2000.

———. *The Modern Poet: Poetry, Academia, and Knowledge since the 1750s*. Oxford: Oxford University Press, 2001.

Curran, Stuart. *Poetic Form and British Romanticism*. Oxford: Oxford University Press, 1986.

Dalrymple, Alexander. "Fragment on the India Trade." London[?], 1797.

Dalrymple, William. *White Mughals: Love and Betrayal in Eighteenth-Century India*. London, Penguin, 2002.

Das, Nandini. " '[A] Place Among the Hindu Poets': Orientalism and the Poetry of Sir William Jones (1746–1794)." *Literature Compass* 3, 6 (2006): 1235–52.

Davies, John. *A History of Wales*. London: Penguin, 1994.

Davis, Leith. "At 'san about': Scottish Song and the Challenge to British Culture." In *Scotland and the Borders of Romanticism*. Ed. Leith Davis, Ian Duncan, and Janet Sorensen. Cambridge: Cambridge University Press, 2004.

Davis, Leith, and Maureen McLane. "Oral and Public Poetry." In *The Edinburgh History of Scottish Literature*. Vol. 2, *Enlightenment, Britain and Empire (1707–1918)*. Ed. Susan Manning, Thomas Owen Clancy, Ian Brown, and Murray Pittock. Edinburgh: Edinburgh University Press, 2006.

de Grazia, Margreta. "Shakespeare in Quotation Marks." In *The Appropriation of Shakespeare: Post-Renaissance Reconstructions of the Works and the Myth*. Ed. Jean I. Marsden. New York: Harvester Wheatsheaf, 1991.

———. "Sanctioning Voice: Quotation Marks, the Abolition of Torture, and the Fifth Amendment." In *The Construction of Authorship: Textual Appropriation in Law and Literature*. Ed. Martha Woodmansee and Peter Jaszi. Durham: Duke University Press, 1994.

DeLucia, JoEllen. "Far Other Times Are These": The Bluestockings in the Time of Ossian." *Tulsa Studies in Women's Literature* 27, 1 (Spring 2008): 39–62.

Derrida, Jacques. *"Speech and Phenomena" and Other Essays on the Husserl's Theory of Signs*. Trans. David B. Allison. Evanston: Northwestern University Press, 1973.

———. *Of Grammatology*. Trans. Gayatri Chakravorty Spivak. Baltimore: Johns Hopkins University Press, 1974, 1997.

Deutsch, Helen. *Resemblance and Disgrace: Alexander Pope and the Deformation of Culture*. Cambridge, MA: Harvard University Press, 1996.

Diderot, Denis. *Selected Writings*. Ed. Lester Crocker. New York: Macmillan, 1966.

———. *Political Writings*. Ed. John Hope Mason and Robert Wokler. Cambridge: Cambridge University Press, 1992.

Dodson, Michael S. *Orientalism, Empire, and National Culture: India, 1770–1880*. New York: Palgrave Macmillan, 2007.

Donaldson, Ian. "Concealing and Revealing: Pope's Epistle to Arbuthnot." *Yearbook of English Studies* 18 (1988): 181–99.

Doody, Margaret Anne. *The Daring Muse: Augustan Poetry Reconsidered*. Cambridge: Cambridge University Press, 1985.

Drew, John. *India and the Romantic Imagination*. New Delhi: Oxford University Press, 1987.

Eagleton, Terry. *Literary Theory: An Introduction*. Minneapolis: University of Minnesota Press, 1983.

Edwards, Hywel Teifi. *The Eisteddfod*. Cardiff: University of Wales Press, 1990.

———. "The Eisteddfod Poet: An Embattled Figure." In *A Guide to Welsh Literature: c. 1800–1900*. Ed. Alfred Owen Hughes Jarman, Hywel Teifi Edwards, Gwilym Rees Hughes, Dafydd Johnston. Aberystwyth: University of Wales Press, 2000.

Eisenstein, Elizabeth. *The Printing Press as an Agent of Change: Communications and Cultural Transformations in Early-Modern Europe*. 2 vols. Cambridge: Cambridge University Press, 1979.

Elbow, Peter, ed. *Landmark Essays in Voice and Writing*. Davis, CA: Hermagora Press, 1994.

Elfenbein, Andrew. *Romanticism and the Rise of English*. Stanford: Stanford University Press, 2009.

Ellis, Frank H. "Gray's *Elegy*: The Biographical Problem in Literary Criticism." *PMLA* 66 (1951): 971–1008.

Elsky, Martin. *Authorizing Words: Speech, Writing, and Print in Renaissance England.* Ithaca: Cornell University Press, 1989.

"Encomiums on Sir W. Jones." In *The Poetical Works of Sir William Jones*. Ed. Thomas Park. London, 1808.

Erickson, Robert. *The Language of the Heart, 1600–1750*. Philadelphia: University of Pennsylvania Press, 1997.

Evans, E. D. *A History of Wales, 1660–1815*. Cardiff: University of Wales Press, 1993.

Fabian, Johannes. "Keep Listening: Ethnography and Reading." In *The Ethnography of Reading*. Ed. Jonathan Boyarin, 80–97. Berkeley: University of California Press, 1993.

Fenning, Daniel . *A New Grammar of the English Language*. London, 1771.

Festa, Lynn. *Sentimental Figures of Empire in Eighteenth-Century Britain and France*. Baltimore: Johns Hopkins University Press, 2006.

Fielding, Penny. *Writing and Orality: Nationality, Culture, and Nineteenth-Century Scottish Fiction*. Oxford: Oxford University Press, 1996.

Fitzgerald, Robert P. "The Style of Ossian." *Studies in Romanticism* 6: 22–33.

Fliegelman, Jay. *Declaring Independence: Jefferson, Natural Language, and the Culture of Performance*. Stanford: Stanford University Press, 1993.

Fox, Adam. *Oral and Literate Culture in England, 1500–1700*. Oxford: Clarendon Press, 2000.

Franklin, Benjamin. *Autobiography, Poor Richard, and Later Writings: Letters from London, 1757–1775, Paris, 1776–1785, Philadelphia, 1785–1790, Poor Richard's Almanack, 1733–1758, The Autobiography*. Ed. Joseph A. Leo Lemay. New York: Library of America, 1997.

Franklin, Michael J., ed. *Sir William Jones: Selected Poetical and Prose Works*. Cardiff: University of Wales Press, 1995.

———. *Sir William Jones*. Cardiff: University of Wales Press, 1995.

———. "Accessing India: Orientalism, Anti-'Indianism,' and the Rhetoric of Jones and Burke." In *Romanticism and Colonialism: Writing and Empire, 1780–1830*. Ed. Tim Fulford and Peter J. Kitson. Cambridge: Cambridge University Press, 1998.

———. "Sir William Jones, the Celtic Revival and the Oriental Renaissance." In *English Romanticism and the Celtic World*. Ed. Gerard Carruthers and Alan Rawes, 20–37. Cambridge: Cambridge University Press, 2003.

———. "The Colony Writes Back: Brutus, Britanus, and the Advantages of an Oriental Ancestry." In *Wales and the Romantic Imagination*. Ed. Damian Walford Davies and Lynda Pratt, 13–42. Cardiff: University of Wales Press, 2007.

———. *Orientalist Jones: Sir William Jones, Poet, Lawyer, and Linguist, 1746–1794*. Oxford: Oxford University Press, 2011.

Fry, Paul. *The Poet's Calling in the English Ode*. New Haven: Yale University Press, 1980.

Garber, Marjorie. *Quotation Marks*. New York: Routledge, 2003.

Gaskell, Philip. *A New Introduction to Bibliography*. New Castle, DE: Oak Knoll Press, 1995.

Gaskill, Howard, ed. *The Poems of Ossian and Related Works*. Edinburgh: Edinburgh University Press, 1996.

———, ed. *The Reception of Macpherson's Ossian in Europe*. London: Thoemmes Continuum, 2004.

Genette, Gérard. *Narrative Discourse: An Essay on Method*. Ithaca: Cornell University Press, 1980.

———. *Paratexts: Thresholds of Interpretation*. Trans. Jane E. Lewin. Cambridge: Cambridge University Press, 1997.

George, Jacqueline. "Public Reading and Lyric Pleasure: Eighteenth-Century Elocutionary Debates and Poetic Practices." *ELH* 76, 2 (Summer 2009): 371–97.

Gibson, Mary Ellis. *Indian Angles: English Verse in Colonial India from Jones to Tagore*. Athens: Ohio University Press, 2011.

Gleckner, Robert F. *Gray Agonistes: Thomas Gray and Masculine Friendship*. Baltimore: Johns Hopkins University Press, 1997.

Glissant, Edouard. *Caribbean Discourses: Selected Essays*. Trans. J. Michael Dash. Charlottesville: University Press of Virginia, 1989.

Goldberg, David Theo, and Ato Quayson, eds. *Relocating Postcolonialism*. Oxford: Blackwell, 2002.

Gordon, George, Lord Byron. *Byron's Letters and Journals: The Complete and Unexpurgated Text of all the Letters Available in Manuscript and the Full Printed Version of All Others*. Vol. 7, *"Between Two Worlds," 1820*. Ed. Leslie A. Marchand. Cambridge, MA: Harvard University Press, 1978.

Gottlieb, Evan. *Feeling British: Sympathy and National Identity in Scottish and English Writing, 1707–1832*. Lewisburg, PA: Bucknell University Press, 2007.

Gouk, Penelope. "English Theories of Hearing in the Seventeenth Century." In *Hearing History*. Ed. Mark Smith, 136–50. Athens: University of Georgia Press, 2004.

Gray, Thomas. *Odes by Mr. Gray*. London, 1757.

———. *Poems by Mr. Gray*. London, 1768.

———. *The Correspondence of Thomas Gray*. 3 vols. Ed. Paget Toynbee and Leonard Whibley. Oxford: Clarendon Press, 1935.

———. *The Complete Poems of Thomas Gray; English, Latin and Greek*. Ed. Herbert W. Starr and J. R. Hendrickson. Oxford: Clarendon Press, 1966.

———. *Poetic Commonplace Books and Manuscripts of Thomas Gray, 1716–1771*. Reading, UK: Adam Matthew Publications, 1991.

Gregory, Elizabeth. *Quotation and American Poetry: "Imaginary Gardens with Real Toads."* Houston: Rice University Press, 1996.

Griffin, Dustin. *Literary Patronage in England, 1650–1800*. New York: Cambridge University Press, 1996.

Griffith, Anne, ed. "Introduction." In *Four Lessons for Harp or Harpsichord by John Parry*. Abergavenny, Gwent: Adlais, 1982.

Griffiths, Eric. *The Printed Voice of Victorian Poetry*. Oxford: Clarendon Press, 1989.

Groom, Nick. *The Making of Percy's Reliques*. Oxford: Clarendon University Press, 1999.

Grundy, Isobel. "*Verses Address'd to the Imitator of Horace:* A Skirmish between Pope and Some Persons of Rank and Fortune." *Studies in Bibliography* 30 (1977): 96–119.

Guillory, John. *Cultural Capital: The Problem of Literary Canon Formation*. Chicago: University of Chicago Press, 1993.

Gunther, Robert Theodore, ed. *Early Science at Oxford*. Vol. 11. London: Dawsons of Pall Mall, 1967–68.

Haggerty, George E. "'The Voice of Nature' in Gray's *Elegy*." In *Homosexuality in Renaissance and Enlightenment England: Literary Representations in Historical Context*. Ed. Claude J. Summers, 199–214. New York: Haworth Press, 1992.

———. "*O lachrymarum fons:* Tears, Poetry, and Desire in Gray." *Eighteenth-Century Studies* 30 (1996): 81–95.

Hagstrum, Jean H. "Gray's Sensibility." In *Fearful Joy: Papers from the Thomas Gray Bicentenary Conference at Carleton University, 1971*. Ed. James Downey and Ben Jones, 6–19. Montreal: McGill-Queen's University Press, 1974.

Hall, Stuart. "Signification, Representation, Ideology: Althusser and the Post-Structuralist Debates." *Critical Studies in Mass Communication* 2, 2 (June 1985): 91–114.

Hammond, Brean. *Professional Imaginative Writing in England, 1670–1740: "Hackney for Bread."* Oxford: Clarendon Press, 1997.

Hartmann, Charles. *Jazz Text: Voice and Improvisation in Poetry, Jazz, and Song*. Princeton: Princeton University Press, 1991.

Havelock, Eric. *Preface to Plato*. Oxford: Oxford University Press, 1963.

Hawley, John Stratton, ed. *Sati, the Blessing and the Curse: The Burning of Wives in India*. Oxford: Oxford University Press, 1998.

Hayley, William. *An Essay on Epic Poetry*. London, 1782.

Haywood, Ian. *The Making of History: A Study of the Literary Forgeries of James Macpherson and Thomas Chatterton in Relation to Eighteenth-Century Ideas of History and Fiction*. Rutherford, NJ: Fairleigh Dickinson University Press, 1986.

Hemans, Felicia Dorothea. *Poems, England and Spain, Modern Greece*. Ed. Donald H. Reiman. New York: Garland, 1978.

———. *Tales and Historic Scenes: Stanzas to the Memory of the Late King; Dartmoor; Welsh Melodies*. Ed. Donald H. Reiman. New York: Garland, 1978.

Hervey, Elizabeth D. *Ventriloquized Voices: Feminist Theory and English Renaissance Texts*. London: Routledge, 1992.

Hess, Scott. *Authoring the Self: Self-Representation, Authorship, and the Print Market in British Poetry from Pope through Wordsworth*. New York: Routledge, 2005.

Hibbert, Christopher. *London: The Biography of a City*. London: Penguin, 1969.

Hill, Aaron. *Gideon; or, The Patriot. An Epic Poem*. London, 1749.

The Holy Bible, Containing the Old and New Testaments. King James Version. New York: Meridian, 1974.

Hudson, Nicholas. *Writing and European Thought, 1600–1830*. Cambridge: Cambridge University Press, 1994.

———. "Oral Tradition: The Evolution of an Eighteenth-Century Concept." In *Traditions in Transition: Women Writers, Marginal Texts, and the Eighteenth-Century Canon*. Ed. Alvaro Riveiro, SJ, and James G. Basker, 161–76. Oxford: Clarendon Press, 1996.

———. "Theories of Language." In *The Cambridge History of Literary Criticism*. Vol. 4, *The Eighteenth Century*. Ed. H. B. Nisbet and Claude Rawson, 335–48. Cambridge: Cambridge University Press, 1997.

———. "Constructing Oral Tradition: The Origins of the Concept in Enlightenment Intellectual Culture." In *The Spoken Word: Oral Culture in Britain, 1500–1850*. Ed. Adam Fox and Daniel Woolf, 240–55. Manchester: Manchester University Press, 2001

Hughes, Meirion. "St. David's Day: Music, Wales, and War in 1800." In *Europe, Empire, and Spectacle in Nineteenth-Century British Music*. Ed. Rachel Cowgill and Julian Rushton, 131–44. Aldershot, UK: Ashgate, 2006.

Hunt, Leigh. *A Book for a Corner; or, Selections in Prose and Verse from Authors the Best Suited to that Mode of Enjoyment*, 2nd series. New York: Derby and Jackson, 1859.

Hutton, Ronald. *Blood and Mistletoe: The History of the Druids in Britain*. New Haven: Yale University Press, 2009.

Inden, Ronald. *Imagining India*. Bloomington: Indiana University Press, 2000.

The Interesting and Affecting History of Prince Lee Boo . . . . Dublin, 1791.

Inwood, Stephen. *A History of London.* London: Macmillan, 1998.

"Iolo Morganwg and the Romantic Tradition in Wales." University of Wales, Aberystwyth. http://iolomorganwg.wales.ac.uk.

Irlam, Shaun. *Elations: The Poetics of Enthusiasm in Eighteenth-Century Britain.* Stanford: Stanford University Press, 1999.

Irwin, Eyles. "Bedukah, or the Self-Devoted: An Indian Pastoral." London: J. Dodsley, 1776.

———. "Ramah: Or, The Bramin." In *Eastern Eclogues; Written During a Tour through Arabia, Egypt, and Other Parts of Asia and Africa.* London, 1780.

Jackson, Virginia. "Who Reads Poetry?" *PMLA* 123, 1 (2008): 181–87.

Jackson, Wallace. "Thomas Gray: Drowning in Human Voices?" *Criticism* 28 (1986).

Jager, Eric. *Book of the Heart.* Chicago: University of Chicago Press, 2000.

Jancovich, Mark. "The Southern New Critics." In *The Cambridge History of Literary Criticism.* Vol. 7, *Modernism and the New Criticism.* Ed. A. Walton Litz, Louis Menand, and Walter Rainey, 210–18. Cambridge: Cambridge University Press, 2000.

Jarvis, Branwen. "Iolo Morganwg and the Welsh Cultural Background." In *A Rattleskull Genius: The Many Faces of Iolo Morganwg.* Ed. Geraint H. Jenkins, 29–49. Cardiff: University of Wales Press, 2005.

Jenkins, Geraint H., ed. *A Rattleskull Genius: The Many Faces of Iolo Morganwg.* Cardiff: University of Wales Press, 2005.

Johnson, Samuel. *A Journey to the Western Islands of Scotland.* Ed. with intro. by Peter Levi London: Penguin Books, 1984.

———. *The Major Works.* Ed. Donald Greene. Oxford: Oxford University Press, 2000.

———. *The Lives of the Most Eminent English Poets; With Critical Observations on Their Works.* With intro. and notes by Roger Lonsdale. Oxford: Clarendon Press, 2006.

Johnston, Arthur. *Enchanted Ground: The Study of Medieval Romance in the Eighteenth Century.* London: Athone Press, 1964.

———. "Gray's Use of the Gorchest y Beirdd in 'The Bard,'" *Modern Language Review* 59 (1964): 335–38.

———. *Thomas Gray and the Bard.* Cardiff: University of Wales Press, 1966.

Jones, Edward. Miscellany. National Library of Wales, MS 169C.

Jones, Rhys [Rice Jones]. *Gorchestion Beirdd Cymru: Neu Floddau Godidow Grwydd Awen.* Anwything, 1773.

Jones, William. *The Works of William Jones.* 6 vols. Ed. Anna Maria Shipley. London, 1799.

———. *The Letters of William Jones.* 2 vols. Ed. Garland Cannon. Oxford: Clarendon Press, 1970.

Jones, William Powell. "The Contemporary Reception of Gray's *Odes.*" *Modern Philology* 28 (1930): 61–82.

———. *Thomas Gray, Scholar: The True Tragedy of an Eighteenth-Century Gentleman.* Cambridge, MA: Harvard University Press, 1937.

Joseph, Betty. *Reading the East India Company, 1720–1840: Colonial Currencies of Gender.* Chicago: University of Chicago Press, 2004.

Josephs, Lewis S. *New Palauan-English Dictionary.* Honolulu: University of Hawai'i Press, 1990.

Julien, Eileen. *African Novels and the Question of Orality.* Bloomington: Indiana University Press, 1992.

Kaul, Suvir. *Thomas Gray and Literary Authority.* Stanford: Stanford University Press, 1992.

———. *Poems of Nation, Anthems of Empire: English Verse in the Long Eighteenth Century.* Charlottesville: University Press of Virginia, 2000.

———. "Provincials and Tropicopolitans: Eighteenth-Century Literary Studies and the Un-Making of 'Great Britain,'" *Diaspora* 9, 3 (2000): 421–37.

Kearney, Hugh. *The British Isles: A History of Four Nations.* Cambridge: Cambridge University Press, 1989.

Kearney, James. *The Incarnate Text: Imagining the Book in Restoration England.* Philadelphia: University of Pennsylvania Press, 2009.

Keate, George. *An Account of the Pelew Islands, Situated in the Western Part of the Pacific Ocean.* London, 1788.

Kernan, Alvin. *Printing Technology, Letters, and Samuel Johnson.* Princeton: Princeton University Press, 1987.

Kidd, Colin. *British Identities before Nationalism: Ethnicity and Nationhood in the Atlantic World, 1600–1800.* Cambridge: Cambridge University Press, 1999.

Kittler, Friedrich. *Discourse Networks 1800/1900.* Trans. Michael Meteer, with Chris Cullens. Stanford: Stanford University Press, 1990.

———. *Gramophone, Film, Typewriter.* Stanford: Stanford University Press, 1999.

Kittredge, G. L. "Gray's Knowledge of Old Norse." In *Selections from the Poetry and Prose of Thomas Gray.* Ed. William Lyon Phelps. Boston: Ginn, 1894.

Kreilkamp, Ivan. *Voice and the Victorian Storyteller.* Cambridge: Cambridge University Press, 2005.

Kristeva, Julia. *Intimate Revolt: The Powers and Limits of Psychoanalysis.* New York: Columbia University Press, 2002.

Kurasawa, Fuyuki. *The Ethnological Imagination: A Cross-Cultural Critique of Modernity.* Minneapolis: University of Minnesota Press, 2004.

Lamport, F. J. "Goethe, Ossian, and *Werther.*" In *From Gaelic to Romantic: Ossianic Translations.* Ed. Fiona Stafford and Howard Gaskill, 97–106. Amsterdam: Rodopi, 1998.

Lass, Robert, ed. *The Cambridge History of the English Language.* Vol. 3, *1476–1776.* Cambridge: Cambridge University Press, 1999.

Lastra, James. *Sound Technology and the American Cinema: Perception, Representation, Modernity.* New York: Columbia University Press, 2000.

Lea, Kathleen M., and T. M. Gang, eds. *Godfrey of Bulloigne: A Critical Edition of Edward Fairfax's Translation of Tasso's* Gerusalemme Liberata, *together with Fairfax's Original Poems.* Oxford: Clarendon Press, 1981.

Leask, Nigel. "Towards an Anglo-Indian Poetry? The Colonial Muse in the Writings of John Leyden, Thomas Medwin, and Charles D'Oyly." In *Writing India, 1757–1990: The Literature of British India.* Ed. Bart Moore-Gilbert, 52–85. Manchester: Manchester University Press, 1996.

Levine, Joseph. *Humanism and History: Origins of Modern English Historiography,* 190–213. Ithaca: Cornell University Press, 1987.

Levine, William. "'Beyond the Limits of a Vulgar Fate': The Renegotiation of Public and Private Concerns in the Careers of Gray and Other Mid-Eighteenth-Century Poets." *Studies in Eighteenth-Century Culture* 24 (1995): 223–42.

Leyden, John. *The Poetical Remains of the Late Dr. John Leyden.* London, 1819.

Lichtenwalner, Shawna. *Claiming Cambria: Invoking the Welsh in the Romantic Era.* Newark: University of Delaware Press, 2008.

Lonsdale, Roger, ed. *Poems of Thomas Gray, William Collins, and Oliver Goldsmith.* London: Longman, 1969.

———. *The Poetry of Thomas Gray: Versions of the Self.* Oxford: Oxford University Press, 1973.

———, ed. *Thomas Gray and William Collins: Poetical Works.* Oxford: Oxford University Press, 1977.

Loomba, Ania. *Colonialism/Postcolonialism.* New York: Routledge, 1998.

Lootens, Tricia. "Hemans at Home: Victorianism, Feminine 'Internal Enemies,' and the Domestication of National Identity." In *Victorian Women Poets: A Critical Reader.* Ed. Angela Leighton, 1–23. Oxford: Blackwell, 1996.

Love, Harold. "Oral and Scribal Texts in Early Modern England." In *The Cambridge History of the Book in Britain.* Vol. 4, *1557–1695.* Ed. John Barnes and D. F. McKenzie, with Maureen Bell, 97–126. Cambridge: Cambridge University Press, 2002.

Lucas, John. *England and Englishness: Ideas of Nationhood in English Poetry.* London: Hogarth Press, 1990.

Luhmann, Niklas. *Love as Passion: The Codification of Intimacy.* Stanford: Stanford University Press, 1998.

Macaulay, Thomas Babington. *Macaulay: Prose and Poetry.* Selected by G. M. Young. Cambridge, MA: Harvard University Press, 1970.

Macdonald, Murdo. *Scottish Art.* London: Thames and Hudson, 2000.

Macfie, Alexander Lyon. *Orientalism: A Reader.* New York: New York University Press, 2000.

Mack, Maynard. *Alexander Pope: A Life.* New York: W. W. Norton, 1988.

Mack, Robert L. *Thomas Gray: A Life.* New Haven: Yale University Press, 2000.

Mackenzie, Henry. *An Account of the Life and Writings of John Home, Esq.* Edinburgh, 1822.

Macpherson, James. *The Works of Ossian, the Son of Fingal. Translated from the Galic Language by James Macpherson.* 2 vols. London, 1765.

———. *Fragments of Ancient Poetry.* Ed. John J. Dunn. Los Angeles: William Andrews Clark Memorial Library, Augustan Reprint Society, 1966.

Mahony, William K. *The Artful Universe: An Introduction to the Vedic Religious Imagination.* Albany: State University of New York Press, 1998.

Major, Andrea. *Pious Flames: European Encounters with Sati, 1500–1830.* New Delhi: Oxford University Press, 2006.

Mani, Lata. *Contentious Traditions: The Debate on Sati in Colonial India.* Berkeley: University of California Press, 1998.

Manning, Susan. "Ghost-Writing Tradition: Mackenzie, Burns, and Macpherson." *Scotlands* 4, 1 (1997): 86–107.

Mao, Douglas. "The New Critics and the Text-Object." *ELH* 63, 1: 227–52.

Marshall, P. J., and Glyndwr Williams. *The Great Map of Mankind: Perceptions of New Worlds in the Age of Enlightenment.* Cambridge, MA: Harvard University Press, 1982.

Martin, Roger. *Chronologie de la Vie et de L'Oeuvre de Thomas Gray.* Paris: Les Presses Universitaires de France, 1931.

Masten, Jeffrey. *Textual Intercourse: Collaboration, Authorship, and Sexualities in Renaissance Drama.* Cambridge: Cambridge University Press, 1997.

McAdam, E. L., Jr., and George Milne, eds. *Johnson's Dictionary: A Modern Selection.* New York: Pantheon Books, 1963.

McCarthy, Eugene. *Thomas Gray: The Progress of a Poet.* Madison, N.J.: Fairleigh Dickinson University Press, 1997.

McCorkle, Ben. "Harbingers of the Printed Page: Nineteenth-Century Theories of Delivery as Remediation." *Rhetoric Society Quarterly* 35, 4 (Fall 2005): 25–49.

McDowell, Paula. "Mediating Media Past and Present: Towards a Genealogy of 'Print Culture' and Oral Tradition." In *This Is Enlightenment.* Ed. Clifford Siskin and William B. Warner, 229–46. Chicago: University of Chicago Press, 2010.

McGill, Meredith. "The Duplicity of the Pen." In *Language Machines: Technologies of Literary and Cultural Production.* Ed. with intro. by Jeffrey Masten, Peter Stallybrass, and Nancy J. Vickers, 39–71. New York: Routledge, 1997.

McKeon, Michael. "The Pastoral Revolution." In *Refiguring Revolutions: Aesthetics and Politics from the English Revolution to the Romantic Revolution.* Ed. Kevin M. Sharpe and Steven N. Zwicker, 267–89. Berkeley: University of California Press, 1998.

———. *The Secret History of Domesticity: Public, Private, and the Division of Knowledge.* Baltimore: Johns Hopkins University Press, 2005.

McLane, Maureen. *Balladeering, Minstrelsy, and the Making of British Romantic Poetry.* Cambridge: Cambridge University Press, 2008.

McLaverty, James. "'Of Which being publick the Publick Judge': Pope and the Publication of *Verses Address'd to the Imitator of Horace.*" *Studies in Bibliography* 51 (1998): 183–204.

McNeil, Kenneth. *Scotland, Britain, Empire: Writing the Highlands, 1760–1860.* Columbus: Ohio State University Press, 2007.

Meek, Donald. "The Gaelic Ballads of Scotland: Creativity and Adaptation." In *Ossian Revisited.* Ed. Howard Gaskill, 19–48. Edinburgh: Edinburgh University Press, 1991.

Merians, Linda E. "What They Are, Who We Are: Representations of the Hottentot in Eighteenth-Century Britain." *Eighteenth-Century Life* 17 (1993): 14–39.

———. *Envisioning the Worst: Representations of Hottentots in Early-Modern England.* Newark: University of Delaware Press, 2001.

Millner, Stuart A. *Thomas Gray's Welsh and Norse Poetry.* Unpublished diss., 1971.

Milton, John. *Areopagitica.* London, 1644.

Montagu, Lady Mary Wortley. "Verses Address'd to the Imitator of the First Satire of the Second Book of Horace." In *The Life and Writings of Lady Mary Wortley Montagu.* Electronic edition. Charlottesville, VA: InteLex Corporation, 2008.

Moore, Dafydd, ed. *Ossian and Ossianism.* 4 vols. London: Routledge, 2004.

Morgan, Prys. "From a Death to a View: The Hunt for the Welsh Past in the Romantic Period." In *The Invention of Tradition.* Ed. Eric Hobsbawm and Terence Ranger, 43–100. Cambridge: Cambridge University Press, 1983.

Morganwg, Iolo [Edward Williams]. *The Gentleman's Magazine* LIX, part 2, 1789.

———. *The Monthly Review of Literature; or magazine de savans.* London, 1792–1793.

———. *Poems, Lyrical and Pastoral.* 2 vols. London, 1794.

Morland, S[amuel]. *Tuba Stentoro-Phonica, An Instrument of Excellent Use, As Well at Sea, as at Land, Invented and variously Experimented in the Year 1670 . . . .* London, 1672.

Mukerjee, S. N. *Sir William Jones: A Study in Eighteenth-Century British Attitudes to India.* London: Cambridge University Press, 1968.

New Literary History 32, 3 (Summer 2001).

Newman, Steve. *Ballad Collection, Lyric, and the Canon: The Call of the Popular from the Restoration to the New Criticism.* Philadelphia: University of Pennsylvania Press, 2007.

Novak, Maximilian. "Primitivism." In *The Cambridge History of Literary Criticism*. Vol. 4, *The Eighteenth Century*. Ed. H. B. Nisbet and Claude Rawson, 456–69. Cambridge: Cambridge University Press, 1997.

Nussbaum, Felicity. *Torrid Zones: Maternity, Sexuality, and Empire in Eighteenth-Century English Narratives*. Baltimore: Johns Hopkins University Press, 1995.

O'Brian, Patrick. *Joseph Banks: A Life*. Chicago: University of Chicago Press, 1987.

O'Brien, Karen. "Poetry and Political Thought: Liberty and Benevolence in the Case of the British Empire c. 1680–1800." In *British Political Thought in History, Literature, and Theory, 1500–1800*. Ed. David Armitage, 168–90. Cambridge: Cambridge University Press, 2006.

"Odes of Mr. Gray." *Literary Magazine, or Universal Review* II, no. XVIII (September 1757): 422–26.

Ong, Walter. *The Presence of the Word: Some Prolegomena for Culture and Religion*. New Haven: Yale University Press, 1967.

———. *Writing and Orality: Technologizing the Word*. London: Metheun, 1982.

Oxford Dictionary of National Biography. Oxford: Oxford University Press, 2004.

Marshall, P. J. ed., *The Oxford History of the British Empire*, Vol. 2, *The Eighteenth Century*. Oxford: Oxford University Press, 1998.

Pagden, Anthony. *The Fall of Natural Man: The American Indian and the Origins of Comparative Ethnology*. Cambridge: Cambridge University Press, 1982.

Parker, Patricia. *Shakespeare from the Margins: Language, Culture, Context*. Chicago: University of Chicago Press, 1996.

Parry, John. *British Harmony, Being a Collection of Antient Welsh Airs, the Traditional Remains of those Originally Sung By the Bards of Wales, carefully compiled and now first published with some additional Variations, by John Parry*. London, 1781.

Patey, Douglas Lane. "'Aesthetics' and the Rise of the Lyric in the Eighteenth Century." *SEL* 33 (1993).

Pennant, Thomas. *Tour in Wales*. London, 1778.

Percy, Thomas. "The Dying Ode of Regner Lodbrog." In *Five Pieces of Runic Poetry*. London, 1765.

———. *Song of Solomon, newly translated from the original Hebrew: with a Commentary and Annotations*. London: R. and J. Dodsley, 1764.

Picker, John. *Victorian Soundscapes*. Oxford: Oxford University Press, 2004.

Pinch, Adela. *Strange Fits of Passion: Epistemologies of Emotion, Hume to Austen*. Stanford: Stanford University Press, 1996.

Pinkerton, John. *Scottish Tragic Ballads*. London, 1781.

Pittock, Murray. *Poetry and Jacobite Politics in Eighteenth-Century Britain and Ireland*. Cambridge: Cambridge University Press, 1994.

———. *Inventing and Resisting Britain: Cultural Identities in Britain and Ireland, 1685–1789*. New York: St. Martin's Press, 1997.

Pope, Alexander. "An Epistle from Mr. Pope, to Dr. Arbuthnot." In *The Poems of Alexander Pope: A One-Volume Edition of the Twickenham Pope*. Ed. John Butt. New Haven: Yale University Press, 1963.

Potkay, Adam. "Virtue and Manners in Macpherson's *Poems of Ossian*." *PMLA* 107, 1 (1992): 120–31.

Potter, Mary, ed. *The Poetry of Nature; Comprising a Selection of the Most Beautiful Apostrophes, Histories, Songs, Elegies, &c., from the Works of the Caledonian Bards. The Typo-*

graphical Execution in a Style Entirely New, and Decorated with the Superb Ornaments of the Celebrated Caslon. London, 1789.

Prescott, Sarah. "'Gray's Pale Spectre': Evan Evans, Thomas Gray, and the Rise of Welsh Bardic Nationalism." *Modern Philology* 104, 1 (2006): 72–95.

———. "'What Foes more dang'rous than too strong Allies?': Anglo-Welsh Relations in Eighteenth-Century London." *Huntington Library Quarterly* 69, 4 (2006): 535–54.

———. *Eighteenth-Century Writing from Wales: Bards and Britons.* Cardiff: University of Wales Press, 2009.

Prins, Yopie. "Voice Inverse." *Victorian Poetry* 42, 1 (2004): 43–59.

"Proclamation for a Meeting of the Bards, *At Midsummer,* 1798" (National Library of Wales, manuscript 164C).

Pughe, W. Owen. *Palestine, a Poem by Heber, and The Bard, by Gray, Translated into Welsh.* London, 1822.

Pyles, Thomas. *The Origins and Development of the English Language,* 2nd ed. New York: Harcourt Brace, 1964.

Rajan, Balanchandra. *Under Western Eyes: India from Milton to Macaulay.* Durham: Duke University Press, 1999.

———. Review of *Tropicopolitans: Colonialism and Agency, 1688–1804.* In *Modern Language Quarterly* 62, 1 (2001): 74.

Rath, Richard Cullen. *How Early America Sounded.* Ithaca: Cornell University Press, 2003.

Ray, Rajat Kanta. "Indian Society and the Establishment of British Supremacy, 1765–1818." In *The Oxford History of the British Empire.* Ed. P. J. Marshall. Vol. 2, *The Eighteenth Century.* Oxford: Oxford University Press, 1998.

Redford, Bruce. *The Converse of the Pen: Acts of Intimacy in the Eighteenth-Century Familiar Letter.* Chicago: University of Chicago Press, 1986.

Rennie, Neil. *Far-Fetched Facts: The Literature of Travel and the Idea of the South Seas* Oxford: Oxford University Press, 1996.

Richards, William. *Wallography; or, The Britton Described.* London, 1682.

Richardson, John. *London and its People: A Social History from Medieval Times to the Present Day.* London: Barrie and Jenkins, 1995.

Roach, Joseph. *Cities of the Dead: Circum-Atlantic Performance.* New York: Columbia University Press, 1996.

Rocher, Rosane. "British Orientalism in the Eighteenth Century: The Dialectics of Knowledge and Government." In *Orientalism and the Postcolonial Predicament: Perspectives on South Asia.* Ed. Carol A. Breckenridge and Peter van der Veer, 215–49. Philadelphia: University of Pennsylvania Press, 1993.

Rose, Mark. "The Author as Proprietor: Donaldson v. Becket and the Genealogy of Modern Authorship." *Representations* 23 (Summer 1988), 51–85.

———. *Authors and Owners: The Invention of Copyright.* Cambridge, MA: Harvard University Press, 1995.

Rosenmayr, Leopold, ed., with Eva Köckeis. *Sociology in Austria: History, Present Activities, and Projects.* Graz, Köln: Böhlau's Nachf, 1966.

Ross, Margaret Clunies. *The Old Norse Poetic Translations of Thomas Percy: A New Edition and Commentary.* Turnhout, Belgium: Brepols, 2001.

Rothstein, Eric. *Restoration and Eighteenth-Century Poetry, 1660–1780.* Boston: Routledge and Kegan Paul, 1981.

Rousseau, G. S. "The Pursuit of Homosexuality in the Eighteenth Century: 'Utterly Confused Category' and/or Rich Repository" *Eighteenth-Century Life* 9 (1985): 132–68.

Roy, Parama. *Indian Traffic: Identities in Question in Colonial and Postcolonial India*. Berkeley: University of California Press, 1998.

Rudy, Jason R. "Hemans's Passion." *Studies in Romanticism* 45, 4 (Winter 2006): 543–62.

Runciman, Alexander. *The Blind Ossian Singing and Accompanying Himself on the Harp*. N.p. 1772.

Saglia, Diego. "'A Deeper and Richer Music': The Poetics of Sound and Voice in Felicia Hemans's 1820s Poetry." *ELH* 74, 2 (2007): 351–70.

Said, Edward. *Orientalism*. New York: Vintage, 1978; reprt. 1994.

Saunders, Davis, and Ian Hunter. "Authorship and Copyright, and Lessons from the 'Literatory': How to Historicize Authorship." *Critical Inquiry* 17 (Spring 1991): 479–501.

Schürer, Norbert. "The Impartial Spectator of Sati, 1757–1784." *Eighteenth-Century Studies* 42, 1 (2008): 19–44.

Schwab, Raymond. *The Oriental Renaissance: Europe's Rediscovery of India and the East, 1680–1880*. Trans. Gene Patterson-Black and Victor Reinking. New York: Columbia University Press, 1984.

Schwyzer, Philip. *Literature, Nationalism, and Memory in Early Modern England and Wales*. Cambridge: Cambridge University Press, 2004.

Scott, John. *The Poetical Works of John Scott, Esq*. London, 1782.

Sharpe, Jenny. *Ghosts of Slavery: A Literary Archaeology of Black Women's Lives*. Minneapolis: University of Minnesota Press, 2003.

Sheppard, Francis. *London: A History*. Oxford: Oxford University Press, 1998.

Sheridan, Thomas. *A Course of Lectures on Elocution*. London, 1762.

Sinclair, John. *The Poems of Ossian, in the Original Gaelic, with a Literal Translation into Latin, by the Late Robert Macfarlan, A.M. together with A Dissertation on the Authenticity of the Poems, by Sir John Sinclair, Bart. and A Translation from the Italian of the Abbe Cesarotti's Dissertation on the Controversy Respecting the Authenticity of Ossian, with Notes and a Supplemental Essay, by John M'Arthur, LL.D*. London, 1807.

Sitter, John. *Literary Loneliness in Mid-Eighteenth-Century England*. Ithaca: Cornell University Press, 1982.

Sitter, Zak. "William Jones, 'Eastern' Poetry, and the Problem of Imitation." *Texas Studies in Literature and Language* 50, 4 (Winter 2008): 385–407.

Sloman, Judith. *Dryden: The Poetics of Translation*. Toronto: University of Toronto Press, 1985.

Smith, Bruce. *The Acoustic World of Early Modern England*. Chicago: University of Chicago Press, 1997.

Smith, John. *Sean Dana; le Oisian, Orran, Ulann &c. / Ancient Poems of Ossian, Orran, Ullin, &c. Collected in the Western Highlands and Isles; Being the Originals of the Translations Some Time Ago Published in the Gaelic Antiquities*. Edinburgh, 1787. National Library of Scotland, Oss. 29.1–2.

Snyder, Edward D. *The Celtic Revival in English Literature, 1760–1800*. Cambridge: Harvard University Press, 1923.

Sorensen, Janet. *The Grammar of Empire in Eighteenth-Century British Writing*. Cambridge: Cambridge University Press, 2000.

———. "Varieties of Public Performance: Folk Songs, Ballads, Popular Drama, and Sermons." In *The Edinburgh History of Scottish Literature*. Vol. 2, *Enlightenment, Britain, and Empire (1707–1918)*. Ed. Susan Manning, Thomas Owen Clancy, Ian Brown, and Murray Pittock, 133–42. Edinburgh: Edinburgh University Press, 2006.

Spivak, Gayatri Chakravorty. "The Rani of Sirmur." *History and Theory* 24, 3 (October 1985).

———. "Can the Subaltern Speak?" In *Colonial Discourse and Post-Colonial Theory: A Reader.* Ed. and intro. Patrick Williams and Laura Chrisman, 66–111. New York: Columbia University Press, 1994.

———. *A Critique of Postcolonial Reason: Toward a History of the Vanishing Present.* Cambridge, MA: Harvard University Press, 1999.

Stafford, Fiona. *The Sublime Savage: A Study of James Macpherson and the Poems of Ossian.* Edinburgh: Edinburgh University Press, 1988.

St. Clair, William. *The Reading Nation in the Romantic Period.* Cambridge: Cambridge University Press, 2004.

Steadman, J. M. "The Asiatick Society of Bengal." *Eighteenth-Century Studies* 10, 4 (Summer 1977): 464–83.

Steele, Joshua. *An Essay Towards Establishing the Melody and Measure of Speech to be Expressed and Perpetuated by Peculiar Symbols.* London, 1775.

Stephanson, Raymond. *The Yard of Wit: Male Creativity and Sexuality, 1650–1750.* Philadelphia: University of Pennsylvania Press, 2007.

Sterne, Jonathan. *The Audible Past: Cultural Origins of Sound Reproduction.* Durham: Duke University Press, 2003.

Stevick, Robert D. *English and Its History: The Evolution of a Language.* Boston: Allyn and Bacon, 1968.

Stewart, Garrett. *Reading Voices: Literature and the Phonotext.* Berkeley: University of California Press, 1990.

Stewart, Susan. *Crimes of Writing: Problems in the Containment of Representation.* New York: Oxford University Press, 1991.

———. *Poetry and the Fate of the Senses.* Chicago: University of Chicago Press, 2002.

Stone, Jerome. "Albin and the Daughter of Mey: An old tale, translated from the Irish." *The Scots Magazine* (Edinburgh, 1756).

Suleri, Sara. *The Rhetoric of English India.* Chicago: University of Chicago Press, 1992.

Sweet, Nanora, and Julie Melnyk. *Felicia Hemans: Reimagining Poetry in the Nineteenth Century.* New York: Palgrave Macmillan, 2001.

Swift, Jonathan. "Thoughts on Various Subjects." In *The Prose Works of Jonathan Swift.* 16 vols. Ed. Herbert Davis and Louis Landa, 273–88. Oxford: Basil Blackwell, 1939–74.

———. *The Complete Poems.* Ed. Pat Rogers. New Haven: Yale University Press, 1983.

Tadié, Alexis. *Sterne's Whimsical Theatres of Language: Orality, Gesture, Literacy.* Burlington, VT: Ashgate, 2003.

Taussig, Michael T. *The Magic of the State.* New York: Routledge, 1997.

Tedlock, Dennis. "Toward an Oral Poetics." *New Literary History* 8, 3 (1977): 507–19.

———. *The Spoken Word and the Work of Interpretation.* Philadelphia: University of Pennsylvania Press, 1983.

Teltscher, Kate. *India Inscribed: European and British Writing on India, 1600–1800.* Delhi: Oxford University Press, 1995.

Trinder, Peter. *Mrs. Hemans.* University of Wales Press, 1984.

Trumpener, Katie. *Bardic Nationalism: The Romantic Novel and the British Empire.* Princeton: Princeton University Press, 1997.

Tyerman, Luke. *The Life and Times of the Rev. John Wesley, Founder of the Methodists.* Vol. 1. London, 1876.

Underwood, Ted. "Romantic Historicism and the Afterlife." *PMLA* 117, 2 (2002): 237–51.

Vendler, Helen. *Invisible Listeners: Lyric Intimacy in Herbert, Whitman, and Ashbery.* Princeton: Princeton University Press, 2005.

Viswanathan, Gauri. *Masks of Conquest: Literary Study and British Rule in India.* New York: Columbia University Press, 1989.

von Kempelen, Wolfgang. *Mechanismus der menschlichen Sprache nebst Beschreibung einer sprechenden Maschine.* Stuttgart: Frommann-Holzboog, 1970.

Wall, Wendy. *The Imprint of Gender: Authorship and Publication in the English Renaissance.* Ithaca: Cornell University Press, 1993.

Wallace, Tara Ghosal. *Imperial Characters: Home and Periphery in Eighteenth-Century Literature.* Lewisburg, PA: Bucknell University Press, 2010.

Waller, Maureen. *1700: Scenes from London Life.* New York: Four Walls Eight Windows, 2000.

Walpole, Horace. *The Yale Edition of Horace Walpole's Correspondence.* 48 vols. to date. Ed. W. S. Lewis, Warren Hunting Smith, and George Lam, with Edwine Martz. New Haven: Yale University Press, 1937–. Vol. 24, letters to Horace Mann.

Warner, Michael. *Publics and Counterpublics.* New York: Zone Books, 2002.

Weinberger-Thomas, Catherine. *Ashes of Immortality: Widow-burning in India.* Chicago: University of Chicago Press, 1999.

Weinbrot, Howard. *Britannia's Issue: The Rise of British Literature from Dryden to Ossian.* Cambridge: Cambridge University Press, 1993.

Wendorf, Richard. *William Collins and Eighteenth-Century English Poetry.* Minneapolis: University of Minnesota Press, 1981.

Wendorf, Richard, and William Ryskamp, eds. *The Works of William Collins.* Oxford: Clarendon Press, 1979.

Wesling, Donald. "Difficulties of the Bardic Voice: Literature and the Human Voice." *Critical Inquiry* 8, 1 (Autumn 1981): 69–81.

Wheeler, Lesley. *Voicing American Poetry: Sound and Performance from the 1920s to the Present.* Ithaca: Cornell University Press, 2008.

Wheeler, Roxann. *The Complexion of Race: Categories of Difference in Eighteenth-Century British Culture.* Philadelphia: University of Pennsylvania Press, 2000.

Wickman, Matthew. *The Ruins of Experience: Scotland's "Romantick" Highlands and the Birth of the Modern Witness.* Philadelphia: University of Pennsylvania Press, 2007.

Williams, Huw. *John Parry (1710?–1782): 'Y Telynor Dall,' The Blind Harper.* Gwasnaeth Llyfrgell Clynd, Wales: Headquarters Library, County Civic Centre, Mold, 1982.

Wilson, Kathleen. *The Island Race: Englishness, Empire, and Gender in the Eighteenth Century.* London: Routledge, 2003.

Wimsatt, William K. *The Verbal Icon: Studies in the Meaning of Poetry.* Lexington: University Press of Kentucky, 1954.

Wolfson, Susan, ed. *Felicia Hemans: Selected Poems, Letters, Reception Materials.* Princeton: Princeton University Press, 2000.

Wood, Robert. *An Essay on the Original Genius of Homer.* London, 1769.

Woodmansee, Martha. *The Author, Art, and the Market: Reading the History of Aesthetics.* New York: Columbia University Press, 1994.

Woolf, Daniel R. "Hearing Renaissance England." In *Hearing History: A Reader.* Ed. Mark Smith, 112–35. Athens: University of Georgia Press, 2004.

Wordsworth, William. *Poems in Two Volumes, and Other Poems, 1800–1807*. Ed. Jared R. Curtis. Ithaca: Cornell University Press, 1983.

Wu, Duncan. *Romantic Women Poets: An Anthology*. Oxford: Blackwell, 1997.

———, ed. *Romanticism: An Anthology*, 3rd ed. Malden: Blackwell Publishing, 2006.

Zaret, David. *Origins of Democratic Culture: Printing, Petitions, and Public Sphere in Early-Modern England*. Princeton: Princeton University Press, 2000.

Zionkowski, Linda. *Men's Work: Gender, Class, and the Professionalization of Poetry*. New York: Palgrave, 2001.

Zuk, Rhoda, ed. *Bluestocking Feminism: Writings of the Bluestocking Circle, 1738–1785*. Vol. 3, *Catherine Talbot and Hester Chapone*. London: Pickering and Chatto, 1999.

Zumthor, Paul. "The Text and the Voice." *New Literary History* 16, 1 (Autumn 1984): 67–92.

———. *Oral Poetry: An Introduction*. Trans. Kathryn Murphy-Judy. Minneapolis: University of Minnesota Press, 1990.

Index

Note: Page numbers in *italics* indicate illustrations.